INSIDE ESPIONAGE

INSIDE ESPIONAGE

*A Memoir of True Men
and Traitors*

David W. Doyle

ST ERMIN'S
PRESS

First published in this form in Great Britain in 2000
by *St Ermin's* Press
In association with Little, Brown and Company

ISBN: 0 9536151 4 6

Typeset in Plantin by M Rules
Printed and bound in Great Britain
by Clays Ltd, St Ives plc

St Ermin's Press
In association with
Little, Brown and Company (UK)
Brettenham House
Lancaster Place
London WC2E 7EN

Contents

Acknowledgements

My thanks to my sister Suzanne Oliver, historian; who used her seniority to 'order' me to write this, and to my editor, Linda Osband, who skilfully but gently pruned off much of the dross.

Illustrations

Just inside Germany, October 1944. John Mowinckel and I had gone to the area around Aachen to do some line crossing.

This photograph was taken in March 1945 as we were preparing for the airborne assault across the Rhine at Wessel.

1949, when I graduated from Princeton and joined the CIA.

Secessionist Katanga welcomes the USA, Elisabethville, 1960.

Moise Tshombe, leader of the Katanga, on his way to the Stadium to give a speech, 1960.

Independence Day, Usumbura, Burundi, July 1962.

Our house in Usumbura, 1962.

With Ann and the children in Dakar, Senegal, 1966.

My Certificate of Retirement from the CIA.

My certificate on receipt of the Intelligence Commendation Medal.

In retirement in Honolulu, April 1992, after the publication of my novel (*Honolulu Advertiser*).

'Loyalty is a malady that afflicts dogs.'
Josef Stalin, 1925

Introduction

The officers of the Clandestine Services (CS) of the CIA are called upon to do some of the most dangerous work in the world. They enter hostile buildings and go down into foul, black sewers in the dead of night to bug the enemy. They do business with Communists and other autocrats, with terrorists and crooks, to seek the truth and try to undo evil. They work endless hours to live their cover as well as to perform their primary duty. They face the fear of exposure and/or death. They are on duty twenty-four hours a day, all year, for their entire careers. All of that and more, but since the work is secret there is no chance of renown or gratitude from the public.

When you've finished this book (unless you are now or have been an espionage professional), you will have learned quite a lot about life inside what is often called the second oldest profession. This memoir is a worm's eye view of spying in war and peace: of what day-to-day espionage was like for some of us during the Second World War and in the depths of the Cold War that followed it.

Part One is about my career in the CIA, especially its Clandestine Services (also known as the DO – the agency's Directorate of Operations). This part of the story chronicles my background and my service in the Office of Strategic Services

(OSS) during the Second World War, including why and how I became a career intelligence officer and what it was like to be one during the Cold War. Part Two looks at the serious damage that was done by some of the very few who did not remain loyal: damage not only to the CIA's image and to its espionage operations, but to the morale of the rest of the Intelligence community. Former CIA officer and convicted traitor Aldrich H. Ames, now in prison for life without parole, is one of those men. So is former CIA officer Harold James Nicholson, a more recent traitor who was jailed for twenty-three years. Their cases illustrate much of what went wrong in the CIA's Clandestine Services as the Cold War was drawing to a close and after it was over. Part Three contains some personal reflections on the dilemma of state espionage in a free society: the merits of spying versus the social or ethical cost. Like it or not, state espionage is vital if our nation is to walk with both eyes open and both hands able in this complicated and dangerous world.

Because the Soviet intelligence and security services have changed names and charters so often, from the Cheka through to the GPU, OGPU, NKVD, NKGB, MGB, MVD, the KGB and finally Russia's SVR, the initials KGB are used in the text to cover the Soviet (and now Russian) state espionage and security apparatus under its various guises. However, its officers are sometimes referred to as Chekists because that's the word the Russians use for them even today. The KGB lives on, relabelled but little changed.

During my espionage career I kept no diary and made no notes, but certain events remain etched in my memory. Also, since retiring I have stayed in touch with DO colleagues – some still serving and some retired. So this story is mostly from my own recollections and from those of former colleagues, although it has been necessary to change some names, places or dates in order to protect operations, methods and specific people. Incidentally, as many memoirs are criticised for being both inaccurate and self-serving – which might be perceived as doubly true for memoirs written by former espionage officers – I have tried not to fall into those traps. However, since no human ego can be completely stifled, hopefully the reader will excuse – and enjoy – what may seem to be the occasional excess.

The CIA Publications Review Board (PRB) has read the manuscript of this book to assist in eliminating classified information and removing any security objections to its publication. However, this review should not be construed as an official release of information, confirmation of its accuracy, or an endorsement of my views. The changes required by the PRB included removing precise indication of certain places and events; I have altered or obfuscated those places and events, but the gist remains.

Why Spy?

I have often been asked, 'What are espionage people and their spy operations really like?' At first that seemed to be an unnecessary question because I assumed that most people had read enough to have a pretty good understanding of the world of espionage. But lecturing on the subject and answering endless questions, it became clear that it was in fact a good question. Most people have no real feel for what espionage actually involves, why and how it is conducted, and how it impacts on the United States and on those engaged in it.

The average spy novel is one of the biggest culprits. Most are written by people who have little or no actual espionage experience. The authors are sometimes very good writers, even excellent entertainers, but they make mistakes that any professional can easily spot, and they usually portray spying as being full of constant danger, gory violence and outrageous sex. As a result, avid readers of espionage novels often ask: 'Did you, too, use a gun and kill people?' My obviously disappointing reply is, 'No, not in peacetime.' Unfortunately, they don't want the vision of James Bond dispelled, although to espionage professionals Bond is a mixture of jaunty policeman, stunt man and comedian. Despite the stuff of novels, guns and murder play no part in normal peacetime espionage operations conducted by CIA officers. The exceptions include defensive weapons kept in an overseas station for protection of files and lives in case of a raid by hostiles, or guns temporarily carried by case officers for their own protection in areas of civil unrest or anarchy. In Africa, in the Congo and Burundi, for example, I kept in the office and sometimes carried a .38 detective special revolver for self-protection, but although I kept in practice, I never once fired it at anyone.

Only rarely were attempts made (always by top management) to have the CS arrange the assassination of foreign leaders. Such attempts were considered ethically indefensible by much of the rank and file, and were thwarted or just dropped in all cases of which I am aware – including those of Fidel Castro and Patrice Lumumba. Despite adverse propaganda, the CIA was from its birth one of the very few espionage services in the world to eschew assassination of opposition elements. On rare occasions agents or informants run by CIA officers have killed people, but almost always for their own reasons and without CIA fore-knowledge. This happened to me once in Burundi, as is described later (see pages 182–6), and it was a very unpleasant experience.

By contrast, the KGB and its allies had no compunction about ordering their agents to murder people who were opposed to their policies. One such agent, a Turk working for the Bulgarian service (which was in effect a KGB subsidiary), shot and nearly killed the Pope at the behest of the KGB. The pontiff, seen accurately as a mortal threat to the Soviet grip on Poland, was badly wounded but survived. Two dissidents, one in London and one in Paris, were also murdered by KGB-sponsored Bulgarian hit men using poisoned umbrella tips. (For a KGB 'confession' to these killings, see former KGB Major General Oleg Kalugin's book *The First Directorate*.)

However, killing opponents was not confined to the KGB and its allies; some of the espionage services of our closest anti-Communist allies routinely rubbed out dissidents and traitors as well as opponents, and some of them still do.

There was a rather unique 'hands off' policy between the CIA and the KGB. We did not physically attack our KGB counter-parts, and, as far as I know, they never took a murderous crack at CIA staff personnel even in the worst days of the Cold War. It would have been wasteful folly to start a tit-for-tat feud between KGB and CIA officers, and we all knew it. The only time our staff personnel would have become really rough with each other would have been if one side caught the other's people breaking into their offices).

Another question sometimes asked is: 'Why do we spy anyway? Why can't our embassy officers and military attachés do the job?' The answer is simple: while most of what we need to know is either overtly available or can indeed be obtained by embassy officers and military attachés, they can rarely obtain the real jewels – the core secrets of those who would harm us. Some of a potential opponent's secrets – invariably the important ones, such as his more obvious capabilities – are closely guarded, but they can be discovered by the use of technology such as secret overhead imagery or communications intercepts. The most important secrets of all are the true intentions, the concealed capabilities or weaknesses, and the secret alliances of a dangerous opponent or rival power. Clandestine communications intrusions can provide some, but usually not all, of the answers. However, humans engaged in espionage are often uniquely able to obtain that small fraction of the truth that we vitally need to know but which is so carefully hidden away. The agents involved, and those who manage them, must be highly disciplined and dedicated, for the risks are great. The CIA has had many such penetrations of hostile services, but unhappily not all the ones needed for our protection. For example, had the CIA had such an agent in Saddam Hussein's inner circle, the Iraqi invasion of Kuwait and the subsequent Gulf War could probably have been averted.

The case for espionage is most compelling if you know how it works and what it can do to help a free society protect itself against a wide array of dangers, such as war, terrorism, foreign espionage and covert action. This book may help those who are uncomfortable with our espionage efforts come to terms with what they have perceived as unjustifiable and unethical government behaviour.

Since our intelligence system was reorganised and the CIA formed in 1947, espionage has done a great deal for the United States. Despite its many critics, the CIA and its Directorate of Operations have been of significant value to the US and her allies during their first fifty years. However, like most human organisations, they have made their share of mistakes. Amos Perlmutter, Professor of Political Science at the American University, who is also editor of the *Journal of Strategic Studies*, puts it this way:

The CIA unquestionably was the major and most awesome tool of American foreign policy in the Cold War, and the judgment of history is that it succeeded beyond its wildest dreams. The CIA has been 'victimized' by the anti-Cold War ideologists. Neither military power nor American security is safe without a serious, efficient, effective intelligence agency.

As is true of all intelligence organisations in open societies, the CIA's errors have been loudly trumpeted while its positive achievements have mostly gone unpublicised. On other occasions failures imputed to the CIA have later turned out to have been more successes than failures. What can be said of our successes – most of which are still classified – must be general, not specific. To identify top-level agents – of whom there were many – would prove the point but would destroy them. To specify methods used would reveal what must remain secret.

Of particular importance to the US has been the CIA's acquisition and processing of a constant flow of vital economic, demographic, technological, societal, as well as military and political intelligence upon which our policy-makers depend. The work that my colleagues and I did in the CS contributed significantly to that flow of intelligence.

The fact that important intelligence information is not always used to good advantage by the analysts and policy-makers is a common problem for all espionage services. Perhaps the single most impressive case is that of Soviet agent Richard Sorge in Tokyo who urgently warned Stalin that Hitler was about to attack the USSR in June 1941. Stalin ignored his warnings (and similar ones from his NKVD's Rote Kapelle network in Western Europe) and lived to regret it.

Most of my CIA colleagues and I were driven by a hatred of state autocracy and repression, and concern that despite their miserable track records they might win in the long run. Since after the Second World War the most dangerous opponent was 'export' Communism, our main task was to work against all forms of it. Naturally the USSR, its European satellites and Red China were the main opponents, and we strove hard to understand – and counter – their activities outside the US. Almost everything we did was to further those goals in one way or another.

Now that the Cold War is over, the dangers are less monolithic but no less serious, and if anything more complex. The USSR, instead of a single opponent, now consists of fifteen separate countries jealous of their independence, plus the intact remains of the military/industrial/security complex. In espionage terms that represents a net increase of nations whose policies often do not mesh with ours. The end of the Cold War has also produced an increase in the activities of terrorists, and in the proliferation of weapons of mass destruction – both serious threats to the US and both best uncovered by sound, inventive espionage; and there has also been the explosion of drugs illegally entering the US. Therefore, the challenges and the excitement in store for young people joining the CS today are immense.

Despite all the recent criticism of the CIA and doubts about its value, the public still generally accept the need for espionage. Whether or not the CIA's Clandestine Services as such have a long-term future, their espionage functions most certainly do. So do the accumulated skills of its people. One of those skills is that of recruiting espionage agents. Persuading people to risk their lives by conducting espionage for another country is one of the greatest challenges to a professional intelligence officer. Espionage using human beings is known in Washington by the dull and humourless acronym: HUMINT.

Unfortunately, those six letters fail to convey that good espionage is one of man's most exciting and productive ventures. Hopefully this book will make that clearer.

PART ONE

TRUE MEN

'The important thing in a military operation is victory . . . to win without fighting is best. To know the opponent's condition is impossible without espionage.'

Sun Tzu, The Art of War

'An army without secret agents is exactly like a man without eyes and ears.'

Chia Lin, T'ang dynasty commentator on Sun Tzu's work

1

Towards Espionage

My espionage career didn't begin until early 1944 when, at the age of nineteen, I joined the Office of Strategic Services – the US espionage and covert action organisation operating during the Second World War. However, several factors in my youth combined to make espionage a logical career choice.

For one thing, my sister Suzanne and I grew up in Western Europe. We were brought up in Belgium and England, and travelled in France, Luxembourg and Switzerland. However, we also had a heavy dose of Africa in our lives because our father, Donald Doyle, an American mining engineer, spent over twenty years (1911–32) running diamond mining operations in the Kasai province of the Belgian Congo or overseeing them from Brussels. Our mother, Joyce, an American and a professional artist, spent from 1919 to 1923 with him in the remote mining town of Tshikapa, which our father had laid out and built. Sue was born at Luebo in the Kasai, but quickly contracted malaria which almost killed her, so our mother decided not to remain in Africa. My father returned to the Congo, while my mother moved in with her mother and grandmother – both widows – who were then living in Harrow, a suburb of London. I was born there in 1924.

In 1925, when I was one, we moved to a house in Brussels.

From when I was three years old, Sue and I walked a kilometre each way to school and back every day accompanied by a governess. The school was run by the redoubtable Mademoiselle Hamaide, was very cosmopolitan and was attended by children from all over the world. The school must have been a forerunner of the Montessori system, with each student being allowed to progress at his or her own speed. Now and then students or visitors would talk to us about life in other countries, some of which were quite exotic.

During our seven years in Brussels, our father remained at his work in the Belgian Congo, coming home only occasionally. He had an office and a secretary in Brussels, but he was never there enough to satisfy his two children. Our maternal grandmother was a regular visitor, and less often our great-grandmother came to keep our mother company. They both had quite an influence on us, as did some of the many visitors who came now and then to stay in or dine at our house – mining engineers who were living and working all over the world. Several of my mother's artistic and literary friends also visited frequently. It was fascinating to listen to exciting stories of prospecting and mining in so many different countries, and to hear or see what some prominent artist had recently said or done. This interesting parade of people through out house continued after we left Belgium in 1932 and went to live in England.

Our parents were as different from each other as an artist and an engineer can be, but they shared a few key characteristics. They were both very well read and widely travelled. They both believed in individual freedom, hard work, honesty and integrity. They both respected other cultures and mixed easily with all social levels from royalty to the poor and downtrodden. Above all, they were both excellent linguists. As a result, Sue and I grew up in a house in which the family spoke English and French with equal fluency. Our grandmother usually spoke English, but lapsed into Spanish now and then to anyone who would listen, while our four servants communicated in French and Flemish. Our parents spoke Kituba and Tchokwe – Congo basin languages – when they didn't want us to understand. Being shut out of their conversations was a frustrating but valuable early introduction to secrecy and the use of codes.

In a sense (and perhaps stretching a point) my progress

towards an espionage career began by the time I was eight, before we left Brussels in 1932. I learned early that adults do not always tell the truth. A rather stuffy Belgian count gave our family several dozen snipe, carefully instructing us that they must be hung in the basement next to the heating system until they were 'ripe', which, he said, would take several weeks. They became ripe all right, and the smell of rotting flesh filled the house. The servants were in revolt, and we children were in tears because the stench was so bad. Finally, Mother had the birds thrown out. Our father, just home from Africa, applauded the decision. When the count came to dinner expecting our cook to have prepared the snipe beautifully, he was given a veal dish instead. Nobody wanted to explain what had happened, so he was told that the cats had eaten them.

Those ashamed of telling such untruths called them 'little white lies', which are somehow considered better than ordinary lies. The conclusion I drew as a small boy having my mouth washed out for lying was that you can lie only if you're an adult. Or if you aren't caught. It took the Bible in prep school to convince me that one must never lie. Five years later, it took Hitler to convince me that one must sometimes lie after all if it helps defend one's nation or ideology. The spy calls it deception, a cover story, or disinformation; the military call it camouflage or concealment; while the average civilian doesn't often admit to deception and, if caught lying, usually denies it furiously.

Our household cat in Brussels was herself a mistress of concealment. One day, without any warning, she led a litter of tiny kittens across the floor of the hallway. It turned out that she had produced the kittens – and tended them until they could see and walk – in a drawer of a large, old refectory table in the front hall. She had made a soundproof nest of playing cards, shredding all the cards in the house in the process. No sounds had come out of the table and nobody had had any idea that she was having kittens, let alone rearing them. In early Cold War parlance, she had 'bunkered' with her litter, to protect them. In the early days of the Cold War, the CIA 'bunkered' agents behind the Iron Curtain to await activation. Thanks in large part to the British traitors George Blake and Kim Philby, the CIA had considerably less success than our Belgian cat.

I learned that Western Europeans differed not only in their

languages, but in some of their fundamental approaches to life. In Swiss trains, for example, there were signs in four languages. The signs obviously reflected the laws most often broken by different nationals. One sign said in English, 'Do not pull the communication cord', apparently because the major infraction of the English-speaking world at that time was trying to stop trains for no good reason. (The same signs are still visible in trains in the United Kingdom.) The French sign warned: '*Ne penchez pas dehors*' ('Do not lean out of the carriage'), a warning repeated in German. The urge to lean out was clearly one of the few traits common to pre-war German and French travellers. The Italian sign was by far the most amusing and, I guess, the most revealing: '*Non sputare in la carrozza!*' ('Do not spit in the carriage!')

The Walloons (French speakers) of Belgium at that time dominated the life of the country and looked down on the Flemish, who spoke their own variety of Dutch. In our Brussels household, Belgian tribalism was clearly expressed by Victorine, the cook, a devoted Walloon. At every opportunity she did her best to make the Flemish members of the staff feel inferior. Our parents took no sides in the eternal sparring between Flemish and Walloons. They had good friends on both 'sides', as well as in many other countries. This early understanding and appreciation of different national or ethnic mores and customs was to be vitally important years later. In espionage work, to understand and appreciate other cultures is a major key to developing, recruiting, training and handling foreign agents.

One of my mother's closest friends was the Baroness Wrangel, widow of the famous anti-Bolshevik General Wrangel. She was a gentle lady dressed always in black, which made her look like a nun. She kept well abreast of events in the USSR and in Europe, and her hatred for, and disdain of, the Bolsheviks had no bounds. She had seen them at work. I was just a kid, but I can recall her telling Mother that Bolshevism was an evil that must be destroyed before it took root. The West, she maintained, must use the Communists' own methods – spying, deceit, brutality and terrorism – or go under like Tsarist Russia had done. I never forgot her descriptions of the horrors of the Bolshevik revolution and the Russian civil war that followed it. I listened very carefully, although without initially understanding what she was talking about or just how bad it was.

My father, like my mother, had a profound influence on me. Whereas she stressed an inquiring mind and obedience to her (she herself obeyed nobody), the fine arts in all their forms and family loyalty, he taught us to respect others, to be kind, to be honest and loyal to principles, and above all to learn as much as we could about everything. I didn't do any of it very well, but at least I knew what I should do.

Despite his high degree of intelligence, my father was rather shy – the exact opposite of my mother. He disliked parties, disdained empty chatter and was quiet almost to a fault. Our grandmother, Boma, who had called Donald 'very sombre, even dull', had been against the match, but after the marriage she quickly became his biggest admirer and supporter. Some people, mostly mother's artistic and voluble friends, thought him dull, even depressing, but actually they bored him. In reality, he was anything but dull. He had a wonderful sense of humour, great energy and a gentle warmth of spirit that he hid behind a diffident facade.

While he was in Tshikapa, the mining camp was visited by Crown Prince Leopold of Belgium. Mother, who was not there at the time, was shocked to see snapshots of Prince Leopold carrying suitcases. When she asked Father about it, he replied, 'Well, he's younger than I am, and he wanted to do it.' A year or so later Father was invited to the palace in Brussels to receive the Order of the Lion from King Albert. He was told to appear in a dinner jacket (which he owned), but refused saying, 'I won't get dressed up in that damned monkey suit just to get a medal, not for anyone.' Crown Prince Leopold liked my father and apparently heard of this. He thought it was funny, and the medal was pinned on Father's business suit instead. 'Royalty are just like anyone else,' he said. 'No better and sometimes a lot worse.'

Mother took pride in being a revolutionary and coached me to follow in her footsteps. I developed a lack of reverence for authority. In the army and later the CIA, that meant being disciplined but not overwhelmed by rank. I obeyed orders because that made things work, but I found that the people who gave orders were not necessarily brighter than those who laboured under their orders. One way or another, my parents, grandmother and great-grandmother tried to teach Sue and me things that were most important to them: loyalty, duty, integrity, truthfulness, appreciation of other cultures and a fierce love of personal freedom. Some of it stuck with me, and some did not. But generally they passed along some characteristics suitable for an espionage career: love of democracy, of travel, of freedom, of adventure and of acquiring knowledge. Our parents in particular taught us to think for ourselves: to think freely, to question almost everything and to seek the truth. They stressed the work ethic and believed that money was far less important than ideals.

A career in espionage is in harmony with such beliefs. Many of those characteristics are vital to the success of a serious free-world espionage service. In-house truthfulness was necessary: in the CIA we lied only to develop and protect agents, operations, methods, or cover stories. We didn't lie to the colleagues with whom we worked, since it was vital to trust one another.

2

London

In 1932, during the Great Depression, Forminière, the Belgian company for whom my father worked, got rid of all foreigners. Despite his senior position, this included my father. We therefore moved from Belgium to England, where he eventually became general manager of a British-American mining company called Consolidated African Selection Trust (CAST). Things were so bad that he offered to work for CAST without a salary for three years. He could afford to, thanks to the three years' severance payment he had received from the Forminière and a modest private income from investments. His offer was accepted, although he was rewarded by being paid a good salary before the three years were up as he had helped turn the company around and make it profitable again.

London was a dirty city then, with coal-burning at its height. We had frequent 'pea soup' fogs so thick that you literally couldn't see six inches ahead of you. My parents put me into Colet Court, a preparatory school. I walked to school and back every day, just a few hundred yards to and from our house on Gunterstone Road. When the pea soups were at their worst, I had to walk slowly with the fingers of one hand brushing along the walls and railings. There were two streets to cross, but without danger since most of the traffic couldn't move at all. Now and then a car would pass, creeping along with a person holding a flashlight or a flare ahead of it. The difficulty for pedestrians was finding the other side of the road. Sometimes it was made easier by some heavy coughing from 'over there'. Most people coughed or sneezed a lot in the bad fogs, and we all had bronchitis every winter. I would arrive at school or back at home with both hands shiny black from the dirt on the walls and railings that were my guide.

Although I had grown up speaking English as well as French, the move across the Channel was traumatic. Justice seemed very hard to find in London. I spoke fluent, unaccented French, but Colet Court totally ignored this and made me 'learn' French. The teacher was a sadistic English bully who spoke appalling French. What little he knew came out with an English accent that, to me, was ludicrous. Mr Downs and his eighteen-inch ruler became my mortal enemies.

When I corrected him, which at first I innocently thought he would appreciate, he became furious and would whack my right hand three or four times with his ruler. He held this weapon like a sword, thin edge down. The pain was severe, and my palm would swell like a balloon. Since in his cunning Downs always chose to attack my right hand, I couldn't grasp a pen to do my homework and was also punished for that. I countered by correcting him as often as I could, but of course this only made matters worse.

I pleaded with Mother to talk to Downs, but it did no good. Downs and I continued to torment each other. I remained a disciplinary problem thereafter, but at least I had learned at first hand about justice. It isn't given to you automatically: you have to work for it. That piece of intelligence would be useful later. So would the new knowledge that to be right and say so can be very dangerous. Best to keep such things to yourself; best, in fact, to listen more and speak less.

There was also the torture of leaving the metric system in favour of England's pounds, shillings and pence. Inches and feet, yards, furlongs, poles and perches, the standard and the nautical mile, ounces, pounds and stones, and the imperial gallon – all were a mystery that my school expected me to know and therefore didn't bother to explain. I had to decipher it *sub rosa* during classes, while pretending to know what it all meant.

Despite these difficulties, life in England had many wonderful qualities. Our family got along well with the British, who never seemed to us to live up to their reputation. They weren't cold, arrogant or condescending. However, there was one serious exception: in pre-Second World War England, speaking French or Spanish in public was considered by the masses to be very odd indeed. Whenever my beloved grandmother took me for a bus ride, an event she loved more than riding in a car, she would speak to me in French or Spanish. The other passengers would stare at us coldly, because we were foreign. I would cringe and eventually I dissuaded her. That experience, added to the depravity of Mr Downs, caused me to bury my French deep down, and when I joined the OSS during the war I had to dig my French back out of my subconscious memory. Fortunately, it came back with a rush, French accent and all.

I escaped from Colet Court school and Mr Downs in 1938, at the age of fourteen, by the miracle of graduating. Then came what in England is called a public school (in reality, a private school). My choice was Gresham's School, outside the town of Holt, in the county of Norfolk. It was founded in the sixteenth century and is still owned by the Honourable Company of Fishmongers, one of the ancient guilds of England. I liked the school, which I had pleaded to go to because my parents said it was the only public school in the UK at that time that didn't allow the faculty to beat its students. That single factor was what persuaded me to pass up the other offers my parents made, including more prestigious schools like Winchester and Stowe. Mr Downs and his eighteen-inch ruler were still very much in my mind. Even those dreadful cold showers at dawn in winter in an unheated bathhouse – which Gresham's insisted made one into a man – were better than another Mr Downs.

Gresham's is a fine school that has – happily – grown and prospered since then. Discipline was strong but not cruel. If possible, infractions were punished by the imposition of instructive tasks. I was caught being very nasty to another boy and had to spend all my spare hours in the library for a week, a clever sentence that widened my horizons considerably.

The school gave its students the choice of joining the Gresham's Boy Scouts, or the school OTC – the officers' training corps. I had been a scout at Colet Court, runny nose and all, but opted for the OTC because it was more exciting. We were issued uniforms, old Lee Enfield rifles, gas masks, and so on. We even had First World War puttees – strips of khaki cloth that you wound around your legs from the ankle to just below the knee. Puttees made good tourniquets, we were told, if we were wounded by the Hun – as our schoolmasters invariably called the Germans. Puttees could also be looped under the armpits of the less fortunate, whom we would drag off the battlefield to be treated or buried as the case might be. Puttees could even be used to hang enemy spies! By 1938, war in Europe was clearly not far away. We dug air-raid trenches, filled sandbags, drilled and even got to fire our rifles during exercises. We were taken to watch army units firing the new .303 Bren gun from Czechoslovakia and the Swedish 40mm Bofors anti-aircraft gun – heady stuff for a fourteen year old. The schoolmasters were almost all veterans of the First World War, so in addition to their instruction in warfare we heard hundreds of war stories. There was no shortage of martial arts advice or of distaste for the Hun in 1938. It was excellent preparation for what was to come.

On one occasion, a group of teenage German schoolboys came to visit Gresham's to play us at field hockey. I can't recall who won, which probably means that they did, but I do recall very clearly that they were steeped in Nazi propaganda, and were terribly arrogant and rude. In the evenings the four assigned to my house, Farfield House, would appear in the dining hall in their Hitler *Jugend* uniforms, salute Nazi style and sit together without speaking to any of us. After each meal, uninvited, they sang songs such as '*Wir fahren gegen England*' ('We're marching against England'). Their performance visibly sickened our housemaster, Mr A. B. Douglas, who had been an infantry officer at the front through much of the First World War. We thoroughly disliked these Nazi boys and the crudeness of their propaganda, and that, too, was a suitable preparation for the future.

When the Second World War began on 3 September 1939, we were still living in England. We had a house in London and a summer cottage outside a village called Strete in South Devonshire, which my parents had bought in 1933. The American Embassy advised all US citizens to go back home, but our parents discussed it with Sue and me. It was our first (and last) formal family conference, and I was impressed with the seriousness of it. I was fifteen by then and innocently thought that the war would be great fun, even if a bit rough at times. We certainly didn't want to appear chicken, and anyway honour mandated that we stay in the UK to help the anti-Nazi war effort. Our father reasoned that we had enjoyed good times in England, that we had a lot of British friends, and that we couldn't run away just because there was a war. We agreed and declined the offer to go to stay with relatives in Pittsburgh. That decision was to cost my father his life in 1942, a victim of overwork and stress.

Well before the US joined in, we all did something to help the war effort. In addition to his very demanding job as general manager of CAST, my father did a lot of voluntary work for the UK industrial diamond control organisation and for the UK Ministry of Economic Warfare. After Belgium fell to the Nazis, he was asked to take over management of Forminière affairs in England because the company's directors and officers had stayed in Nazi-occupied Belgium. He also served as a volunteer in the Home Guard's US platoon in London: 'Old men in their fifties trying to act like boys,' he said laughingly. On top of that, he was a volunteer firewatcher during the Luftwaffe's night bombing of London. For months he had very little sleep and became totally exhausted. The stress severely damaged his already weakened heart and hastened his death.

My mother joined the WVS (Womens' Voluntary Service), helping bombed-out people, driving an ambulance briefly during the air raids, and later (with Nancy Cunard) meeting, feeding and settling refugees from Dunkirk and Gibraltar, and merchant mariners from the Caribbean who had been torpedoed at sea. Sue, while still a schoolgirl, was a firewatcher and did various jobs in the WVS, and later as a university student helped with the harvest in the holidays. Although still at school, I joined the Home Guard.

The so-called 'phoney' war (3 September 1939 to 10 May 1940) began quietly in England. Nothing serious happened in France, where the Germans and the Allies glared at each other across their frontiers and bombarded each other with propaganda leaflets. The popular song in Britain said it all, with wildly misplaced optimism: 'We're going to hang out our washing on the Siegfried Line, if the Siegfried Line's still there . . .' In fact, the Allies didn't reach the Siegfried Line until late 1944.

For us life went on much as usual. Norfolk, including Gresham's School, was peaceful – even serene. All that changed radically soon after the May 1940 German *blitzkrieg* that swallowed up Norway, Denmark, Holland, Belgium, Luxembourg and a large part of France. The Battle of Britain started, and life in the British Isles changed. Our family spent the summer of 1940 partly in London and partly at the cottage in Strete. My parents were outwardly indifferent to the daylight bombing of late August and early September, but they did pay attention to the night bombing which began in the second week of September. However, the family rarely went to a shelter – even during the first fifty-seven-day non-stop bombing onslaught.

As the coast of Norfolk was one of the possible German landing sites for the planned invasion of the UK, Gresham's School was evacuated to the seaside town of Newquay in Cornwall. Farfield House was on the top two floors of the Pentire Hotel, which still exists very much as it was then. Being out of London during most of the night bombing was a relief; one could study and not worry about being killed or wounded. For me, the wild countryside around Newquay was a joy, with the sea, beaches, cliffs and caves to explore. At home for Christmas and the school holidays, I realised what Sue, our parents and the other full-time residents of London went through during those night bombing raids.

Father used to meet very mysterious men from some government office, and they would talk in his library at home in whispers. One of his regular contacts was Colonel Sir Claude Dansey, who was in fact a very senior member of the Secret Intelligence Service (SIS) and who, it seems, thoroughly disliked the US and Americans, although we knew none of that. However, we did know that their conversations had something to do with the war effort and were very secret, but Father never gave us any details. We learned later that he was able to delay a large shipment of copper from Africa to Germany until war broke out and the British could impound it.

In May 1940, he undertook a very risky trip for the British: he visited France as it was falling to the Germans to rescue whatever Dutch and Belgian industrial diamond cutters he could find and bring back to the UK. They were needed desperately by the UK war industries, and saving them from the Germans would be a real contribution to the war effort. Unfortunately, he was unable to find any diamond cutters and just managed to escape the Germans as they came into St Malo. He was arrested briefly as a suspect alien in Exeter, England, when his aircraft landed there, but Dansey's men quickly sprung him. The result of this was that the Nazis blacklisted him as a state enemy to be captured or killed. I was intrigued by my father's role in whatever it was, but it never occurred to me then that I had anything to offer an intelligence service.

During the London raids, I used to watch in admiration as the females in my family listened to the German bombs, dropped in sticks of four or so, exploding nearer and nearer. They showed no emotion. I don't believe they were as scared as I was, for I dreaded sitting there helplessly with no way to fight back. My mother, citing her First World War experience, used to calm our two remaining servants by telling them to stick 'close by me, and you'll be just fine . . . this house won't be hit'. Several maids and charwomen in the neighbourhood used to spend the nights in our kitchen and hallway because Mrs Doyle had said that it was 'safe' there. They had more faith in my mother as a shield than I did, and probably more than she herself did.

One of the greatest pleasures I remember in England was the time we spent at the cottage in Strete. It was a three-storey house with a small garden, looking out over the cliffs to the Channel. It was there, on the sea and in the fields in the early years of the war, that I learned to have patience. I accompanied fishermen trolling the sea for fish and helped when schools of mackerel swarmed near the beaches. Watchers in special little huts on the cliff tops would sight the fish and raise the alarm. We would all go down from the village to help dig a long trench in the coarse sand, usually on the long beach called Slapton Sands (where in 1943–4 our troops practised for D-Day). A fishing boat would put out from shore towing a long net. Six or eight men bent to the oars because it was impossible to use a sail for this. When the net surrounded the school of fish, we would haul both ends so that the net tightened and the fish were eventually brought ashore, where they could be scooped up and put into the trench. The entire process might take an hour or two, especially if the school of fish was large. Sometimes there were thousands of fish, each weighing some two to four pounds, rarely more. Sometimes fifty of us were there, twenty-five on each side of the net, pulling like mad.

Someone would rush up to the village and telephone the buyers, who arrived in lorries and bid on the fish. Before the bids, however, each person who had helped was allowed to take whatever he or she could carry on foot up the cliffs. The gimmick was that we had to carry the fish with a thin string looped through their gills and around one finger of one hand. You couldn't wrap a handkerchief or banana skin or anything else around that finger. It was a matter of honour, and everyone played by the rules. On the first occasion, after a half mile in soft, gravelly sand along the beach followed by a mile-long climb up some 400 feet above sea level, I found myself wishing I'd been less greedy. The string was cutting into my finger, right down to the bone. The next time I only took four medium-sized fish. Even that was a long and painful uphill trudge, but the family's excitement over a wartime dinner of really fresh mackerel made it well worth the small sacrifice.

Sadly, at night we could sometimes see ships burning a couple of miles or so offshore, after being torpedoed by German submarines or motor torpedo boats (Eboats). Through our ancient telescope we could see the crews struggling in the water, backlit by burning oil, but of course we were unable to help them. When a tanker blew up, the survivors struggled briefly but were quickly overcome by the oil which covered the surface of the sea – whether or not it was burning.

Sometimes alone, sometimes with a neighbour my age, I stole eggs from seagulls' nests in the cliffs. They were fishy, but food was short even in the English countryside and they were a welcome change of diet for those who could bring themselves to eat them. Besides, each one was at least twice the size of a chicken's egg – almost enough for two very hungry people. Rabbits also abounded because hunting them had diminished. I used to borrow a ferret from a neighbour to flush rabbits out of their burrows so that I could shoot them. But ferrets are nasty tempered little creatures who bite and scratch, and shotgun ammunition was expensive, so I learned to wait in a bush and watch for hours at a time. Then I would shoot rabbits with a .177 calibre pellet air rifle. A shot in the head did the trick, although the range had to be less than fifty feet. The rifle loaded only one pellet at a time.

Waiting motionless for hours to get off one shot taught me not only patience but how to make sure that each shot counted. A miss, and all the rabbits bolted for their holes: and the long wait started again. Twenty-five years later when I was attending a course at the CIA training area in Virginia known as the Farm, we had a refresher session on the firing range. I was still able to shoot a perfect score.

Strete was fairly safe from German military attention until a radar station was established on a hill just behind the village – about a half mile from our cottage. Then we had the occasional bomber or fighter plane flying over, low to the ground. I recall no bombs being dropped nearby, but one German bomber's tail gunner fired his machine-gun at Sue and me as we walked up the vicarage lane. He missed. Curiously, the next German bomber's tail gunner merely grinned and waved at us. One day a German ME-109 was shot down and landed in a field a quarter mile from the cottage. As it came down, it fired and sprayed our garden with tracer bullets. Sue was outside and didn't realise until later that she had been strafed – without result, luckily. When the radar station commander, a lady WAAF (Womens' Auxiliary Air Force) officer, came down to inspect the wreck, she took one look at the pilot – who had been burned to a crisp in his cockpit – and threw up. A rumour went around that the ME-109 was actually shot down by a lucky accident: an army cook near Torquay had run out of the cookhouse when he heard the aircraft coming and tripped, falling over a machine-gun which had gone off and hit the aircraft quite by chance.

Meanwhile, things went well at Gresham's School. I got good grades and for once behaved myself. I was promoted to Prefect and was put in command of the school OTC (officer training corps). There was little doubt in my mind that I would soon be commissioned in the armed forces. I applied to be a fighter pilot in the Royal Navy's Fleet Air Arm, but was turned down because I was an American. The next bet was the Royal Engineers, and I went to the small town of Redruth in Cornwall to sign up in the British army. This time I made no mention of being an American. As I shall recount later, this turned out to be a big mistake.

3

In the Army

Since I had been born in the UK, but of American parents, by US law I had dual nationality until the age of eighteen. Then I would have to decide whether or not to keep my US citizenship. The British Government, which viewed British citizenship as a duty, didn't care which nationality I chose. I could only lose my UK citizenship by foreswearing it in court. The US, on the other hand, considered citizenship a privilege and was quick to relieve you of it for a number of reasons: one was voting in a foreign election; another was swearing allegiance to a foreign head of state, which is what I did – unaware of the consequences.

When I had volunteered for the British army, the recruiting officer in Redruth was interested only in feeding the cannons with fodder. He didn't ask if I was American, because my birth certificate said only that I had been 'born in Harrow, Middlesex'. He assumed that I was British, and since I could speak both British and American English with different idioms and accents, I spoke British English with him. I wanted to have a go at the Nazis, so I didn't mention my dual nationality. I'd no idea it mattered, but it was to cost me my US citizenship. It took a transfer to the US army to get it back.

My appointment to the Royal Engineers came through in September. They sent me to Cambridge for a year of study

crammed into six months, to be followed by entry into the officer cadet training system. I duly reported to King's College and
became a student in what was called the RE short course. We
studied such things as explosives, surveying, bridge design and
building, design of defensive works such as tank traps, and so on.
Some of us were transferred to Selwyn College for the last part of
the course; as Selwyn specialised in religious studies, we were
there for rations and quarters only, and there was little interaction
between us and the 'normal' divinity students and faculty.

Sue was a student in Cambridge at the same time. She
remembers that although I was in the British army, since I was
under eighteen (and therefore still classed as a child for food
rations) I was able to bring her bananas and oranges, which I was
issued because of my tender age. Adults hadn't seen those fruits
since 1940. Looking back, I was indeed still a child: a lot of my
spare time in Cambridge was spent with friends exploring the
beauties of the river, the stunning architecture, the college 'backs'
and the town's many pubs, rather than in studying. However, I
did apply myself to learning what was of interest to me: surveying, field bridge-building and the military uses of explosives.
Apart from that, the RE short course was pretty much a standard
engineering course, which I found boring.

Not long after I had started with the RE in Cambridge, my
father became very ill. Overwork and a weak heart had finally
brought him down, and he was put into a London nursing home.
I visited him there once, on what was called compassionate leave.
He was in a hospital bed, looking pitifully weak and thin. He held
my hand and apologised for being a rotten father, away so often,
too busy, and so on. It was silly, because he had been a wonderful father. I said so, trying to reassure him by saying how much
he was loved by us all, and how much I loved him and appreciated all he had done for us. But we were both ill at ease, and it
was a very stilted conversation – one I often wish could be
repeated without the stumbling clichés. It was the last time I saw
him alive. The next time they called me to visit him – this time in
an emergency – was on Thanksgiving Day, 1942, but he died
just before I got there. It was a body blow that took years to
heal. He was gone before I had really got to know him as a friend
as well as a father. We had only just begun to have adult talks, to
discuss our feelings about life and its funny sides.

Back at Cambridge it was hard to follow the routine. I kept thinking of the loss of my father, and I went to more pubs and parties than were good for me. Twenty years after I had left Cambridge, Sue and I were visiting the city and walking across the College grounds. When I pointed to an unfamiliar building and asked her what it was, she was shocked. It was, she explained, the university library!

My class finished the RE short course in April 1943, and we were sent to a pre-OCTU (officer cadet training unit) in the south of England. I did well for several weeks, but I was suddenly advised by my mother to apply urgently for transfer to the US army in order to recover my US citizenship, which I did. The colonel commanding the pre-OCTU was furious, and I was expelled from the OTC cycle and reverted back to being a sapper, a private soldier, pending transfer to the US army. I was assigned to clean the unheated latrines at an engineers' camp in Clitheroe, Lancashire, which was a cruel form of punishment in the bitter winter of 1943. I became so ill that I was hospitalised for a month, three weeks of it in bed.

When I was well enough to be discharged, I returned to Clitheroe, where the CO told me that my requested transfer to the US army had been approved. That was fine with me, and I told him so. His response was: 'We'll be glad to see you go, Doyle. You've been a lot of trouble.' I was still young and silly enough to think that that was a compliment.

I was given a travel voucher and took a train (unescorted) to London, where I reported to the British Military Police at the railway station. They were relaxed, cheerful and friendly. The sergeant gave me a cup of tea, sat me down and made a phone call. A few minutes later, two burly US army MPs showed up, armed with .45 calibre automatics, which they slapped suggestively in case I had any ideas about making a run for it while being escorted from one army to the other. I was delighted, however, to be going to my own army and went along peacefully when they marched me to their office. Next, I was put on a train to the US army's infamous 10th Replacement Depot at Lichfield Barracks in Staffordshire, near Birmingham.

Lichfield was both interesting and depressing. What interested me was to take basic training again, in a different army. Everything was different. The uniforms were much more comfortable, the food was better and more plentiful, and the humour was equally funny but based on a very different way of life. The pay was some three times more than the British army thought I was worth. The drill and weaponry were new and strange, and it took time to get used to them. The military jargon was different, as were the customs, the curses and the discipline. And, suddenly, I had to wear a ribbon – the European Theater of Operations (ETO) ribbon. Thirty days later, despite my congenital insubordination, I was given another ribbon – for good conduct. A week or so later, I was given a stripe and made a Private First Class. Then I got a weekend pass to visit my family in London.

I was the instant laughing stock of everyone. My family and friends had last seen me in British army uniform without any ribbons or stripes. Now, a few weeks later, without doing anything, I was – as the British used to say of the US troops in the UK – 'over paid, over dressed, over sexed, and over here'. Those tough ladies in my family and among my friends who had endured the savage bombing raids on London without a murmur, and certainly without earning any ribbons, needed something to laugh at.

It was during this visit that I learned why I had been urged to apply for transfer to the US army. My parents had been entertaining their friend, US Consul General Carlson, for dinner in mid-1942, when he had politely asked where I was. In camp, they replied. 'What camp? Boy Scouts?' When they told him it was a British army camp, Carlson questioned them further and discovered that I had sworn allegiance to the King of England. 'All right,' he told my parents. 'I'll get the dummy his citizenship back if he'll agree to a transfer to the US army.' In fact, the process took almost a year, from early to late 1943. I got my citizenship back, but with a six-month lacuna, the best Carlson could do. That gap was to haunt me. Even decades later, each time my US diplomatic passport went in to be inscribed for a new overseas post, the six-month gap in my citizenship caused last-minute delays. The computers, or whoever did that sort of thing, never got it right.

Lichfield Barracks was bleak enough in winter, but it had other unpleasant sides. I was awakened at dawn one morning by a ragged salvo of rifle shots nearby. I asked the barracks commander what it was about and was told that Lichfield was the principal execution station for the US army in Europe. Every week or two, I think on Thursdays, GIs were executed in Lichfield before dawn by firing squad. They were executed for such things as rape, murder, or desertion in the face of the enemy. These men were put to death right in the middle of the camp, so that we could all hear it and learn a lesson. This was a real surprise to me. Executions were almost unheard of in the 1939–45 British army, where discipline was tighter but sentences much lighter and almost never fatal.

Lichfield was commanded by the infamous Colonel Killian. He was reputed to run his 10,000-man camp with singular brutality and complete unconcern for the most basic human rights. As a result, the suicide rate was high, especially among GIs who had been wounded in action, nursed back to health and were awaiting reassignment to combat units. They were treated with contempt, as if they were new recruits. On one occasion, Killian had ordered a GI to be badly beaten for some minor infraction. The GI and a buddy then lay in wait for him and beat him up. The Colonel managed to tear a dog tag off one of them, and they were caught and severely disciplined, which was logical enough. But that incident was part of Killian's downfall. He was so notoriously unpopular that after the war he was hauled up before Congress and duly punished.

Not long before I left Lichfield, a shipment of teenage Irish boys arrived. Each one had a claim to US citizenship, either from a father or mother who had emigrated back to Ireland from the United States. The US army gladly accepted them as volunteers and gave them basic training at Lichfield. They arrived looking miserable in brand new uniforms that didn't fit, and they literally smelled as bad as skunks. They could barely speak English, but words weren't needed to understand that not one of them had ever had a bath in his life. Not only that, but they were mortally afraid of water, which, they had been taught, would surely give you your death of cold. The non-commissioned officers took them as fair game and set up a shower line. These unfortunate Irish recruits – some fifteen terrified men were in our barracks alone – were ordered to undress. Then they were manhandled into the shower room, where they were scrubbed with stiff brushes and yellow soap until their skins were bright red and virtually flayed. They were then given hot showers, which must have been very painful as well as frightening. They howled like banshees, and that night most of them had nightmares. The next day, for good measure, they had their teeth brushed for the first time, a process that had them howling again. When it was all over, the air in the barracks was again fit to inhale.

The experience of growing up in the British officer 'class' but serving in the wartime ranks of two armies as an enlisted man turned out to be good training for understanding, appreciating and getting on with people at all levels of society. This was to stand me in good stead in my later career.

4

The OSS

I was surprised one day to be singled out at Lichfield by an officer who provided travel orders and special instructions for me to report to a building just off Grosvenor Square in London. He seemed quite annoyed that my orders told him nothing about my new assignment, only an obscure London address to report to.

When I arrived there, US Navy Commander Van Der Poel, a friend of the family, informed me that I was being transferred to the Office of Strategic Services. The OSS had been officially established in June 1942 under General 'Wild Bill' Donovan, a Congressional Medal of Honor winner from the First World War. Donovan headed the OSS until it was dismantled after the Second World War. I had never heard of the OSS, which was pretty much an unknown quantity not only to the general public, but also to the rest of the US armed forces. There, it was often referred to sarcastically by those who had heard of it as 'OSS – Oh, So Social!' In fact, it was anything but social. The OSS undertook many difficult and risky espionage and covert action operations that saved many thousands of Allied lives.

Van Der Poel was very friendly and sent me to another building near Grosvenor Square. There, I took a fairly exhaustive French test and then handled some agent reports from occupied Europe for a few days while living at home and waiting for orders. Mother told me that I had been selected for the OSS by Van Der Poel and US navy commanders Norman Armour from Chicago and Halam Tuck from Maryland, two officers who had been family friends for many years. Their decision had mainly been based on my languages (French, German and Spanish) and my supposed knowledge of the Continent.

The OSS was a dream compared to Lichfield. Everyone was friendly, regardless of rank (which didn't seem to be important). My initial few days of work – translating and processing espionage and action agent reports from Nazi-occupied France – were interesting enough, but after I was posted to the SUSSEX Plan, life became fascinating.

SUSSEX was the cryptonym for an OSS operational plan based on the assumption, which happily turned out to be too pessimistic, that after we landed on the Continent, the Germans would jump on the Dutch, Belgian and French resistance movements and cripple them. This would deprive our commanders of vital intelligence. The French part of the SUSSEX Plan was partially to replace dead or captured French resistance 'assets' (intelligence jargon for resources). The plan was to drop about fifty two-person intelligence teams – mostly French men and a few women – into key places, where they could observe and report on German military installations, transportation, troop movements and so forth. The SUSSEX Plan, a joint Allied operation, trained the teams and parachuted them into their various assigned operational locations in France, Belgium and Holland. By the time I joined SUSSEX, most of the agents had been dropped and no more were needed. Our unit, therefore, was assigned to support them after we landed on the Continent.

Although it turned out that the Germans did not have enough penetration of the French resistance to destroy its reporting resources or its fighting capabilities, the SUSSEX Plan was a success. A great deal of intelligence – over and above that which we received from the various French resistance movements – was acquired by the teams and radioed back to us. OSS London relayed it to the Allied armies and air forces. Only half a dozen of the hundred or so SUSSEX agents were identified, caught and executed by the Nazis. The rest survived, and some are still members of The OSS Society.

I joined SUSSEX in February 1944, at the spacious estate of

the American playwright, Gilbert Miller, near Horsham in the beautiful rolling hills of Sussex. I was one of several men designated driver/interpreter. Everyone in the unit could both drive and speak French, so the designation was meaningless. We learned such things as the German order of battle, codes and ciphers, clandestine communication methods and equipment, aircraft identification, unarmed combat, line-crossing techniques, and enemy uniforms and insignia.

The job of the unit to which I was assigned was to establish and maintain radio contact with the agents in France. Once we landed in France, we were to meet, recover and debrief the SUSSEX teams when our advancing forces in France approached or overran their positions. We were also to recruit new agents and infiltrate them through the Allied and German lines where possible. We were to use whatever other sources (including our own unit's reconnaissance capabilities) might provide intelligence on the Germans.

In May 1944, we moved to Bristol, entering the 'sausage' from which we went to Normandy. Now we were incommunicado – no visits, letters or phone calls to or from the family were allowed.

Our unit sailed from Plymouth on a US navy cargo ship as part of the immense invasion armada from England. The sight of all those hundreds of ships and little boats as far as we could see was incredible. Only then did I really understand the size of the venture. The only incident on the crossing to Normandy was when somebody 'accidentally' let his carbine fire a round that neatly shot the camera out of the hands of a major in our unit. The major, who was taking a picture of the surrounding ships in the evening light, was by far the most unpopular person in our unit, so of course the man who fired the carbine was never identified.

We arrived off Omaha Beach before dawn and lay there well offshore for a while, listening to the naval shelling. I was in a hold of the ship and was brought out of a deep sleep by booming whumps of air that seemed about to crush in the boat's sides. I went up on deck and was treated to a fantastic sight. Close behind us was a US navy battleship firing her huge guns at steady intervals. Each time the battleship fired, the resulting compression wave hit our ship broadside so hard that an immense burst of hot, smelly, gritty air was forced up out of the hold through the large open hatch. We couldn't see the strikes of the shells on shore, where thick smoke was rising hundreds of feet in the air, but when eventually I got back to Omaha Beach by road a few days later, the shell holes left by those naval guns were incredible. You could fit a large house into each immense hole.

Our army's hold on Omaha Beach was still shaky, so our ship was waved off and we went north-west along the coast and finally hove to off Utah Beach. The landing there had gone off much more smoothly than at Omaha. After a climb down boarding nets to a small landing boat called a buffalo, which contained one tank and maybe a dozen men, we landed dry footed on the wide sandy beach near the town of Carentan. We quickly formed up our OSS/FI unit and drove inland as far as practical.

That night we slept in a small field surrounded by hedgerows. It was a peaceful enough night for us, although the poor guys up front were having a hell of a time winkling the Germans out of the fields and hedgerows. We lay on our backs watching the pyrotechnics in the sky. German aircraft were supposedly overhead, and the sky was literally filled with Allied tracer shells. Long streams of red and yellow tracers arced up lazily from what seemed like a thousand anti-aircraft guns. The larger shells exploded in the air, with the same effect of a multitude of flashbulbs going off constantly. I went to sleep with my head on a nice, springy tuft of grass. In the morning, however, I discovered that the tuft was a large cow pat. Luckily, it was pretty much dried out.

We moved off after dawn and camped in an apple orchard, which we quickly discovered was in front of a battery of 105 millimetre guns. Each shell had a driving band, a ring of fairly soft metal that bites into the gun's rifling grooves and gives the shell the spin required to stabilise its flight, thus increasing its range and accuracy. The driving bands had a habit of coming off as they left the gun barrels, and they would whiz through the orchard, cutting off branches full of ripening apples. We kept our heads well down, and eventually our commander, Lieutenant-Colonel Kenneth Downs, got us out of there to another orchard behind the guns.

A few days later, there was a gas alarm throughout the beachhead: the Germans, we were told, had started shelling with mustard gas. Everybody went to find his gas mask and put it on in case the news was accurate, but mostly we thought that the Germans would be very unwise to start an escalating gas war. I had been told by an 'authority' that we had a new kind of weapon that was much worse than gas, and it was only later that it was clear that he had been referring ambiguously to the atomic bombs that were later to be dropped on Japan.

The same major whose camera had been shot couldn't find his gas mask and he quite literally panicked, running around in circles and squealing that he would die. Our top sergeant, snorting in disgust, took off his own mask and gave it to the major. To our astonishment, the major took it and – without a word of thanks – put it on. We all turned away, ashamed for him. The 'gas attack' turned out to be a false alarm, based upon some GI's sighting of unusually coloured smoke from a set of incoming artillery shell bursts. The major paid once again for his unpopularity not long afterwards. One of our drivers, the late Ralph Kessler, 'by mistake' drove the heaviest vehicle we had over his barracks bag, flattening all his breakable worldly goods. Soon after, the major disappeared from our unit.

Some of our work in Normandy consisted of contacting and working with the French resistance to acquire intelligence on the German armed forces. We also interviewed escapees from the part of France still occupied by the Germans. Among our best sources were several firemen (*pompiers*) from Paris. They had left Paris of their own free will, crossed 100 miles of Nazi-occupied countryside and managed to filter through the German lines into our beachhead. There, they asked to be taken to US intelligence and were sent to our unit. On the way to Normandy, they had made it a point to observe and remember rail and road traffic, and installations used by the Germans or their French collaborators. Their information helped our air forces find many prime targets. Those firemen from Paris were among the most courageous and observant people I have ever met.

The SUSSEX agents, whom we slowly recovered as our lines advanced, performed heroically, as did many members of the various French resistance movements. While we were still in Normandy, and as our beachhead expanded, our unit contacted more and more French resistance units and got them to organise reporting sources among the resistance groups in the parts of northern France that were still in German hands. The product from these sources was very useful to the Allies, right down to the tactical level. Some of the French resistance sources reported on the location of German platoons, squads, artillery pieces and the positions they were defending. It made a great deal of difference to our infantry to know ahead of time just what they were up against. Unhappily, there weren't enough reporting sources for us to be able to help all of the line units. But still, our intelligence saved many Allied lives and cost the enemy a lot of people, time and equipment.

The French civilians and resistance fighters who had accused women of consorting with German soldiers, or of otherwise collaborating with the Nazis, took their revenge in a particularly humiliating way. They shaved their victims' heads, removed their shoes, and then paraded them, women of virtually all ages, through the streets of Normandy. I remember seeing my first such group in the suburbs of the town of Caen. There were maybe eight to ten women escorted by a dozen silent men variously armed with modern and ancient weapons. The women were forced to walk in single file, while most of the onlookers jeered and shouted obscenities at them. Because of their shaven heads, the women looked for all the world like men; they were eerily unattractive. Their faces were mostly grimly uncommunicative, although a few were red with embarrassment. Now and then a few tough cookies shouted back at the crowd, which redoubled its insults and jeering. One of the women was in her late teens. She had a beautiful face and was weeping. She caught my eye with a look of utter despair, but there was nothing to be done even had we known she was innocent (which we didn't). It was a purely French affair and our orders were not to interfere. It turned out later that some of the women were indeed innocent – victims of men who had been scorned by them or who held other grudges against them.

We lived off K rations – flat cardboard cartons containing small cans of spam or cheese, or what looked and tasted like cat food, along with four crackers, four cigarettes, a tiny supply of toilet paper and a packet of instant coffee. Sometimes we had C rations, which were larger cans of food than the K ration miniatures. Even more rarely, if one fell off a tank, we scrounged Ten-in-One rations – a carton of meals for ten men – a treasure if you were hungry. The D ration was a bar of unmeltable, tropicalised chocolate for emergencies; about six ounces of it held you together until you could get something more substantial. We each had a 'shelter-half', which when buttoned together formed a two-man pup tent, but the weather was wonderfully sunny and the nights were mild so we slept mostly in the open.

SUSSEX Plan casualties were light. Where the teams acted the way they had been trained, they got away with it. However, two incidents were caused by members stepping out of their cover roles. To be blown, in espionage jargon, means to be exposed – one's cover has been penetrated. It can be a disaster and can even cause death. That almost happened to one of our SUSSEX Plan observers, who became careless and was spotted by a German officer while he was leaning casually against a haystack reporting by walkie-talkie to his radio operator in a nearby town. The observer was beaten almost to death by the Germans, and lived only because his position was overrun by our advancing troops.

Sadly, the second occasion was fatal for three of our two-person SUSSEX teams. Their official mission finished, they made the mistake of getting together and trying to join (and spy on) the German retreat, rather than letting themselves be overrun by our troops. They stole a German army vehicle and drove off with the retreating Germans, in order to continue reporting. Courageously, but unwisely, they had no German uniforms or documents to cover their activities. They were easy to detect, and the wary German Feldpolizei picked them up, beat them and shot them.

Before the US army broke out of the Normandy beachhead, there was a gory prelude: Operation COBRA, in which almost two thousand American and Allied bombers flew from UK airfields on 25 July to smash the German defences in the St Lo area. They made a majestic, even stupendous, sight as they rumbled and growled through the bright blue sky and began to attack the German positions. We lay on our backs in the grass and watched the lead bombers of each formation shoot their smoke markers towards the ground. The markers arched down, leaving long lines of white or coloured smoke, which were intended to lead the following bombers to their precise targets.

Then we noticed that the smoke markers were slowly drifting back towards our position. We chatted idly about this, convinced that the bombers would detect the drift and correct for it, but in fact that was not the case. The bombers went with the drift, and slowly the bombs came closer and closer to our lines. Smoke and dust rose hundreds of feet in the air, obscuring the air crews' view of the ground. Before the end of the air strike, our own 'friendly' fire had killed over a hundred men of the US 30th Division.

However, the huge raid, coming on top of weeks of heavy shelling of the Germans, did the trick. The US army was able to break through the German lines west of St Lo. Our OSS unit – a dozen men in 'soft' vehicles, jeeps and a small truck – drove through the gap shortly afterwards. Everything was covered with a thick layer of white dust, the result of the bombing and shelling. The smell of thousands of dead people and animals was horrible. You could tell the difference between all the sad sources of the smells: German soldiers, French civilians, US army dead, cattle, swine, goats, donkeys (there were so many of them!), sheep and dogs; each had its own peculiar smell. The stench stayed in our nostrils, even in our clothes, for days afterwards. Today, over fifty years later, I can still conjure up those fearsome smells and can recall reacting to the carpet of death with, 'There but for the grace of God, go I.'

At last we were free and clear of the crowded beachhead. It was a beautiful summer and the German army seemed to have been broken. I remember one sight that seemed to symbolise their condition: a German soldier who had been blown up into the air and whose body was hanging on some telephone wires, blood still dripping down his legs.

We drove south in high spirits, eager to see Paris again. A surprising number of elderly Frenchmen – probably veterans of the First World War – took off their hats as we passed and placed them over their hearts. It was a very touching gesture. At other times French children flagged us down to tell us where the Germans were and how many there were. Usually they gave us greatly inflated figures, but the locations were often correct.

When the Germans almost cut through the US Third Army's armoured breakthrough from Normandy, near Avranches at the base of the Cotentin Peninsula, our unit was in among our advancing armour. We had only 'soft' vehicles and small arms, and would have been sitting ducks for the Germans at night if they had managed to intercept the US force – as seemed possible. At dusk, our unit commander, Lieutenant-Colonel Downs, began searching for somewhere to hole up for the night. There seemed to be no suitable place to hide in the sparsely populated countryside until he spied a convent. He knocked at the small visitors' door, and to our relief the Mother Superior invited us in to shelter for the night, 'provided you behave correctly'. The huge main doors swung open and our little column drove into the courtyard, out of sight of anyone outside.

We had a very prim dinner with the nuns. We produced K and C rations and the convent provided bread and wine. The youngest nun, who was perhaps still in her late teens, was one of the most beautiful women I have ever seen. Almost everybody in our unit had his eyes on her throughout dinner. She showed no signs of noticing it, although the Mother Superior did.

After dinner we were shown to a dormitory, where, as far as I know, we all spent a peaceful night. I slept well, and neither heard nor saw anything. Early in the morning, we learned by radio that the German attack had failed and that our advance could continue down the coastal corridor. After a hurried breakfast we left the convent, cheered on by the courageous nuns.

That morning, driving along a small coastal road near Mont St Michel, we came across a large German unit that had been demolished, probably within the hour. There were horses, carts, military Volkswagens and bodies strewn over a long stretch of road between tall hedgerows. Nothing moved, although they had clearly just been shot up. We thought that it was the result of an Allied air strike. Unhappily, due to the high hedgerows, we had to drive over the slippery, wheezing mess. There was no way around it for soldiers in a hurry.

Almost twenty years later, in Burundi, I learned what had actually happened. The tri-service military attaché at our embassy, Colonel A. A. Alexander, and I were on a routine trip to the neighbouring country of Rwanda. We spent the night at a small government inn halfway between Burundi's capital – Usumbura (now known as Bujumbura) – and Kigali, the capital of Rwanda. After dinner, sitting on the lanai of the inn as the moon rose over the gorgeous mountains of Rwanda, I told Alex about that incident. He started as if I'd given him an electric shock. It seems that a lieutenant in his command had returned from a trip that same morning and reported that he had lost his way, and then stumbled upon and massacred the remnants of a battalion of German soldiers. However, nobody in his unit had believed the story, which was this: as he and his driver had come over a crest in the road, they spotted this large enemy unit strung out along a kilometre of country road, hemmed in by the ubiquitous tall hedgerows. The road in front of them dipped down and rose again, so they could see the entire German force as though in a bowl. The officer yelled to the driver to turn their rig around because they had a three-quarter-ton truck with a quad fifty in tow. A quad fifty is a set of four .50 calibre machine-guns and is a very powerful weapon. The gunner sat between the guns and had a ground-glass screen in which his illuminated sights overlaid the target. The weapon had been designed as an anti-aircraft piece, although in Normandy it was sometimes used to destroy hedgerows and hopefully everyone behind them. It had a fearsome effect up to a mile away. The driver managed, backing and filling, to turn the rig around so that the quad fifty faced down the road. The Germans continued on stolidly, unaware of the danger behind them. The lieutenant jumped into the gunner's seat and simply mowed the Germans down, starting at the near end, then the far end, and finally the middle of the column. The Germans didn't have a chance. Presumably some survived, but by the time we got there they had gone.

In late July 1944, shortly after our breakout from the Normandy beachhead, two of our French agents actually sneaked into a German Panzer tank park and stole a Tiger. They brought it through the lines, found our unit and proudly showed it to us as though they were car salesmen showing off a new model. These two very resourceful and brave young men were deeply disappointed when it was decided that there was really nothing we could do with the Tiger except turn it over to the nearest US tank unit (part of Combat Command A, if memory serves). The agents weren't even allowed to go back and get another one, which is what they really wanted. Debriefing them fully was more important.

With the SUSSEX operations starting to wind down except for the physical recovery of the agents, it was about this time that part of our unit was converted into long-range reconnaissance. We reported to 12th Army Group and London via large radios on the rear deck of our jeeps; these jeeps, plus a few without a radio, became known as 'Phantoms'. We rode ahead of the forward US and French armoured vehicles, trying to pinpoint just where the Germans were and in what numbers, with what weapons, and so on.

The most adventurous of our 'Phantoms' was Lieutenant John Mowinckel, a US Marine officer attached to our unit. He and his driver-interpreter (and friend from Princeton), Reginald Camille Dussaq, were sometimes as much as fifty miles ahead of the US and French forward elements. I was driver-interpreter of another of these jeeps, with several different partners, of whom the most colourful was Sergeant Peter Wolkonsky, a royal prince from a Polish/Russian line. Pete was a fearless character of great optimism who saw the funny side of everything – including the war.

Reggie Dussaq, my best friend in the unit, was mortally hurt in a dumb accident on 22 August 1944, just before we got to Paris. He and John Mowinckel were coming back from a reconnaissance patrol when a US army truck crossed into their lane and smashed into the jeep. Reggie, who was driving, had his chest crushed, but John was unhurt. I replaced Reggie as John's driver/interpreter from then until after the Battle of the Bulge.

Weeks later, in northern Belgium, we caught up with the US army field hospital which had tended Reggie in his struggle to live. It had apparently taken him three days to die, but he had been cheerful to the end – joking with the nurses and never downcast despite the pain.

The last time I had seen Reggie was when we occupied Le Mans, where the famous car rally takes place. It was a beautiful summer's day, and we stopped long enough to go to the local bath house and eat a civilised meal at a restaurant in the town's central square. Feeling clean and fresh, we had a quiet meal and promised to meet up again in Paris. I have never been in Paris since without tipping my hat to that very special and courageous young man.

Before we reached Le Mans, Wolkonsky and I had been working the landscape ahead of the French 2nd Armoured Division. Our job was to go along with – often ahead of – their reconnaissance probes, to help find any retreating Germans and to report their numbers, activities and location directly to 12th Army Group and London. Although organised German resistance had just about collapsed, there were still instances of armed confrontation. The Allies virtually controlled the air, and our armoured forces identified themselves to friendly aircraft by tying brightly coloured plastic or cloth panels on the rear deck of each tank, behind the turret. A different colour was prearranged for each day. One day however we rounded a bend on a small country road and saw half-a-dozen French 2nd Armoured Division Sherman tanks on fire. Nearby, a German Tiger tank was burning and its ammunition exploding. The surviving Frenchmen explained that they had encountered the Tiger and shot it up. Almost instantly, however, they had found themselves being strafed by a flight of US fighter planes because they had mistakenly put up the wrong colours for the day. We looked at the mess and asked if we could help. Fortunately, we were told that the French medics were on their way, so – having work to do – we drove on. We were at the scene for no more than five minutes, but the useless waste of those men and their equipment was sickening.

Twenty years later, while attending a cocktail reception in Dakar, the capital of Senegal in West Africa, a fellow guest introduced himself as Count de la Vigne. Both of us, at the same moment, realised that we had met before. After a few minutes of questioning each other, we hit on the answer: he had been one of the wounded officers in that unfortunate French armoured unit. To illustrate what had happened to him, he rapped on the table with his right hand. It was made of wood. When he did that, I recalled seeing him having his arm bandaged. I had caught his eye in 1944, and we had smiled at each other. That brief glimpse of each other had been vivid enough in both our memories to bring us together twenty years later.

As Wolkonsky and I neared the town of Alençon in the early afternoon of a hot, windless August day in 1944, our jeep needed water. We stopped at a village pump to water the jeep and have a drink ourselves. There was not a soul around, and the silence was a welcome change from the dust and wind of driving with the windshield down. A mile or two behind us, a French armoured column was grinding along, stopping now and then to take care of small isolated pockets of German troops, or sometimes to have a quick drink in some wayside bar. It was curious how many tanks threw their treads, and had to be repaired, just outside a bar. Mowinckel used to stop and go in after them, reminding them that there was a war to be won.

While we milked the village pump, some shouting and laughter started up nearby, breaking the quiet. We investigated, and through a gate in the hedgerow we saw why the village was empty of people. A large group of youths and older men were playing soccer in a pasture, watched by a chattering, shouting line of women. The game seemed to be rather undisciplined, the main purpose being to kick the ball rather than scoring a goal. Only after a couple of minutes did we realise what we were watching: the 'ball' was actually the head of a German soldier. His uniform was behind a makeshift goal, with his headless body in it, and his rifle, bayonet mounted, was pinning his body to the ground. His helmet was perched on top of a stick marking the other goal. The villagers invited us to play with them, but we declined. We hadn't had four years of Nazi occupation, so we could afford to be nauseated by their callous revenge.

Pete and I walked back to the pump and cranked up the jeep. We drove until we could see the next village, stopped and lay in a shallow ditch watching for Germans. In a minute, if we saw nothing, we would clamber out of the ditch and drive into the village. If we found a French man or woman, we'd ask for information about Germans. We usually received accurate information, although now and then we got a small boy who'd push forward eagerly and say something like, 'Oh, I saw hundreds of Boches a few minutes ago in farmer Vachement's field.'

'How many?' we'd enquire.

'Well, maybe five hundred.'

'How big is the field, and what were they doing?'

'The field is huge, maybe a hectare [about two acres]. They were eating something.'

'Five hundred Boches in one hectare? And all of them eating?'

'Well, maybe a hundred.'

'How many, really?' we pushed.

'Well, maybe ten, I think. Any candy for my sister?'

This time however there was nobody in sight. Just as we were about to get up, the ground started shaking and a Sherman tank pulled up on the road, right beside our jeep. Behind it were a line of other Shermans. The turret hatch of the lead tank opened and a dusty figure shouted down to us in French: 'Any Boches in the village?'

'We've seen nothing,' Pete shouted back. 'We're on our way down there now. Which way are you going?'

The man, a French officer, pointed to the left fork of the road. 'We're going that way. We heard there were no Boches that way. We're in a hurry to get to Paris.' He waved to us and closed his hatch.

'Surprisingly,' said Pete, 'he's a full colonel. Must be the regimental commander. I wonder why he's in the lead tank? Crazy or something?'

At that moment another jeep skidded to a halt and a French general, the acting division commander, hopped out. He was a lean, elderly man who carried a walking stick. He walked over to the tank and slapped his stick several times on the bow plate. The hatch opened again and out peered the colonel. The two men stared at each other, and the general asked the colonel where he was headed.

'The left fork, my General. In the direction of Alençon.'

The general beat his stick slowly on the bow plate, making a hell of a racket, and shouted, 'No, no, you'll take the right fork, towards Ballon.'

Pete and I realised that we had ringside seats at a confrontation, and we hunkered down, keeping quiet. The bow hatch of the Sherman opened, and the driver looked up at the general, a grin on his face. Clearly he'd seen this before. They both argued the point for several minutes, neither giving ground – nor watching out for Germans. They shouted their difference of opinion as though they hated each other, then suddenly, to our surprise, the general conceded, smiled and waved the colonel off on the road towards Alençon – which the French division took unopposed a couple of days later. We branched off then and rejoined the US advance towards Le Mans.

Once we came across a tank platoon of the French 2nd Armoured Division which had stopped in a field outside a farmhouse. The men were getting water from the farm pump, but the farmer's wife was greedy. She stood by the pump as each man came with his canteen, and she made each one pay for the water. She didn't charge a lot of money, but it was the principle of the thing that was so surprising. She had no shame. The men, unlike US soldiers, meekly paid her.

Sometime during our 'Phantom' jeep's progress between

Chartres and Rambouillet – where we rejoined Lieutenant-Colonel Downs and the rest of our OSS/FI team – we passed unopposed through the sleepy farming village of Authon-la-Plaine. There was a skirmish there later in the day, but in the early morning we saw no Germans. I remembered the village because, true to its name, it was on a very flat plain that seemed to stretch for ever. Decades later I learned that some old friends had a house there. When my second wife Hope and I visited them in about 1990, we were treated as celebrities by the mayor and his assistant. We talked about the liberation of the village, which everyone of our age or older remembered vividly since nothing as exciting had happened in Authon since August 1944.

Some of our unit reached Paris the day before it was officially liberated, ahead of our armoured columns, meeting very little resistance except for a few snipers – none of whom I encountered directly. Members of the French resistance had in effect cleared the city of organised German resistance. John Mowinckel, armed with a .45 pistol, took the surrender of a large number of German officers and men at the Crillon Hotel. (He survived to represent the Veterans of OSS in person at the fiftieth anniversary of the liberation of Paris.)

That first night in Paris was a tremendous thrill for those of us who had been to Paris before the war. A few cafés and bistros were open, although mostly with their shutters half closed because of the sniper fire. We went from bistro to bistro celebrating with the Parisians, who were overwhelmingly happy to see us. When things began to circle around me, I went 'home' to a very large, elegant mansion in the Square Monceau that Downs had borrowed from a friend.

The day after the fall of Paris, all resistance was over. A complete US combat infantry division paraded in victory down the Champs Elysées. I joined the wildly enthusiastic French crowd lining the broad avenue. The huge crowd was unrestrained in their enthusiasm for their liberation as well as for their liberators. They cheered and hugged us, dancing with us and singing happy songs. Amid the noise, however, there were expressions of surprise on all sides because the US troops, marching some twenty abreast in massed formation, made virtually no sound. The French, accustomed to soldiers with iron in the toes and heels of their boots, were amazed that the Yanks had rubber-soled boots.

We left the Champs Elysées (where the celebration went on late into the night) and visited a French convent in the city. The Mother Superior and her nuns had been actively and very effectively helping the OSS, and some of us went there to thank them. After all this time I have no memory of where the convent was or what order it belonged to, but the sense of peace in that quiet courtyard was extraordinary after the flurry of our entry into Paris and the wild welcome which we had received. The aura of calm courage that emanated from the Mother Superior and her nuns was very impressive. That they could have taken the awful risks that they did, day after day for years, knowing that the Germans executed everyone they caught helping their enemies – even priests and nuns – was a testament to their faith. Just one informant, or one word overheard, or one radio message intercepted and the transmitter pinpointed by triangulation, and the Gestapo would have been on them like a pack of wolves. Yet those cool ladies seemed to think nothing of what they had done.

We rested in Paris for three days, most of which I spent in the company of Madeleine L., a stunningly beautiful French girl about my age. Her ready laugh with her head cocked slightly on one side, and the way she grasped my arm when she laughed, are with me still. Madeleine taught me French songs, fables, poems and jokes. She showed me museums and art galleries, and charming corners of Paris I had never heard of. We fell in love, and she laughed at my innocence while she taught me how to behave with a girl you love both in bed and out. I had never been so happy.

Suddenly it was time to head back to the war. I rushed out for a quick lunch with Madeleine, who wept quietly and I had a hard time not joining her. I gave her my APO address and she wrote down her telephone number, which I had already memorised, and her address. We also agreed that if all else failed, we would each check with the bartender in a small hotel off the Champs Elysées where we had had our first drink together. She walked me to our take-off point and drew admiring glances from my colleagues. She waved, wet-cheeked but smiling, as we drove off, but that was the last time I saw her. No letters came through the APO system, and my letters to her were returned with 'wrong address' on them. Every time I returned to Paris, I tried her telephone number, but it had been disconnected. The bartender in the hotel had been replaced and the new man had never heard of her. I walked around our haunts endlessly, without result. I'll never know what happened to her, but it was years before I got over it.

Leaving Paris on the last day of August 1944, our OSS unit joined a task force with the uninspired title T-Force, for an unopposed drive north to Luxembourg, where our unit's headquarters joined General Omar Bradley's 12th Army Group. It was a beautiful and peaceful drive in warm late August weather. Only one Luxembourger – a bent old man in his seventies or eighties – offered some resistance. He was manning a horizontal pole blocking the border between France and Luxembourg. The pole, which was striped red and white like a barber's pole, was insubstantial and could have been easily brushed aside by any of our vehicles, but the column commander ordered us to stop and got out to talk to the old man. Without written orders, he refused to raise the pole. The commander nodded gravely and decided to humour the old man. He sent back word down the line to see if anyone could negotiate our entry into Luxembourg.

Fortunately, three Luxembourg soldiers – the only ones I met in France – had been assigned to our OSS unit before we left Paris to do reconnaissance and to contact the minuscule Luxembourg resistance organisation. One of them – an indomitable man named Wenzel Profant – went up front and began to talk to the old man. Shortly, a piece of paper was procured and some words jotted on it (I suppose it was a request for passage), which was signed by the American column commander. Profant handed it tenderly to the old man, as if it were the Magna Carta. The old man read it, nodded slowly, never cracking a smile, and slowly wound up the pole. He then placed his hat over his heart as a token, I thought, of his grudging respect for *force majeur*. Once more his tiny country was being invaded.

As our column started forwards, Profant and his two compatriots shouted to the villagers that the Luxembourg army had arrived. The crowd of fifty or so villagers, who had been watching the old man's performance, bellowed its approval. The result thereafter was hilarious. Each time we entered a village, the three would shout '*Die luxemburgischer sind hier*', or words to that effect, and the villagers, under the impression that the entire column was made up of their own gallant soldiers, cheered madly. And so we crossed Luxembourg until we reached the capital city.

John Mowinckel and I then went off to the area around Aachen, just inside Germany, to carry out one of our unit's functions: the business of recruiting men and women agents to be line crossers. Unlike the SUSSEX agents who were parachuted in, these line crossers went in overland. The mission of these men and women was to go on foot through the enemy front lines and, once 'inside', to collect intelligence and transmit it back to us by radio. Usually they were sent to obtain tactical military information. For example, where were the Germans deployed, and in what depth? In what regimental or other units? Where were they solidly dug in? How many were there? What kinds and quantities of weapons and ammunition did they have, and what vehicles, fuel, clothing, food and other stores? And, above all, what were their intentions, their readiness, experience and morale? The list of questions was long, and new agents had to be given some training in observation, elicitation, reporting and Morse code before they went through the lines and into enemy territory.

Getting the answers we needed meant that the line crossers took severe risks. We escorted them through our lines going in, but not coming back out again, and so they had to survive our own, often trigger-happy, troops on their way through the Allied lines. They also had to survive the dangerous business of infiltrating through the German lines, hopefully unseen; or, if seen, without arousing undue interest. Once in there, the Germans were suspicious, quick to challenge civilians, ready and willing to shoot on sight. They often executed low-level spies after a brief, brutal interrogation. The agents had to risk sending Morse code radio messages to us, hoping to evade German direction-finding detectors. When their mission had been accomplished, the surviving agents then had to negotiate the equally dangerous return voyage, or – if circumstances were right – go to ground and wait to be overrun by advancing Allied troops.

During the period from our breakout of the Normandy beachhead until the Allied advance ground to a halt from the North Sea to the Swiss border, line crossing was impractical. Those few agents that the OSS dispatched through the rapidly retreating

German lines were quickly overrun by our own troops – if they hadn't been detected and shot by the Germans. Later in the war we dressed some of our agents and even our own OSS officers and men in German uniforms, and infiltrated behind enemy lines to acquire short-term tactical information and transmit it back to our field units. Success was at best limited, and at worst we had some notable failures. One such failure (discussed later) was the airborne crossing of the River Rhine at Wesel, Germany.

How did we find people to take these risks, to volunteer to venture into the unknown, against all odds, when they didn't have to? And to risk their lives in the coldest blood imaginable in order to achieve what often turned out to be small gains that a moment of front-line battle by uniformed troops might render useless? The answer is that we had a cause, a crusade against the German Nazis and the Italian Fascists, and – for most of us – against all other forms of autocracy. Most Western Europeans submitted to Fascism, but a small, highly motivated sprinkling of patriots and ideologues resisted the Fascists actively. Many of them agreed to help OSS despite the risks. Each such helper had an intense personal desire to free his or her country, usually coupled with a hatred of the German or Italian leaders. It was that simple. Many of those who survived, incidentally, went on to spend the rest of their active lives fighting the savage forms of autocracy developed by the Soviet Communists and their satellites. Others, convinced Communists, reverted to their previous efforts to make the world safe for the various Communist versions of dictatorship and autocracy.

Line crossing was an art. Each actor had his way of acquiring and handling agents, and slipping them through both our lines and through those of the Germans – and hopefully recovering them at some later date. It required not only recruiting the agent, training him, motivating him, equipping him and trusting him to do what we wanted, but also escorting him on his surreptitious journey to the German lines, as he carried his radio in a battered suitcase. Each agent who survived one trip developed his or her own approach to the next trip, and honed his or her own way of handling the risks and the fear of being caught and executed.

One such case was a Belgian of German origin whom John Mowinckel recruited to act as a line crosser. He was a middle-aged bachelor, who had only two or three discoloured teeth left in his mouth. I've long forgotten his cryptonym, but as he had a lot of guts as well as bad teeth I'll refer to him as FANGS – a five-letter cryptonym would have been suitable for one-time pad coded radio transmissions. FANGS was a remarkably brave man, but he had perfect cover because he looked like a wimp. Trying to convince him to risk his life in the Allied cause wasn't easy. All he had to do, John said, was to cross the front lines and spy for us. It was simple – well, not really, and FANGS knew it.

John did most of the talking. I watched, assessing FANGS and waiting to chime in if needed. John was good at his job, very persuasive, and the Belgian was listening carefully. Soon, FANGS was mentally performing his mission, and the sweat beaded on his face and neck as he weighed the chances of success and the consequences of failure. I sweated with him, imagining it. To infiltrate agents through the lines was becoming much more difficult. The Germans, as their perimeter shrank and they neared home, became more nervous and trigger-happy. It was becoming more difficult to find holes in the German lines through which to slide our agents.

The scene at the little table was like a Rembrandt painting. We talked by flickering candlelight in FANGS's cottage just inside the Belgian border. Two young American soldiers and one very mature Belgian, who knew the border area like the palm of his hand. FANGS was a small man, maybe five feet five, skinny and dark haired. He was what was called a Nouveau Belge – a German-speaking inhabitant of the portion of Germany given to Belgium after the First World War. He was still in his late forties, but his ruddy face was deeply lined. He didn't look like a hero, even in the light of the single kerosene lamp on the sideboard. All his relatives were either dead or had been dispersed, and he lived a lonely, almost monastic, existence. That had been a factor in our choice of him for the mission into Aachen: there were no dependants to worry about. And, if he didn't come back, there would be nobody but us – John and I – to mourn him. Even his few drinking friends at the local bar would quickly forget him. *C'est la guerre.*

He had served in the Belgian resistance since 1943 and had a good record as a courier, but when he finally agreed to cross the lines for us, I found no pleasure in his decision. A human being, a man who could easily refuse the mission and go right on living, had made a pact with us to put his life very much on the line. He hated the Nazis, and that was enough to tilt him in our favour.

Line crossing usually required 'recruiting' a US infantry or combat engineer platoon leader to provide us with a squad of men for extra protection until we got through the US lines. It had to be a good squad, with bright, gutsy guys who were willing to help. The squad had to be familiar with the terrain and with German positions and patrols. It was best if there was only limited, sporadic contact between the opposing forces in a relatively quiet, stable portion of the front. Forested or broken terrain, and the suburban gardens of a city, lowered the risk of detection by the Germans.

Our method of recruiting a platoon began well behind the front, where two of us drew rations for a platoon – D, C, or K rations for forty or so men. We gave away most of the food to other troops as we drove back towards the front. We kept the cigarettes, the chocolate, the more edible canned food and the toilet paper. With these, we 'bribed' the platoon leader and the squad of men he picked to help us. The bribe helped, but their real incentive was that they, too, needed the information we hoped the spy would produce. Otherwise they never would have volunteered to face extra risks – including being shot by the Germans for espionage. It was a given that we OSS types would be shot (after SS style 'interrogation') on the basis that we were spies, but regular infantrymen also faced execution for helping infiltrate an enemy spy through the lines.

At this particular time in the autumn of 1944 we were besieging Aachen and our forces in the immediate area were in sporadic (patrols only) contact with the Germans. The front lines were static. The scene was as good as it could get for line crossing. All we had to do was to find a suitable platoon to help us infiltrate our agents.

The division headquarters suggested a platoon headed by a particularly memorable sergeant: a very tall Texan, who increased his height with a Lincolnesque, shiny black top hat which he had liberated somewhere. Inevitably, everyone called him 'Top Hat'. His platoon commander, a second lieutenant, had been shot by a German sniper three weeks before. The bullet had hit him squarely in the head and had gone clean through his helmet. He hadn't yet been replaced.

So Top Hat now commanded the platoon. He was blessed with enormous common sense. His platoon, his lair, was dug into a heavily wooded hillside that faced a southern suburb of Aachen. The men in his platoon were living temporarily in a collection of dug-outs scattered among the trees which had been furnished comfortably with loot from nearby houses. Drab olive blankets were used for every conceivable purpose: shielding dug-out doors, as extra bedding, and hung up among the trees to camouflage equipment.

Top Hat took good care of his men, and they loved him for it. He had cattle carcasses strung in the trees, so that they always had fresh meat, and even on the move he found a way to feed his men a hot meal almost every day. His men responded by obeying him as if he were the division's commanding general, perhaps more willingly. Top Hat seemed to have no fear and appeared to thrive in the misery and danger of front-line life, and his attitude was infectious. He believed implicitly that God walked with him, and the platoon sheltered under the umbrella of his confidence and faith. Top Hat was their salvation and, as a result, his platoon routinely took the fewest casualties of any company in the entire division.

Top Hat listened to our spiel about running line crossers and getting hot information that everyone needed. In exchange for an escort through the lines, an area with which he and his men had become very familiar, we agreed to give him cigarettes and candy and toilet paper, which he could distribute to his men. We showed up the next morning with FANGS, having timed his infiltration to hit the slow hour. At that time the German early morning patrols were back from their dawn sightseeing and had finished their reports, while the enemy soldiers were cleaning weapons, washing, shaving, talking, eating, but mostly sleeping wherever they could find shelter.

John and I waited for Top Hat to arrive. Far off in the distance there was the muted clatter of a fire fight, a small one with just a few weapons in action. Nearby, all around us, there was an eerie silence; not a shot was fired, no squealing of tank treads or the distinctive whine of a military Volkswagen engine, and no far-off voices. Even the wind had died completely and the rain had stopped. It was time to go.

Top Hat had his group ready, a squad of six 'volunteers'. We set out with our intrepid agent, who was dressed in civilian work-men's clothes, with his radio in a scruffy old cardboard suitcase. If he were to be stopped and searched by the Germans, the radio would be his certain death warrant. We walked slowly and care-fully north into the southern suburbs of Aachen. Three of Top Hat's volunteers led the way, followed by Top Hat; then came John and FANGS, followed by another two volunteers. I was at the tail end with the sixth volunteer, an older man who looked quite incapable of providing us with extra protection from the vigilant Germans. His eyes were wide, with a haunted look, and the sweat poured down his face and neck despite the cold. I've never seen a trained veteran soldier more scared, but he managed to control his despair, which in my book made him a very brave man.

The trip through our lines was, in fact, uneventful. We passed the last US machine-gun pit with its two-man crew, who both stared at FANGS in surprise: a civilian on a patrol? With a suit-case? But Top Hat winked at them and it was OK. We crawled as much as we walked after that, for maybe half a mile through gardens, past empty houses, down narrow lanes and across orchards, until finally we had left the last US outpost well behind us. Still there were no Germans. We stopped and listened every now and then, scanning the windows of the abandoned houses, behind which a sniper could be hiding, but luckily we met no resistance.

Top Hat and John scanned a garden ahead and saw nothing. We went on another hundred yards and stopped again. There was nobody in sight, and no noise. Top Hat whispered that from here the risk of all of us being spotted together was too great and that it was time to send the agent on his way. We whispered 'Good luck' to FANGS and watched him crawl off into the next garden and out of sight. We waited for five, maybe ten minutes, and then crawled back to our lines and waited for about an hour, which seemed a very long time indeed. Then we heard what we had dreaded: a single shot, coming from the direction FANGS had gone.

We never actually knew what happened to him. FANGS never transmitted by radio and never reappeared, so we presumed that the Germans had caught him and executed him on the spot. A week later, heavy street fighting broke out as the US forces worked their way into Aachen. We went along, too, on other OSS business, but we never caught up with Top Hat and his platoon again, so we never knew what happened to them either.

John and I were active in the Aachen area, with a couple of side trips into France, through most of the winter of 1944 and the early spring of 1945. At one point we worked with a unit of the 35th Infantry Division near Morhange in northern France. I recall vividly that as we progressed up a village street, soldiers spaced out along both sides of it and small arms going off in all directions, a huge Percheron cart horse – a stallion – escaped from his stable and galloped down the street in terror. Sparks flew from its steel horseshoes and his breath steamed in the cold air. He looked like an apparition from hell, and the battle-weary GIs scuttled out of his way – more fearful of the beast than they were of the Germans.

On another occasion we got caught up in a fire fight, with small arms going off all around us. Yet, in the middle of it all, a beautiful blonde French woman dressed in black was wandering around with a basket full of ripe apples, offering them to our troops. When we asked her why, she replied: 'My husband was like these young men. He was killed at the front in 1940, not far from here. He would be pleased that I care enough to give these men apples.' That was a scene I will never forget.

Some time during that winter our small team was visited by the late Colonel David Bruce, head of the OSS in Europe and later Ambassador to the United Kingdom. He put me up for a commission (which John Mowinckel had also done), and I flew back to London to go before the commission board. I turned up in a grubby uniform and was asked what I thought were some dumb questions. I made some cheeky responses, was rejected and returned to my unit.

5

The War Nears its End

At my own request I was reassigned to the OSS unit attached to the 18th Airborne Corps of the First Allied Airborne Army and was sent to Ringway in England for jump training. Everybody who took his or her parachute training at Ringway will remember some of the events for ever. I still recall clearly my first encounter with The Windmill, which was at the peak of a large warehouse, about thirty feet high. Sticking out from the building was a wooden platform, which you climbed up and jumped from. Above it, a wooden drum was attached to the wall of the house. It had four large, flat, wooden paddles on short wooden poles sticking out of it, rather like short canoe paddles. Their pitch could be changed to alter the rate of fall. A rope was wound around the axle of the drum and attached to the parachute harness, where the 'chute pack normally was. After you jumped, the instructor explained all too casually as we sat around the jump hole, legs dangling, the drum's whirling paddles slowed it enough so that when you hit the mat three floors below, you would not be crippled – if you landed according to training, rolling over on one shoulder.

'You're kidding,' said one Frenchman as he stood up on the platform. 'That thing can't work. Is this April the first?'

'I never kid,' replied the instructor. 'This is a real exercise. Get on with it, there are five men waiting behind you.'

'I'll go last,' said the Frenchman. 'If the others make it.'

'You'll go now, old man,' said the instructor, pushing the fellow out. The odd thing was that The Windmill worked. Nobody was hurt.

There was an old barrage balloon at Ringway for night jumps, one of those balloons that used to float over London during the Blitz and over ships at sea. Ringway used the balloon to avoid flying aircraft at night, so that they didn't have to light up the air-field and the drop zone after dark – which might have attracted loitering German aircraft. The first time I went up in the balloon, I was dismayed. This big, ungainly gas bag had a tiny gondola hanging beneath it on frail-looking cables. The gondola had low canvas sides, but no roof. Four trainees and a jumpmaster could only just squeeze in and sit with their backs against the canvas sides, facing each other. There was a Joe hole (a hole through which agents, or 'Joes', jumped) in the middle of the wooden floor, which you jumped through when your turn came. Before jumping, you hooked your parachute's 'static line' on to a hori-zontal metal bar above the hole; the line's webbing strap with its steel safety hook connected the top centre of the parachute canopy to the stationary bar. When the canopy (and its riser lines and the breaker cord) were pulled out of the 'chute pack and reached their full combined length, the breaker cord would snap and the parachute would automatically open – if it had been packed correctly.

'We'll be up at six hundred feet, so it's wise to hook up before you jump,' the instructor reminded us laconically. 'You won't be able to afterwards.' We were jumping without reserve para-chutes – none were issued at Ringway – so everyone hooked up very carefully when his turn came. As the parachutes were packed by the staff, the trainee had no control over what hap-pened. There were nasty stories circulating of roman candles (the British word for streamers, i.e. parachutes that don't open), and of 'chutes opening with a hand-grenade type explosion, throwing out assorted shot bags and folding irons used to fold and pack parachutes properly.

The first 'night of the balloon' was cool and still, and I was sur-prised that we could clearly hear people talking and dogs barking from 600 feet up. I was number two to jump. The first trainee went through the hole, and we could hear everything: the static line whizzing out of the top of his parachute pack, the canopy hissing out after it, the breaker cord snapping, and finally the canopy opening with a soft 'wump' and a 'huff' from the parachutist as his descent was suddenly slowed. Sure enough, a folding iron was ejected at high speed from the opening canopy, and for a moment it whined on its way down to the ground. We could even hear the jumper's second 'huff' when he hit the ground. I went next, praying for a good opening and a good landing. Everything went well until I misjudged the ground. Tensing my legs before loosening them to land, I hit the ground almost straight-legged and was lucky not to be badly hurt.

Next day, we jumped from a Whitley bomber, an ancient wood and fabric machine held together with the proverbial glue. In the centre of the cabin (which had no windows) was the Joe hole. It was in fact a cylinder through the bomb bays, just wide enough for a man and his parachute pack – if he jumped perfectly upright with his face upturned. If he jumped short, the parachute pack hit the edge of the hole and the jumper was propelled against the far side of the cylinder. The result was a bloody cut under the chin. If he jumped too long, his chin hit the other side anyway. Many of us earned little scars, known as Ringing the Bell, and mine was still visible for many years after the war.

The next night jump – our second – was a different story. A cold, drenching English rain poured down the sides of the bag and straight into the gondola, like a waterfall. We were soaked, but the instructor just said, 'A bit of rain never hurt anyone . . . we go on with it.' We did, and he was right – nobody even caught a cold.

Our last training jump was from a C-47, which the British called the Dakota. (The civilian version is the DC-3, which is still in use today. The newest are over fifty years old, but still certifiable to fly.) Compared to the primitive, rattling Whitley, the C-47 was a Rolls-Royce. The jumpmaster explained that we would go out in a stick of eight men, after we had all hooked up our static lines to the overhead steel cable which ran down the centre of the cabin. On his command, we stood up and hooked up, and the first man in our stick jumped through the open rear door. The second man stopped in his tracks, and the jumpmaster yelled at him, 'Go!'

'He's hung up under there,' shouted the trainee. 'It's killing him.' Sure enough, we could all hear the flapping and thumping under the aircraft, despite the engine and slipstream noise.

'Hung up, my arse,' shouted the jumpmaster. 'That's his parachute pack down there, slapping under the tail. He's on the f.....g ground already. Out you go,' and he pushed the jumper out the door.

After Ringway, I went straight back to my unit in France. We were stationed at a country estate near Poissy, outside Paris, in rather palatial quarters. I was issued with an OSS tear-gas pencil – a single-barrel one-shot cylinder that looked like a thicker-than-usual fountain pen. You unscrewed the top, inserted a cartridge into the barrel and screwed the top on again. Then, when you pressed the ball at the end of the pocket clip, the pencil fired. However, nobody had told me how to use the pencil – it was, supposedly, obvious – so when I took it up to my room and fired it out of the window, I got a full dose of tear gas, whose effects lasted for half an hour. I'd overlooked the fact that a warm house on a cold evening draws air into the window. I told nobody in the unit, and it was not until some years afterwards that I told that story against myself.

My OSS airborne unit's last operation of the European war was in the huge Allied landing at Wesel, on the Rhine. It also turned out to be the last Allied airborne landing in Europe before the war ended – and the biggest. It was also the best planned and executed, although our part of it was not a success. We had seven agents in our unit, a collection of tough French, Belgian and Luxembourg men, who had survived five years of war. One of them was my old friend Wenzel Profant, who had negotiated with the old guard on the Luxembourg border in September 1944. These agents were dressed as forced labourers, and as each man carried half a radio, they had to work in pairs. They were due to be dropped just short of the German lines, at the very outer perimeter of the drop zone. Once on the ground, they were to scurry from the landing site on the drop zone's outer edge, slip through the confused German lines, set up concealed observation points and radio back tactical intelligence. Then they were to 'retreat' with the German forces as far as they could with reasonable safety, reporting as they went.

We also had two captured German military Volkswagens. Each

car was crewed by two German-speaking OSS men (mid-westerners), who were dressed as German soldiers, an officer and his driver. They were packed into gliders and also landed at the edge of the drop zone. Their job was to drive like hell through the German lines, acting as if they were escaping the Allied attack. Once behind German lines, they would cruise about collecting short-term tactical intelligence and radio it back to us.

The 18th Airborne Corps' commanding general gave us space on two gliders for our Volkswagens; our agents and the headquarters of our small unit, which was under the command of Captain Vinciguerra, were found room in a C-47. After the landing, we established our headquarters inside the drop zone and prepared to receive the intelligence by radio from the agents and the two VW crews. We were then to sort it out and pass it along as quickly as possible to the G-2s of the 17th Airborne Division and the 18th Airborne Corps.

However, Murphy's Law ('If something can go wrong, it will') was king of our unit that day, 24 March 1945. It was an operation in which everything that could go wrong did just that. One glider received German cannon fire and the Volkswagen's driver – Sergeant 'Easy' Stelterman – was wounded before they hit the ground. The other glider landed safely, but, as I recall, the engine of the VW failed to start in time to allow credible passage through the German lines. The agents, to a man, apparently holed up in haystacks and abandoned buildings and reported nothing. They later claimed that intense small-arms fire had made them go to ground. We all thought that they had decided to survive the war, which was obviously drawing to a close. Since they were civilians, there was nothing that we could do to them anyway except to fire them.

One vivid memory I have is of the German farm outside Wesel where we spent the night of the 24th after rounding up our stragglers. The farmer had turned his pigsty into a jail for Russian prisoners of war. There were no beds, or blankets, or heat, only one wooden peg driven into the stone wall on which each man hung his clothes. The pig run was fenced with barbed wire, which was also stretched across it two feet off the muddy ground, and the prisoners had to crawl in the mud and pig droppings to get fresh air. This was the first time I saw evidence of the standard Nazi treatment for Russian prisoners of war doing forced labour.

Although our OSS unit had not distinguished itself at Wesel, the Allied armies as a whole had. For the first time an entire airborne army, 22,000 men of the US 17th and British 6th Airborne Divisions, had landed on German soil as a fighting unit: the First Allied Airborne Army. The jump met all its objectives and thus became, I believe, the only completely successful Allied jump of the war. Finally, we were now crowding the Nazis into the Ruhr, their industrial heartland, and nothing could stop us.

An interesting anecdote on parachutes: our personnel parachutes were camouflaged silk, while our reserve and cargo 'chutes were made of nylon. Both were in great demand in Paris, and the soldiers who followed behind the parachute drop at Wesel to clean up the battlefield also gathered up the 'chutes which littered the ground. Thousands of them 'found their way' to Paris, where they became the first wedding dresses made of decent material since the German occupation began in 1940.

Our diminutive twenty-man OSS parachute unit returned by road to Poissy, from where we had left on 24 March. We immediately started to refit and prepare for the next operation. We were still officially attached to the 18th Airborne Corps, and its commanding general was very gentlemanly about our failure at Wesel. He scheduled aircraft space for us on the planned Allied jump into Czechoslovakia in May 1945. That jump was to reduce the so-called Nazi Redoubt in the Czech mountains, which was thought to have been selected for a last stand by Hitler's SS fanatics. There, too, we were to undertake tactical intelligence operations, and this time we were all determined to make it work.

The Redoubt jump was cancelled because of VE Day – Victory in Europe – on 8 May 1945. We felt particularly lucky because the 18th Airborne Corps had projected over thirty per cent casualties on the Czech landing alone, mostly due to the rough, steep, partly wooded and partly rocky terrain.

It was my twenty-first birthday, and we were paid and given a weekend pass to Paris. Four of us took a jeep as far as Versailles, where we decided to begin celebrating. We parked the jeep and began bar crawling. We became quite rowdy, wildly happy to have survived so many gruelling years of war, and one man got a bit rough. 'For fun', he broke the antenna off an MP jeep which happened to be parked outside a bordello. Two MPs, who were just leaving the bordello, pulled their .45 automatics and ordered us to freeze. We ran, but they chased us into an unlit alley and fired, hitting the culprit in the head. When we stopped to help him, we were of course caught. Luckily, he was not badly hurt. However, we had to spend the night in jail. Our very angry CO – Captain Vinciguerra – rescued us in the morning, chewed us out and gave us the choice of staying in Europe in the army of occupation or going to the Far East. I chose the Far East because I believed that almost all Germans had supported Hitler, and the idea of living among them was very distasteful.

My orders came through sending me 'home', to a country I had known about and loved all my life, but had never seen. I was to report to OSS headquarters in Washington DC, then to Area F – an OSS training and rest camp better known as the Congressional Country Club, in Potomac, Maryland.

The Atlantic crossing was interminable. On a US navy C-2, we plodded slowly along the north Atlantic in a huge convoy, which only broke up as we neared land. Rumour had it that the Japanese navy was sending submarines into the Atlantic to knock off US troops before they could be transferred to the Pacific. In the opinion of the more cynical soldiers, however, the US navy had simply forgotten to release its ships from convoys. Our convoy station was right astern of a small and incredibly smelly banana boat, which must have been carrying bananas from North Africa to the US. The little ship bobbed up and down like a cork even in the smallest waves, filling the air behind it with the stench of rotting bananas.

Our ship had about 400 American prisoners of war just released from Nazi camps – US soldiers, sailors and airmen. They were still trying to get used to what was relatively good food compared to their prison rations, and were prone to sea-sickness. They had to file past the open engine-room door on their way to meals, inhaling the hot oil and diesel fumes that bil-lowed up from the bowels of the engine room. Many men couldn't take it and went back on deck to be sick; they then retired to their berths to recuperate in cots a dozen or so high in the hold. The stalwart souls who got through the chow line and managed to eat, and who went up on deck to try to find some fresh air, were then done in by the banana boat. I felt for them, but thoroughly enjoyed many of the 'luxuries' I had barely seen for years: fresh milk, butter, bacon and eggs. However, my stomach had shrunk and, try as I might, I couldn't eat that much.

When we finally broke convoy and got away from the banana boat, the torment of those unhappy ex-prisoners of war didn't end. We sailed due west with a following wind that was exactly the speed of the ship. A relentless summer sun and the cloud of smells that we dragged along with us were too much for most of them. Fortunately, a couple of dozen men, including me, were immune to sea-sickness and were healthy, so we played poker, told war stories and did our best to enjoy the trip. I did however learn one lesson on that journey: some foolish men lost their entire back pay for all the years they had been prisoners of war – the poker sharks saw to that – and to this day I never gamble more than a few dollars at a time.

The first time I saw my own country was on the fourth of July 1945, when, with great relief, we arrived in Boston harbour. I was paged on the dock by a Red Cross lady, who said that I must get on a train to New York immediately because my sister was waiting there. It turned out that Sue had joined the OSS and was leaving soon for a posting in England. We had a couple of days together with Mother before she left, and I was tremendously impressed by New York.

I rested and was debriefed at Area F. While I was there, some strange things happened. The first was a visit to the camp psychologist – a requirement whose value I couldn't see at the time, or since for that matter. He wanted to know which parent I liked best, my father or mother. I couldn't answer, since, although they were both so completely different, I loved them equally. He shrugged irritatedly and continued, 'Did your palms sweat when you jumped out of airplanes?'

I was dumbfounded. How could a person remember that, and why did it matter? 'I never noticed . . . why do you ask?' I replied.

'I do the questioning, Doyle. You do the answering. Did you soil your pants under enemy fire?'

'No, sir.'

'Can you still get an erection?'

I suddenly realised how to end this ridiculous interview: 'Yes, sir. But not now, thank you.' The implication that he might be gay and had made an improper advance was clear, but he obviously couldn't make anything of it without others wondering, too. He gave up, wrote something in a little booklet and dismissed me with an angry grunt.

Another strange happening at Area F concerned a professor of European history at an Ivy League college, who had been recruited into the OSS by General 'Wild Bill' Donovan. The professor had made a name for himself in the OSS by using his considerable imagination to conceive and run a successful operation into occupied Europe. With the war in Europe over, the professor turned his attention to Japan, a nation about which he knew next to nothing. He read up on the country and learned that a fox seen at night was, to the superstitious Japanese, a symbol of catastrophe to come. Thus, several foxes seen at various places would, the professor concluded, cause widespread fear and erosion of the will to continue the war. On top of that, if they glowed, they would appear to be ghosts of foxes, symbols of utter calamity for Japan. The professor went so far as to claim that the effect might even be a Japanese surrender.

The US navy fought the assignment, even hinting at the merits of a parachute drop (which would pass the buck to the air force), but the professor wanted a beach landing and he won. A dozen foxes in cages were transferred aboard a submarine as it approached Japan. While they lay off the landing beach, the OSS man handling the foxes combed fluorescent paint into each fox's fur, loaded them into a rubber dinghy and rowed them to the beach, where he let them loose. He began to row back out to sea, and hadn't gone more than a few yards when, to his horror, the bright moonlight revealed that the foxes were sitting casually on the beach licking the fluorescent paint off themselves and off each other.

The very same professor had what he modestly called another brilliant idea: to drop a string of OSS parachutists, ten miles apart, across the waist of the Thai Peninsula (Thailand was then called Siam). The parachutists would then work their way north, recruiting and training the locals until they had raised an army of resistance capable of dealing damaging blows to the Japanese troops in Siam.

A group of French-speaking OSS parachutists were asked to

volunteer. There were about fifty parachutists in the briefing room, and the professor outlined his plan to a silent, very sceptical group. At the end of his presentation, one of the officers raised his hand and said, 'Sounds like quite a plan, sir, but most of us in the audience know each other and I note that we're all French speakers.'

'Of course,' replied the professor. 'That's because the Siamese speak French. It's their national language.'

'Not at all,' replied the officer. 'I grew up in Siam and never met a soul who spoke French. I believe you're thinking of Indochina . . .'

This time, General Donovan sent the professor back to the Ivy League. The lessons learnt from the professor's performance, however, were invaluable: always do your homework and acquire all the information that bears on an operation before you set it in motion. But above all expect Murphy's Law to dominate operations. In fact, it sometimes seemed to me that Murphy's Law was, on balance, rather optimistic.

The atomic bombs dropped on Japan ended the war before our rest and training were finished, which was a stroke of luck for me as well as for countless other Allied servicemen. The Allied armies were projecting very heavy casualties on landing in Japan, and we had been told that half a million of us – especially those scheduled to land by parachute – would be casualties in the first month. Whether or not that was an exaggerated estimate, it's little wonder that so many Americans welcomed the news that we had brought the war to an end by dropping the bombs on Japan. Like many thousands of other US troops slated to parachute into Japan, I probably owe my life to those two atomic bombs.

I was at Area F for only a couple of weeks and then went on leave. My mother and grandmother had by then rented an apartment at the Governor Shepherd building, which was, by chance, very close to OSS headquarters, so I moved in with them.

The time had come to leave the OSS and the US army. The OSS had taught me the value of intelligence in general and of espionage in particular, in war. It was clear that the United States would need a good espionage service in peacetime as well, but my first priority was to resume my interrupted education. A college degree was a must. I had more 'points' towards a discharge than most, counting my time with the British army, my service overseas and my four battle stars, so I was notified that I could escape at once. Having joined the US Army overseas, I could be discharged at any army post in the world.

I chose Fort Logan in Colorado – the nearest post to Golden, where my father had attended the Colorado School of Mines from 1906 to 1909. He had enjoyed Golden and had often spoken about it and the sleepy little town of Boulder to the north along the edge of the Front Range of the Rockies. It was just as beautiful as he had said, so I decided to attend the University of Colorado in Boulder. No sooner had I signed up, got rooms in a fraternity and a job washing dishes in a sorority, than a long, black limousine pulled up outside the fraternity house. Inside was one of my father's Princeton classmates, 'Ducky' Swann, who owned and operated a music store in Denver. Ducky was very insistent that I go to Princeton instead of UC. He had even talked to my mother, who agreed with him. 'We all want you there. The class will give you a scholarship.' He handed me a train ticket to New York City, which, in a moment of weakness, I accepted, knowing that I would miss the wild mountainous beauty, the clean clear air, the skiing and the ice hockey that Colorado offered.

At Princeton, I was interviewed by the Dean of Admissions, who was another classmate of my father's. He was a gruff but friendly, straightforward man who told me that I was to enter the university as a second-term freshman. I pointed out that I had already completed an academic year at Cambridge and had expected to be accepted at Princeton as a first-term sophomore, if not a junior. The war, I added, had been a learning experience in itself. He smiled and said that I could either take the entrance exam or accept his offer. Since I had done no formal studying for over two years, the exam looked a bit risky, so I accepted. He then advised me that the scholarship I had been promised by Ducky Swann was to be $100 per term, something of a disappointment.

Once admitted to the class of 1949, I studied foreign policy, history, and French and Spanish literature. I also sang in the choir and, for the first time in my life, read as much as I could. The new Firestone Library opened at the end of my junior year, and it was a thrill to have a carrel of my own in which to study. I did well enough in Princeton, majoring in economics and graduating cum laude. I should have done better, but in an eerie repetition of my experience at Colet Court, I tangled with a French literature professor, a former Frenchman who was now a naturalised American. He insisted that the French words for the blow of a fist (*coup de poing*) was pronounced '*coup de pogne*', whereas I insisted that the French pronounced it '*coup de point*'. I was right, but when he finally looked it up in *Larousse* and realised his mistake, he was so infuriated that he reduced my grade in his course to a simple pass (4), which cost me Phi Beta Kappa and Summa Cum Laude.

The subjects at Princeton which were later useful in my espionage career included history, economics, literature, anthropology and international relations. I was an early attender at the university's School of Public and International Affairs (SPIA). I was also exposed to US national politics for the first time, and realised that I had known literally nothing about this area of American life.

It was normal to wonder if mining engineering would be an appealing post-college career – after all, my father had been very enthusiastic about it – and events quickly gave me the chance to see one aspect of mining from close up. During the Christmas break of 1945–6, I applied for a passport to go to the UK the following June to visit my mother, who was still spending her summers in the house at Strete. Ruth Shipley, the well-known chief of the State Department's Passport Division, was a family friend and had the reputation of a tigress. She called me into her office and said: 'I'm not going to give you a passport this year, David. You've lost too much time during the war. Keep going at Princeton and I'll give you one next summer.' The look on her face when I started to protest told me that next summer might be in the balance as well.

Without telling her, I applied to the Kennecott Copper Company via a former protegé of my father, Russell Parker, who was then senior vice president. He arranged for me to go up to a large ilmenite prospecting camp in northern Quebec. I went by train to Quebec City, by river steamer to Havre St Pierre, and by bush pilot to the prospecting camp. We lived under canvas, cooking outdoors, eating fish and small game we caught locally, and enjoying twenty or more hours of daylight every day. I learned how to build a canoe and how to handle it properly, how to build a log cabin, how to pack a huge load using a 'tump' line, and how to tickle for trout in a stream. The work wasn't all that stimulating, but it was gruelling. Each day we broke into parties of four, took a canoe and went to the starting point of our team's prospect line for that day. Sometimes we had to portage from lake to lake, so it paid to be in shape. Only out on the water could we get away from the plagues of mosquitoes and black flies that formed cones around our heads. We also had to walk dead straight lines carrying a magnetic dip needle over terrain which was all old glaciatic moraine with huge, moss-covered boulders. It was a wonder that we found our way back to camp in the evening, let alone any ilmenite deposits – from which titanium is extracted.

As there was no future in mining without a university or mining school degree, and as espionage still called more strongly to me, I decided to return to Princeton early, and left the prospecting camp after only two months.

I had kept in touch with Lyman B. Kirkpatrick Jr, my CO in the SUSSEX Plan, who had joined the CIA the day it was formed in 1947. Through him, I was able to join the CIA shortly after my graduation from Princeton in January 1949. The reasons for choosing an espionage career were simple: I already had friends in the CIA, or who were planning to apply for admission, and I knew what the work would involve. The idea also appealed because of Princeton University's motto: 'Princeton in the Nation's Service', which reflects my own attitude. Such sentiments may seem old-fashioned today, but they were very much a part of the country's mood back then.

Before joining the CIA, however, I went to see General Donovan in his Wall Street office. As former OSS chief, I wanted his advice. As well as the job in the CIA, I had been offered a job in Chicago, where a well-known industrialist who was an ex-OSS officer was forming a private espionage service. The purpose was to use barter trade to finance operations, a necessary activity at that time because there were only three 'hard' currencies in the world trading arena: the Swiss franc, the Portuguese escudo and the US dollar. I was a nobody in the OSS, but Donovan was gracious enough to agree to see me.

'Should I join the private intelligence organisation that's forming up in Chicago, sir,' I asked Donovan, 'or go down to Washington and join this new thing called the CIA?'

The General was silent for a moment, pondering my question. Then he said, smiling, 'The Chicago idea is fun, but it won't work. No serious government will bank on getting its intelligence from a private firm. When you graduate from Princeton, go on down to Washington and join the CIA, young man. But I fear that within ten years it will begin to look like the Department of Agriculture.'

So the CIA it was, but unhappily that was one of 'Wild Bill' Donovan's more accurate predictions.

6

Joining the CIA

'What is called "foreknowledge" cannot be elicited from spirits, nor from gods, nor by analogy with past events, nor from calculations. It must be obtained from men who know the enemy situation.' This was written by Sun Tzu, who then remarked that, 'Now there are five sorts of secret agents to be employed. These are native, inside, doubled, expendable, and living.'

Tu Mu, expanding in the ninth century AD on Sun Tzu's explanation that, 'Inside agents are enemy officials whom we employ', said:

> Among the official class there are worthy men who have been deprived of office; others who have committed errors and been punished. There are sycophants and minions who are covetous of wealth. There are those who wrongly remain long in low office; those who have not obtained responsible positions, and those whose sole desire is to take advantage of times of trouble to extend the scope of their own abilities. There are those who are two-faced, changeable and deceitful, and those who are always sitting on the fence. As far as all such are concerned you can secretly inquire after their welfare, reward them liberally

with gold and silk, and so tie them to you. Then you may
rely on them to seek out the real facts of the situation in
their country, and to ascertain its plan directed against
you. They can create cleavages between the sovereign and
his ministers so that these are not in harmonious accord.

There is no better thumbnail sketch of the need for, and methods
of, espionage than those Chinese words written so long ago. Had
Europe's officials been influenced primarily by Sun Tzu and his
many Chinese commentators, rather than Clausewitz's exhorta-
tions to total warfare, the First and Second World Wars would
have gone very differently. By 1947 this was apparent to
Washington, and national preventive espionage in peacetime at
last came into fashion. I joined the CIA in March 1949.

Whereas the OSS had taught me the value of espionage in
wartime, a career in the CIA was convincing as to the value and
the realities of peacetime espionage. The effort, difficulties and
cost of seeking protected knowledge about world affairs and
acquiring foreknowledge of events soon became clear.

I served those first eighteen months in Washington in Lyman
Kirkpatrick's domestic operations division – the segment of the
CIA that collected intelligence from various sources in the US. I
worked at first in what was called the Aliens Branch, which handled foreign defectors – mostly Soviets and Eastern Europeans –
after they reached the United States.

Edward Fitch Hall, the Branch chief, was one of the finest
men I have ever known. A former *New York Times* editor, he had
a quick wit, a wonderfully rich stock of stories, and a gentleness
of character that one rarely finds. Eddie set me thinking again
about Communism, Fascism and democracy, and to ask how
we – my colleagues and I – could counter the first two and help
save the third. He showed me how theory fitted in with practice
in peacetime, and especially how to match what had to be done
with what we were able to do – and make it work. He mixed the
abstract with the practical, describing a world I knew well but
had never quite seen that way. And he laughed both with me and
at me, teaching that while God may watch every sparrow that
falls, He always has another to replace it.

Eddie worked me hard, forcing the pace of editing field
reports and interrogation results. I'll never forget those first long

days, when eight hours' daily reading files at a desk seemed like an infinity – a torment I would never be able to survive. He laughed, saying, 'Within a month the days won't be long enough.' He was right. The work was so fascinating that the days were soon far too short, and we often worked well into the night.

The work in the Aliens Branch was particularly interesting because of the trickle of defectors from the USSR and the Soviet Union's Eastern European satellites. We continued friendly interrogations that had begun overseas, where most of them had defected, and we tried to resettle them successfully in the US or elsewhere in the West if they preferred. Some of the interrogations lasted for months and even years, if the defector was particularly knowledgeable. Defectors from the KGB, for example, would be asked to identify and describe the jobs, competence, personal details and defectability of as many of their former colleagues as possible from passport, surveillance and other photos of all Soviets serving abroad. As photos became available, we would show them to each KGB or GRU defector. That process could take a very long time.

The Director of Central Intelligence (DCI) had the statutory authority, as I recall, to permit 110 authentic intelligence defectors to be given US citizenship each year, but the CIA did not accept defectors automatically. Each defector had to demonstrate his or her bona fides. If we already knew who the defector was and what he or she did, his or her bona fides were quickly accepted as qualified for asylum and resettlement in the US, or elsewhere, with our help. Others gained acceptance by giving us so much good information that a) it was clear they were who they said they were, and b) their intelligence and related information was of such great value that it was highly unlikely that the other side had 'sent' them to us as doubles.

Most Cold War defectors from the Communist side had no apologies to make: they were acting in the noblest tradition of defying autocracy. They changed sides for various reasons, including political dissidence, revenge, to escape danger, to seek freedom or to make a statement, but rarely for money or other personal gain. Those who defected from the Soviet Union were a special breed of people who deserve particular mention. They did immense damage to the USSR. The early defectors of the 1920s and 1930s provided the first revelations of what life was

really like in what was then the world's most closed society. To
the Soviet leaders they were traitors, but to the West these defectors were true men who had turned their backs on one of the
greatest frauds in history – the so-called Peoples' Paradise.

From the start of the Cold War, a trickle of defectors from the
KGB and its immediate predecessors arrived in the free world,
people like Golitsyn, Myagkov, Petrov, Rastvorov, Deriabin, and
more recently Gordievsky and Sheymov. They provided a series
of updates in our knowledge of the Chekists, and our first real
look at the organisations that had made the USSR the world's
biggest counter-espionage state. Through them we received
information on how the KGB was structured, who worked where
in it, what their plans and targets were, what their budgets were
and what they knew about us.

Defectors from the KGB or GRU generally needed a sense of
'belonging to', and being appreciated by, the US Intelligence
community. Unfortunately, some were not treated in the manner
they felt they deserved, and in some cases they were quite right.
Some either went sour or re-defected back to the USSR. Some
were prima donnas and there was no way to please them. Some
spent too much of their energy (and our time) feuding with each
other but, by and large, they were by far the West's best window
into the KGB and the GRU, and their allies around the world.

That rare breed of brave men, defectors-in-place, must also
be given a mention. They are defectors who agree to remain
ostensibly loyal employees of their country's intelligence service,
but who are in fact reporting to the 'enemy' services such as the
CIA. Oleg Gordievsky was just such a hero. So were some of the
dozen or more Russians executed as a result of fingering by
Ames (see page 247). Defectors-in-place often recruited themselves. Being fully trained and well aware of what interested the
US Intelligence community and how to accomplish their tasks,
they were particularly valuable. The risks they ran were of
course horrendous, and CIA traitors such as Ames have had a
very negative effect on potential defectors-in-place. Nobody in
the former KGB or in today's Russian Intelligence Service is
going to defect and stay in place if he knows (or feels he can
assume) that there is a mole inside the CIA who will unmask
him.

Defectors, especially those from the KGB, tended to be

mavericks. Some – particularly those with protectors in the hierarchy – lived out their nonconformity and got away with it. Most, however, survived (until they physically defected) by pretending to conform and not showing any of their real feelings about the system. This produced a severe strain that could lead to violent releases of tension after they were in safe hands. Very few defectors were easy to handle, and unhappily too many were handled badly and without adequate consideration for their feelings.

Victor Sheymov wrote a book called *Tower of Secrets* (Naval Institute Press, Annapolis, 1992), which is one of the most fascinating and valuable accounts of life in the KGB that I have ever read, especially in its description of the persistence, emptiness, brutality and danger to the free world of a regime that we in the CIA knew about but were unable to convey adequately to the US public.

Although Sheymov's book leaves a few important questions unanswered – for example, what were the results of the KGB 8th Chief Directorate's successful 'star wars' effort (which long preceded ours and may have led to the US massive Strategic Defense Initiative)? And how did the USSR acquire the U-2 flight plans at all, let alone three to four days before the flights? – one assumes that he passed along his ideas on these subjects to his CIA debriefers. In any event, his book is a must for anyone interested in the KGB and its successors.

He makes a case that the CIA felt it had to exercise rigid control over its agents, whereas the KGB did not. In my experience, the German branch early on did try to exercise rigid control and tried to convince all of us of the need for it, but in my real world, and that of most people I worked with, one had to be flexible. The 'perfect' agent, for example, was so deeply motivated and skilled that one worked with him, not over him. To cajole, urge and argue was all right, but to try to play gauleiter with a star agent was a ticket to failure. On the other hand, the Ames case is a perfect example of what sloppy control does to an imperfect, sloppy agent.

Sheymov's book tells how the KGB recruited (often under threat of physical harm if refused) one informant for every three Soviet citizens – a figure other defectors have also given. The severe difficulty of recruiting Soviets and other Communists was of course due to the extensive protective measures they took to defend against such recruitments – as Sheymov so well describes.

The first defector case I was involved in was in 1949. An elderly Russian geologist had defected in Turkey. He was full of fascinating trivia – such as how to fry eggs on blazing hot desert sand without their getting gritty – and he had a stock of amusing Russian anti-Stalin stories, but he didn't qualify as a bona-fide intelligence defector, so we advised that he be accepted into the US on a green card as a political refugee not as one of the DCI's quota.

The next defector I handled was a Russian cross-country skier, who knew the Finno-Soviet border and its guards very well. He proudly showed me his invention – a pair of folding skis – and explained at length how he had designed and built them. They were very compact and were hinged in the middle, so that they could be folded back against each other. Being a skier, I was thoroughly intrigued and began to ask him a lot of questions: how secure were the recessed locks that kept them in the open position? What metals had he used to make the hinges and the locks strong enough to endure tremendous forces? He quickly interrupted, saying that I was going off on a tangent. The skis were merely his means of getting out of the USSR so that he could defect. He had been able to hide them under his clothing when he got close to the border, then miss the mines by skiing on deep snow. Would I be good enough to put him in touch with whoever wanted to know about the Finno-Soviet border area? I did so at once, and of course the folding skis were considered interesting potential border-crossing devices.

The most interesting case while I was in the Aliens Branch was the double defection of two Soviet air-force pilots, Anatoly Barsov and Pyotr Pirogov, who had defected in Linz, Austria, bringing their aircraft with them. There was a good deal of international publicity about the affair, as well as the usual outrage on the part of the USSR. The safe-house in which they were interrogated had already been selected and rented before I was brought onto the case. It was a very nice town house in Georgetown, which was far bigger than was needed, and the senior officer who chose it had his wife redecorate it at great expense to the taxpayer. Incredibly, however, they had failed to notice that there was no rear entrance. The kitchen entrance was down some stone stairs and under the front door. As a result, all traffic into and out of the house was visible for a long way up and down the street. I commented that it hardly seemed like a safe-house and was invited (because of my youth and 'inexperience') to stick to things I knew about. Luckily the interrogations went well, and there was no sign of KGB surveillance.

Eventually, the two defectors were resettled in New York. Pirogov stayed in the US and wrote a book about his experi-ences, *Why I Escaped* (Duell, Sloan and Pearce, NY, 1950), but Barsov opted to return to the USSR. He knew that he would be executed, but didn't care. He told Pirogov that he couldn't stand freedom and planned to re-defect. Pirogov then informed us. One officer reacted by proposing that we arrange a terminal 'accident' for Barsov so that he couldn't tell the Soviets anything about us. Somehow this proposal reached Dick Helms (then Chief, FI [Foreign Intelligence], an ancestor of the DO). Dick, who later became DCI, exploded, saying that we weren't like the Soviets and didn't kill people who disagreed with us. The officers I knew in the Agency were almost all of Dick's opinion. There was occasional talk of doing away with someone, but in my expe-rience it was mainly the letting off of steam. Barsov was duly executed by the Soviets after his return to the USSR.

After two years in the Aliens Branch, I accepted an offer to go out to California to work in the overt San Francisco office. It took two more years, 1950–2, before I was able to get a transfer into the covert side, which had been my goal since early 1949.

Ann Forbes, my bride of two months, and I arrived in San Francisco in late 1950 and rented a two-bedroom apartment in the Sunset district, which was still being developed. It had paper-thin walls and a military neighbour, who became known as 'Colonel Burper', for obvious reasons. Although he performed noisily each evening after dinner, we stayed in that apartment for the two years we were there; it was our first child Katherine's initial home.

Although there was no sign on the outer door, the office in San Francisco declared to all who asked that we were a CIA office. Our job was to go out and seek intelligence and related informa-tion from people with foreign knowledge, connections or travel. We had no cover and we carried identity booklets (called cre-dentials), which identified us in true name as CIA officers. It was

an interesting job, spotting, meeting and interviewing businessmen, missionaries, journalists, pilots, ships' captains and others
who worked overseas or had regular foreign contacts. Our office
gathered positive intelligence (political, military, economic,
socio-demographic, topographic, agronomic, and so on) from all
over the world, with special emphasis on exploitation of overt
sources with knowledge of the USSR, its satellites, and Red
China.

There was no time for boredom: in one day I might interview
a missionary forced to leave Red China about his experiences
there, followed by a businessman about bauxite deposits in West
Africa; the next day I might talk to an author close to the Dalai
Lama and an Armenian who had managed to flee the USSR, and
then in the evening a journalist who had befriended Yugoslav
President, Josip Brosz Tito. We produced a large flow of intelligence that was much appreciated by headquarters. We also
successfully supported certain headquarters' elements: for example, by arranging non-official cover for staff agents (i.e.
intelligence officers under non-official cover).

Among many other things, this tour of duty taught me how to
convince US businessmen to co-operate with what many even
then called the enemy – the US Government and its hated
Internal Revenue Service (IRS). We had to explain that although
we CIA officers were government officials, we were not from the
IRS or the FBI. We only wanted information and had no intention of blowing the whistle on malefactors who – despite their
crimes – had significant intelligence about events overseas. When
they understood that we didn't want to know about any of their
peccadilloes, they almost always became very co-operative. Some
even became close personal friends. Only once in twenty months
was I given a flat 'No' response from a potential source.

The office chief was retired US Navy Rear Admiral Marion C.
Cheek, who had been fleet intelligence officer for Admiral Halsey
during the Second World War. Cheek's face was seamed with
lines, to the point where someone remarked that he looked as if
he'd spent his life in a frying pan. He was ostensibly crusty and
old-fashioned, but below the surface was a warm-hearted,
fatherly man of great sensitivity and wisdom. His guidance
helped me to become a successful gatherer of raw intelligence
reports.

One day we got a message from Washington requesting us to send an officer to interview a famous cartoonist. The cartoonist was of Russian origin, and his cartoons were full of jibes at the Soviets. The material he put out indicated a pretty good under-standing of the Soviet system and daily life under the Kremlin. We were to ask him if he had any contacts inside the Soviet Union. If so, would he care to tell us about them? If he agreed, we would of course like to send his sources ostensibly innocuous questions through the cartoonist's good offices.

Cheek selected me to go to see the cartoonist. We agreed that it was probably a very long shot, but orders were orders. Stan Delaplane, a very well-known columnist who was a good friend of mine, telephoned the cartoonist to introduce me and explain my CIA role. Shortly after, I telephoned the cartoonist, who invited me to come right over. We met in his office, high up in a large building overlooking San Francisco Bay. I was wearing a business suit, with my prescription sun glasses in my pocket, and I showed him my CIA credentials. He heard me out, laughed and said that he had no such contacts. In fact, he said, the notion was absurd – a reaction I privately shared. We chatted for about ten minutes about inconsequential things, and then I left.

Waiting at the elevator, I put on my glasses and turned to look out of the windows at the gorgeous view of the Bay. There he was. He had followed me into the hall and was looking in my direction with an amused gaze. We waved goodbye to each other. I thought little of it at the time, since in those days CIA people passed virtually unnoticed in the West, and we were certainly not the targets of media hostility that we later became.

The next week an interview with the cartoonist appeared in a national magazine. In the article, he made much of the fact that a CIA 'spook' had recently visited him to ask if he had sources inside the USSR. That, at least, was accurate. But his story dressed me in a trench coat, with scarf and hat, and my sun glasses became sinister peepers through which the 'spook' had stared at him suspiciously. My questions had been ridiculous – that much I agreed with from the start – and the tone of the tale could not have been more slanted if it had been KGB disinfor-mation. Not long afterwards, CIA headquarters sent us a message asking what idiot had made such a fool of himself in front of this most famous and influential man. The message arrived at the end of the working day. When my secretary showed it to me, I recall feeling that maybe my new career was over before it had really begun.

Admiral Cheek invited me to meet him in his apartment that evening. It was still light, and we stood on his fifteenth-floor balcony looking out towards Sausalito and the Golden Gate Bridge. As I arrived, one of San Francisco's many small earthquakes occurred and the apartment swayed like a ship at sea. Cheek swayed with it, a huge grin on his face as he clasped the balcony railing with both hands.

'Just like being at sea, David my boy,' he said. 'By the way, I sent a message back telling Washington that I was the idiot who saw that silly cartoonist. And I reminded them that the idea was theirs in the first place. They haven't responded.'

Usually the chief executive officers (CEOs) of large corporations were intelligent and well educated, but now and then I ran across one who was not as lettered as one might have expected. I visited the CEO of a very large, successful US agricultural corporation, which traded internationally, including with the USSR. In my effort to tell the CEO what the CIA did and how broad our interest in the USSR and the other Communist countries was, I made the mistake of assuming that a man in his position was erudite. 'We're interested in everything,' I told him. 'In fact, we have very catholic tastes.'

'That's all right,' he replied, looking a bit uncomfortable. 'I have no prejudices, you know. My daughter dates a Catholic.'

John Edgar Hoover, the man who put the FBI on the map, hated the CIA because it was his competition. The CIA had 'usurped' (his word) the FBI's rightful prime area of foreign operations: Latin America. It had been given the job of collecting intelligence in what had been, until 1947, an FBI intelligence and counter-intelligence fiefdom. Despite the fact that President Harry S. Truman and Congress had ordained that the CIA do the job, Hoover had his boys make life as difficult as possible for us.

On one occasion, I approached a lady business executive in San Francisco and asked her to provide the CIA with copies of those reports from her company's overseas activities that contained foreign intelligence. I also asked her to introduce me to any colleagues who might have useful information obtained overseas. She quite naturally wanted to know how she could believe that my CIA credentials were real. Unaware of Hoover's standing orders against helping the CIA, I gave her the number of the FBI office in town and suggested that she call them to verify that I was indeed a CIA officer. We had what was supposed to be liaison with the local FBI office – they knew our names and had agreed to vouch for us – but the agent she got on the phone listened to her request and then replied, 'Well, you asked.'

'Is he really with the CIA?' she repeated.

'You asked, didn't you?'

He was unwilling to say any more. She gave up, but fortunately he had angered her so much that she decided to tell me about the call. I explained the uneasy relationship we had with the FBI, and she decided to trust me. She became a very useful source.

On another occasion, I was acquiring sources among the Armenian community in the Fresno area. I called on the FBI agent in charge in Fresno and got a surprisingly warm welcome. We became friends, and he was very helpful pointing me towards those Armenians with family or friends still in the USSR. But he made the mistake of telling his superior that he was helping the CIA. The superior told Hoover, who promptly sent my friend a communication: 'You have twenty-four hours to move, with your family, to Puerto Rico, or your career is terminated.' The poor man had to move his wife, several children and all his effects in that short space of time.

The fear of being too close to us was so great that when one of my closest OSS friends who had joined the FBI was transferred to San Francisco, he didn't dare pick up our friendship again.

To give another example of the lack of co-operation between the two Services, the CIA domestic operations base in one US port city was keeping a low profile in order to do its work better. However, its office was in a building that also housed the local FBI office, which was on the ground floor, whereas the 'secret' CIA office was tucked away on the tenth floor. Nobody was supposed to know it was there, and the FBI had agreed to help protect that security. One day a Soviet sailor from a fishing trawler decided to defect. He walked into the FBI office and, in a thick Russian accent, asked for the CIA. One of the FBI agents told the sailor to go up to the tenth floor, walk east along the corridor and go into room 1010. The Soviet duly did as he was told. The CIA station chief, who was the soul of operational discretion, almost fell off his chair in horror when an unknown, unexpected Soviet not only found the 'secret' CIA office, but walked unannounced through the outer offices into the chief's own room.

People we wanted to interview usually glanced at our true credentials and asked how they could help. Even here, Murphy's Law could be operative. One of our officers showed his credentials for the first time to the chairman of the board of a large oil company. The chairman started to laugh, and when our man looked at his credentials, he discovered that his wife had slipped in an 'I love you' note on the inside lower half of the plastic holder. Fortunately, the chairman was very understanding in spite of our fellow's red face.

I once had to visit a Californian farmhouse in which a recent defector, a former senior Hungarian army colonel, and his family lived. He was reputed to have some sensitive military intelligence which we needed, but which his earlier interrogators had somehow missed. I arrived mid-morning, to find only his wife at home. She spoke almost no English and I spoke no Magyar, but I was able to communicate by signs that I wanted to speak to someone other than her.

'Ah,' she said. 'My husband?' I nodded.

She called to a small boy of about five who was playing outside, and who rushed to his mother's side. She briefed him in rapid-fire Magyar. The boy asked me in very broken English, 'Do you want to speak to "my husband", sir?' I nodded, and off he ran behind the house.

I waited on the porch with the wife. Twice she murmured soothingly, 'My husband, he come.' I asked her if she liked living in California, but she shook her head. She didn't understand. The little boy came back in a couple of minutes, followed by a sight I can still see clearly. The colonel was driving a tractor with which he had been ploughing a field. His back was ram-rod straight, both hands on the steering wheel, and he was looking straight ahead, in a very military fashion. He was dressed in a black business suit, white shirt, blue tie, highly polished boots and a black bowler hat. The little boy introduced his father, proudly, 'Sir, this is my husband.' I managed to keep a straight face.

We talked for an hour, the colonel's broken English being adequate for our purpose. At midday I was offered lunch: a meat stew swimming in fat, but which tasted delicious. During the meal, the son occasionally joined in the conversation with unusually adult remarks for a boy of five. Each time he referred to his father, however, he called him 'my husband'.

The colonel and I talked all afternoon. He was a very formal man, but friendly, very knowledgeable and helpful. The visit was well worth it. As I drove down the lane on the way home, I looked back and saw him once again on his tractor, bowler hat and all.

7

The Clandestine Services

In 1952, I was finally able to get back into the overseas espionage business by transferring to what was then called the Directorate of Plans, also known as the CIA's Clandestine Services. (It is now known as the Directorate of Operations [DO].) The CS was staffed by highly patriotic, motivated, loyal men and women with a strong sense of purpose and integrity. Many were the products of Ivy League colleges and spoke more or less the same ideological and social language. Others were new citizens from various European and other foreign areas, often socialists who had spent the war fighting Fascism first and Communism later. We were variously short or tall, thin or fat, amusing or dour, bright or dull – but we were not the normal run of government bureaucrats. Honesty was taken for granted, as were regular twelve-hour working days and six-day weeks. We were engaged in one of the world's most exciting ventures: using bright and devoted people, and some primitive technology, to find the hidden truth about, and to counter the activities of, a worldwide and very hostile Communist camp.

The great majority in the CS were, and still are, a remarkable collection of highly skilled case officers that took years to build. For example, there are specialists in the recruitment of Russians as agents. These officers know the Russian language, are at ease among Russians, are personally appealing to them, and know enough about Russia to be able at least to talk politics and preferably also Russian history, literature and the arts. They must be able to judge personality and elicit information on the basis of which a successful recruitment pitch can be engineered. The trick is to be outgoing, amicably persuasive and obviously intelligent, the sort of person people want to befriend. Others, who don't have this ability, may instead be expert managers of agents who have already been recruited by someone else. Then there are case officers who become specialists in a particular area, in foreign languages, or in editing reports. The largest pool is of generalists, multi-skilled case officers and managers who combine most, if not all, of these characteristics in one way or another.

Still others are referred to in the CS as technicians. They are a very special breed of experts in such fields as breaking and entering, installing microphones, matching the colours of paint by artificial light, opening locked doors and cracking closed safes, and so on. Other technicians have special skills such as originating secret writing methods and electronic communications techniques, designing and making disguises and concealment devices, and devising ways of invading hostile computer systems.

One of the generalist case officer's jobs is to plan and conduct audio/video operations. He must conceptualise the operation, case the target, draw up the operational plan and get it approved up the line as far as necessary. He must also know the capabilities and limitations of the technicians, and ensure their safety when a planned operation might endanger them. He must be prepared to go into the target with them and share the risk. In fact, he is usually first in and last out.

The following examples give an idea of how very hard it would be, should the CS be badly mutilated or even dismantled, to rebuild this valuable repository of unusual skills and of highly motivated men and women unafraid to use them.

My first job in the CS was in the Projects Branch of the Foreign Intelligence Staff. This small group of half-a-dozen officers screened every espionage project submitted to the Chief, FI (at that time a scholarly man named Gordon Stuart), for his approval. Each one of the hundreds of FI projects came up

annually for approval. Our job was to do the initial vetting for the
FI staff, making sure that each project was properly documented
and performing well, or (if it was a new one) likely to perform
well. We then summarised each project and sent it to various FI
staff elements for further analysis by specialists. Projects requiring commercial cover went to the Cover Branch; those requiring
specialised equipment or disguises went to the Technical Branch,
and so on. Some of the submissions were a few pages in length,
with a few supporting documents relating the project's history,
personnel, product, cost and dangers. Others, especially large
projects with years of activity, arrived in huge files that took days
to read and summarise. Eight years was generally the maximum
project age, from 1947 to 1955, although a few were built on old
OSS operations from the Second World War.

We often called on case officers and/or their managers to come
to the FI staff offices and defend their projects, or explain them
better. After two and a half years, during much of which I ran the
Branch, I was familiar with every espionage project we had and
just about every case officer in the CS. The totality of what we
were doing, less than ten years after the CIA had been formed,
was formidable.

One of my most painful memories was the embarrassment of
having been selected to run the Branch despite the fact that
Maggie X was much older and much more experienced in FI
projects than I. She had laboured in the Branch for three years
and outranked me. Despite the still solid vestiges of a glass ceil-
ing, there were quite a few women in senior and mid-level
managerial positions (as there had been in the OSS), and Maggie
should have been there too. But during a long tour in Europe she
had put the fear of God into too many young officers, who had
later managed to block her upward progress. To her great credit
she never once complained or tried to make me feel uncomfortable, and we became good friends.

During my first years in the CS things began to change for the
worse. Someone stole from the blind man who sold sandwiches
and soft drinks in one of the corridors. The thief bought a sandwich and told the blind man he'd given him a $5 bill. The blind
man gave him back his $4 change, but that night, when his wife
counted the money, he was short of $4. The idea that one of us
would stoop to robbing a blind man was shocking.

Then one of our station chiefs in Asia robbed the till of his own station and, it was said in the corridors, was caught having taken 200,000 operational dollars. Then another senior officer was caught with his hand in the confidential funds' till. The result was an influx of hundreds of finance officers, hired to make sure that no more thefts occurred. Now everything took much longer, and paperwork mounted up. Some saboteur also brought in a whole lot of the brand new Xerox copying machines and paperwork skyrocketed.

Anyone with a building pass could copy classified documents. Worse, we all felt vaguely under suspicion, which in turn further eroded adherence to the rigid code of honour which had been an integral part of the spirit of the early days. All this diminished, but happily did not come close to extinguishing, our remarkably high spirits and strong sense of adventure. We still had mavericks and cowboys – some of great value, plus a few who did damage – but not so many of them. Donovan's prediction was slowly taking shape.

8

The Far East Division

In early 1955, a controversial and expensive project was submitted by the Far East Division to the FI Staff for renewal. There was considerable opposition to this because it would be very costly, and eventually the proposal was put before a large meeting between senior staff members and the FE Division brass. I liked the project, which was producing well and was cost-effective, and defended it vigorously. Shortly thereafter – as a sort of unexpected reward – I was offered a job as head of a Far Eastern country desk

The 'desk' was one of the largest in the CS, with some forty personnel located in one of the temporary buildings (long since torn down) beside the Reflecting Pool. Those ramshackle First World War era two-storey buildings were on President Lincoln's right as his statue gazes towards the Capitol. The CS occupied all four of the 'temporary' buildings in a row there, named J Building through to M Building by some imaginative bureaucrat many years before. They were in a perfect location: a two-minute walk to the Lincoln Memorial in one direction, a five-minute walk to the Jefferson Memorial and the Tidal Basin with its glorious cherry blossom trees, a two-minute walk to the Potomac River, a ten-minute walk to the State Department and fifteen minutes to the Smithsonian complex.

Occasionally we had visits from officials of Far Eastern intelligence services. One such group of four security officials came to the CIA headquarters and, as desk chief, I was in charge of them while they were in Washington. I didn't yet know if I'd be going overseas to serve in their country in a liaison capacity, or under cover, so I chose the crafty (I thought) operational alias Dale Dougal. As I escorted them to the Director's briefing room, a very senior CIA officer came out of the door we were about to enter. We had served in the OSS together and were good friends. He waved cheerfully to me and said in a clear, loud voice, 'Well, David Doyle, good to see you!' The four visitors looked at each other and grinned knowingly.

Next day, in the men's room, I was accosted by the new Far East Division chief, a man with minimal field experience. He asked me, quite gruffly, if I had already recruited one or more of them. When I told him that I'd only met them for the first time yesterday, he shook his head in disapproval. 'I believe in fast, firm recruitments,' he said. 'You should, too.'

I replied, questioning his judgment, 'Are you instructing me to ignore standing orders, waive the clearance process, and ask a foreign security official about whom I know next to nothing to risk his career as a CIA spy? Will you come with me in case he throws a fit?'

The chief looked surprised, as if the idea of first getting to know what makes your potential recruit tick was a new thought. Perhaps it was. Anyway, he dropped the subject.

Ann and I took the same officials to a Georgetown restaurant called l'Espionage. They thought the name was very funny, which is what we had hoped. After dinner, to atone for the purely Western food, I offered them cordials. They put their heads together and decided to go to the bar rather than stay at the table. We sat on stools, and they ordered one of every liqueur the bar had. The astonished bartender complied. As fast as he served the drinks, they were polished off with appropriate giggles and commentary. The predictable happened: the visitors passed out. The bartender helped us carry them to our station wagon, where we put the rear seats down and laid them out like logs in the back. It was a strange drive back to their hotel, where these four snoring men had to be helped to bed by the hotel night staff.

As soon as they had recuperated, they visited us for lunch at our house. We chatted about the differences between our two cultures. At one point I asked them what was the trait they found most widespread amongst Americans. Their spokesman answered, with a straight face, 'You are inscrutable.' On cue, the four men giggled, while Ann and I exploded with laughter.

Another group, this time of VIP foreign security officials from the Far East, were given special treatment at the request of the CIA station in their country. The desk officer in charge of their visit arranged everything, all of which went well until their last day which included a visit to a turkey farm in Pennsylvania. I hadn't paid much attention to this, having never seen a US turkey farm, until we got out of the cars and were almost overcome by the smell. The sight of tens of thousands of turkeys huddled together under the low roof of an enormous building – their lives spent in filth without room to move – was even more depressing than the stench of their collective urine and droppings. The VIPs looked at me in disgust, wondering why we had brought them there. The desk officer whispered that it was to impress them with the size of the operation. I translated this lamely, explaining that it had been a mistake made by someone down the line who thought they might be interested. They looked relieved and began to joke about it. Other than the turkey farm, their visit was a success. It helped cement relations between our two services and, as far as I know, we are still exchanging valuable intelligence with them.

Although I didn't much like the desk work, it did provide a detailed view of the operations of a large field station. There were an impressive number of espionage and covert action operations against our primary targets – the Soviets, the Chinese Communists and their allies. By 1957, however, I was ready for my next assignment, in the field in the Far East.

I am still not permitted to say which Far East station it was, for security reasons, but for over three years I was deputy chief, and for long periods acting chief, of the station's Soviet branch. We ran operations against the Soviet presence in the country and into the Soviet Far East. The main purposes were to gather intelligence on the USSR and its satellites, and to recruit Soviet and satellite personnel stationed in or visiting the country. However, at that time Soviet and satellite personnel were so paranoid that it was tough work, and operating against them in a large city was very difficult.

Stalin had died four years before, but his harsh imprint was still to be found all over the Soviets and their Eastern European allies. Every non-Soviet they met was a presumed provocation, so they stayed in their embassies unless they had an official or housekeeping reason to go out. Even then, they went in groups, almost never alone. KGB and GRU officers going out to meet agents, or otherwise engaged in operations, were an exception, as were the 'journalists', most of whom were KGB anyway. The local national security people tried to keep them under surveillance, but the city was a mass of people and vehicles, so it was fairly easy to slip away from anything except a lock-step surveillance – one where the watchers stay up close to the target so as to be noticed and thus deny the target any chance of operating unobserved. As a result, lock-step surveillance causes the target to abort and not meet his agent. We did manage to meet and assess some of the Soviets, but it was an uphill struggle; eyeball-to-eyeball conversations tended to degenerate into polemics, which led nowhere, and it would be a decade before they loosened up a little with Americans.

One solution was to recruit non-Soviets who had frequent dealings with the Soviets. However, it was not easy for a non-Soviet to discover what made a Soviet tick: fluent Russian helped, but only so far. The Soviets of that period trusted almost nobody and were at ease only with each other, and even then very selectively. A Soviet who contemplated defection dared not give any hint of it beforehand, not even to his wife or his best friend.

Despite the difficulties, we did manage to recruit some people who knew various Soviet officials well. And we succeeded in producing one vital piece of Soviet naval intelligence that had the Pentagon singing. Helped by information from liaison as well as from our own operations, we built up a fair idea of which Soviet intelligence personnel were doing what, but we didn't recruit any KGB or GRU officers while I was there. To that extent our mission was not a great success.

The chief of station (COS) held weekly staff meetings, some of which had their humorous sides. The COS held these meetings in a large conference room, and all branch chiefs and acting chiefs were included, so I had to attend what were normally quite boring and uninstructive sessions. There were a few light moments, however, like watching to see who would flinch during one of the many earthquakes that hit town (ten or so a day, although most were not noticeable except to instruments). The COS was an elderly man, who usually kept what was in fact an active sense of humour well hidden. He was often grumpy and had frequent fits of operational and bureaucratic over-caution. One meeting in the late 1950s still stands out after headquarters issued a new instruction: henceforth, on all dispatches, an asterisk would be used to flag basic biographical information on new names, for entry into headquarters' files. Right after the asterisk, information – i.e. the full name and any aliases, the date and place of birth, citizenship, profession, address, and so on – was to be typed into the document in a certain format.

The result of this new instruction was an increased workload for the case officers, so it was discussed in a staff meeting. Predictably, the COS said that in his opinion there was no point in contesting the instruction; we would just have to bite the bullet. One station officer, however, challenged the instruction, claiming that it dumped more work on the field operators in order to ease the load at headquarters, which was not a fair exchange.

'Besides,' he added at the end of his statement, 'my typewriter doesn't have an asterisk.'

The COS responded instantly, 'But you do, Bert.'

One of these weekly staff meetings was interrupted when a stranger – an Asian – burst into the room and dashed over to accost the COS, who looked quite startled. When the stranger made some off-beat remark like, 'Why don't you get things right, John?', the COS replied, 'Well, you're a new face . . . or are you?' Then he burst out laughing and introduced the stranger, who began to dismantle his disguise. He was one of our own case officers, a Caucasian well known to everyone in the room, who had been made up to look older, smaller, fatter, less fit and oriental. It turned out that a famous theatrical make-up expert from the US mainland had been brought over to show our technicians the latest tricks. His work was amazingly good, for nobody in the room – apart from the COS, who had been persuaded to permit the event – had recognised the 'stranger'.

Some years later, under disguise myself, I discovered how difficult it can be to get into and out of a disguise under operational conditions. In one case, I changed my identity and went into a full disguise in one European country and then flew from there to another country, where I was to have an operational meeting. It isn't practical to change into full disguise in most European hotels, where the staff have good memories and security is fairly tight. I have done it in airport and railway station rest rooms, but it wasn't easy. The switch to spectacles and the implanting of cheek pads were simple in a locked toilet, but changing the colour of one's hair, or giving oneself heavier eyebrows, or a moustache and/or beard, was much more difficult. Combing in the dye and gluing on hair pieces with a small hand mirror and inadequate lighting were very difficult. It was a job that was best finished, brazenly, at washbasins with bright lights and large mirrors, but then one had to suffer the surprised stare of the washroom attendant, who always seemed to realise what was happening and who just might pick up a telephone and call airport security.

The Alberge X in a Spanish city offered a unique solution. It was one of my favourite watering holes: an immense two-storey rustic suburban inn that had been a rambling country farmhouse until the rapid growth of the city enveloped it in the 1960s. There was no formal reception area and the doors were unguarded all day. After a leisurely breakfast on the balcony, I only had two things to do in the city: to change identity and to catch the afternoon plane to the city where my meeting was scheduled. After eating, I repacked my bags and paid the bill. The bags went into the trunk of my rented car, which I drove around the corner, out of sight. I parked and walked back to the inn, through the empty front hall and into the huge kitchen, where I said goodbye to the owner and his wife. Then I walked casually back to my room, which I had left unlocked, and went in, locking the door behind me. There, I put on my disguise and then left the inn through the front door. One of the maids passed me in the hall, but, taking me for some other guest, smiled and wished me a good day. Five hours later I was in another city with a completely new identity.

One incident in the Far East was outlandish and quite foreign to a secret service. Soon after the Allied occupation ended, a CIA surveillance team was following a Soviet intelligence officer known to be actively working against the Allies. The team was a mixed one, consisting of some locals and some CIA officers, and its leader was a former Texas small-town sheriff, a man steeped in the traditions of the Old West.

The Soviet either suspected that he was being followed, or knew it, and he pulled all the old tricks that irritate surveillance teams. He tied his shoe lace, taking advantage of it to sneak a look behind him. He used shop windows as mirrors. He entered a phone booth and pretended to make a call, then went into a bookshop where he browsed, now and then casually looking out of the windows at the street. He had a long, leisurely coffee in a restaurant, and made sure that he walked around the place and nodded or talked to a few people so that the surveillance would have to check them all out. When he came out, he walked on a bit, then doubled back and walked straight through the surveillance team. Then he turned and doubled back again.

Unfortunately, the Texan had a short fuse and he did the unforgivable: he fell in behind the Soviet, shortened the distance between them and calmly shot the man in the legs. When asked why on earth he had done such a stupid thing, he replied with a snort: 'Well, fellas, it stopped the bastard.' The CIA had no further use for his services.

Another misfit in the field was Nick, a CIA case officer in the Far East under diplomatic cover. He was a former newspaper reporter and had great difficulty distinguishing informants from agents. Sources – media style – are known as informants in the espionage world. An informant does not usually go out of his field and seek protected information; he or she already has it, and shares it with his or her contacts. Informants may or may not be paid, but they are not controlled, trained, disciplined agents. An informant doesn't have to have the deep conviction for a cause which propels a full-blown agent to put himself at great risk of suffering torture or death, as well as endangering the lives of his family and friends. If informants do have such a conviction, and are willing to accept operational discipline, they then qualify to be recruited as fully fledged agents.

Whatever Nick's view of his profession, he carried it intact into the CIA. In the early 1950s, some brilliant headquarters' type assigned him as a case officer to the Far East – probably because he spoke fluent Italian. Nick took over six or so agents from his predecessor, who had always met these agents separately, in various different safe-houses. Nick however decided to change the pattern. He met his agents clandestinely at first, but in a stunningly weird lapse of operational security he established 'Pay Day', when all his agents came to his embassy office on Friday mornings to collect their weekly salaries and expenses.

The reluctant agents did as he instructed, and this astounding new way of doing business went on for several weeks. One fine Friday morning, however, the COS happened by Nick's anteroom and was horrified to see half-a-dozen very uncomfortable Asian gentlemen sitting in twisted postures, trying not to see or be seen. Nick was shipped home forthwith and made a reports' officer at headquarters, a job for which he was much better suited.

Murphy's Law is always at every espionage officer's side. I was developing an agent in the Far East, a man who was in close contact with the Soviets, and we usually met in a safe apartment. However, this man adored a local delicacy – which I also happened to like – so after each clandestine meeting we broke the rules and went out for a midnight snack. To reduce the risk, we went to out-of-the-way bars, mainly in the working districts of town, and tried to be as inconspicuous as possible.

This worked for about a year, until one evening my friend was spotted by a colleague in his government ministry. When the colleague joined us at the bar and sat next to me, he immediately asked me who I was and what I did. Not realising that he was a friend of my contact, I gave, to what I thought was a stranger, a phoney name and told him that I was Mexican. I felt it highly unlikely that this stranger had ever been near Mexico, and at least my contact would not have been 'caught' with a US citizen. Since my maternal grandmother was half Mexican and I spoke fair Spanish, I thought I could carry it off.

But luck wasn't with me that night. The stranger had just returned from Mexico, where he had served some years in his country's trade mission! He listened to my Spanish, asked some pointed questions about current Mexican politics and economics (of which I knew next to nothing), and laughingly suggested that I was not a Mexican but a Spaniard posing as a Mexican. I dug him in the ribs and cackled my agreement, while my agent tried not to faint from relief. The stranger was so pleased by his coup that he forgot to ask why a Spaniard in a Far Eastern city would masquerade as a Mexican.

One of the more interesting events that took place while I was stationed in the Far East concerned the shooting down of the U-2 by the Soviets on May Day 1960. The very distinguished ambassador from Pakistan was a personal friend, but not an agent. He was a big man in every way, with a generous nature, an infectious laugh and a huge stock of funny stories. However, he was so incensed when President Eisenhower admitted that the U-2 had been a US espionage operation that he called me to his office and chewed me out royally.

'I'm going to make a statement you won't like, Colonel Doyle,' he began, making it clear from the use of my surname that he was being formal – he had bestowed on me the title of colonel when we had first met, despite my protestations, saying, 'That's OK, we'll make you a colonel in my country's army.' 'No sophisticated nation ever admits to espionage,' he went on. 'This will cause a break between Pakistan and the United States, and your country will regret it for ever.'

I was mystified and asked what this was all about. When he told me, I was still mystified because I knew nothing about the U-2 affair – nor even the fact that it existed. I assured him, quite truthfully, that I had known nothing about this operation, but he responded by shouting at me, 'Nonsense, how can you lie to me when your President admits it?'

At first, he wouldn't believe me, even though I agreed with him that sophisticated nations should not admit to espionage. In addition, I told him that our operations were always strictly compartmented, so I really knew nothing about the U-2 flights. I think he thought that this was so strange that it might actually be true. Eventually he laughed, relented and accepted my explanation. We returned to using first names.

At the end of the meeting, the ambassador invited me to a reception he was giving for one of the royal princesses, a very well-known member of the imperial family. He was clearly impressed that she had accepted his invitation. 'Bring your wife,' he urged me, 'but be sure you get there before Her Highness. It's very bad form to arrive after she does.' I already knew this and promised to be there early. The reception was to be held in a palatial former royal residence.

For reasons best left undisclosed we got there late, at precisely
the same time as Her Highness arrived. She walked into the
entrance hall just as we did. We recognised her from her photographs, and she nodded in a friendly way and started chatting to
us. She wanted to know more about us and was eager to practise
her excellent English, so we stood talking in the hall for about five
minutes. Then the three of us mounted the long, very formal
staircase together – chatting casually all the way – and were
announced by a fancy footman, who shouted out our names as if
we were a party of three. The ambassador was visibly astonished.

'My word, David,' he whispered later. 'I had no idea that you
and your wife were friends of hers. How nice for you.'

I responded that she was 'a wonderful woman. God knows
what she sees in us.'

'Nonsense,' he replied. 'Why hide your light under a bushel.'
We laughed and the conversation moved on to something else. I
never confessed that we had only just met. In espionage, it's best
never to give away anything that you don't have to.

The result was that thereafter he introduced me to dozens of
his friends and colleagues, again calling me 'Colonel David
Doyle, my very good friend'. I tried to correct him several times,
but he repeated that he had decided that I was an honorary
colonel in his army. My friendship with Her Highness was clearly
a very important matter.

Not long afterwards, he asked me if I could arrange for him to
use the PX (post exchange) store, where members of the military
could purchase general goods. 'I just want to buy a few little
items,' he said. 'I know you can arrange it, David, for a good
friend.' I spoke to the PX manager, who issued a card that named
my friend 'Sergeant X'. The ambassador agreed to be discreet,
the only restriction put on this irregularity by the PX manager.
The next day the manager telephoned me and asked me to come
over. It took me about fifteen minutes to get there, but 'Sergeant
X' and his wife were still there, buying furniture, kitchenware,
sporting goods, cigarettes and food. They had already spent several thousand dollars and, not unnaturally, were the main
attraction in the store. Everyone was staring at them. The ambassador's handsome Canadian wife was dressed in a beautiful sari,
and he was very impressive in a dark suit and tie. Outside was his

enormous official black limousine complete with chauffeur and flag flying proudly. Nobody in the PX had seen anything like it. When I asked him to be more discreet, he laughed and said, 'David, that's as discreet as I can get . . .' That ended any thoughts I might have had about eventually recruiting him.

Liaison with foreign intelligence or security officials is one of the most productive sources of high quality intelligence and counter-intelligence, for both sides. Some of our officers enjoyed being in daily contact with their foreign counterparts. Others, including me, appreciated the 'take' from liaison but preferred to operate independently. Liaison with foreign services is too sensitive to portray in any depth because of what it says about the secret international dealings of sovereign nations, but liaison does have its funny aspects.

The immigration authorities in one Far Eastern country knew a number of our people and noticed that most of them used official passports (as distinct from diplomatic or regular passports). They used to tease our undeclared people at the airport by taking our official passports, looking them over, nodding that we could enter the country, offering us the passport but then holding on to it. When, surprised, our man would tug at the passport but still find it being held by the immigration officer, his eyes would automatically fall to the passport itself, where the officer's thumbs were blocking certain letters on the cover of the passport, so that instead of reading 'OFFICIAL PASSPORT', it read 'CIA PASSPORT'. The officer would then roar with laughter.

Although much of my time in the Far East was spent on desk work – the Soviet branch of the station was quite large, and my role was essentially to supervise operations and do paperwork – I did recruit and handle a few agents, and ran some audio operations. I learned there that these were the most exhilarating parts of espionage.

9

Recruiting Agents

Although it was later, in Africa, that I did most of my recruiting, it's worth digressing a little to comment on the core activity of espionage using humans: recruiting agents. Agents are the keystone of operations in the world of espionage; they fill only a small gap in the overall collection of intelligence, but it is a critical gap.

The use of humans – as opposed to satellite imagery, for example – to collect protected information can be divided into two general categories. The first and most obvious is acquisition of knowledge by direct observation or elicitation, without resort to espionage. Diplomats and military attachés on post abroad collect intelligence, and they are declared to the host government. So, too, are media foreign correspondents. These trained and skilled people dig up guarded information from sources they exploit as part of their job. They may offer their sources a *quid pro quo* – perhaps lavish entertainment, information exchanged both ways, reimbursement of expenses, or even cash rewards – but, in seeking to acquire sensitive or protected information, they do not usually hide their work, or their own identities, or who their sponsors are. Their sources are informants, not trained agents. Informants are used by CIA case officers, but they generally play a secondary or supporting role. They provide information or services voluntarily. Unlike fully fledged agents, informants produce information they themselves select, and when they want to. Most of what we need to know about a dangerous opponent's capabilities can usually be obtained through open sources.

However, the rest of what we need to know, especially the all-important categories – an opponent's true intentions and hidden capabilities – can often be obtained only through stealth, deception and cunning: in a word, espionage. Here the identity of the sponsor, the real goals of the work, and the methods and people used are masked. The real identity of the operator (a CIA case officer, for example) is often disguised. He or she may operate using an alias, provided it is worth the extra time and effort that an alias costs.

Whereas informants are neither controlled nor disciplined by the people they help, espionage agents are both. They have been recruited and are then managed by intelligence officers; they have accepted to be trained in tradecraft when feasible, to submit to direction, to always be on target, to be conscious of surveillance, to report covertly, to tell the whole story, to meet clandestinely and, above all, to switch basic loyalty and keep it that way. Through such agents we can discover what a nation's leader really has in mind, not what he wants those outside his inner circle to know. So one prime goal is to assess, develop, recruit and manage selected movers and shakers in power and out – not just to pin cryptonyms on them and scoop up what they want to say, but to recruit them as our agents. If a troublesome foreign leader talks to confidants about his ambitions, opponents, worries and plans, then we need either to recruit one of those confidants and task him or her to report back to us accurately, or we need to have a carefully placed microphone hidden by a human being. If the leader communicates mostly in writing, we try to read his mail, perhaps by recruiting his personal secretary or aide. The same is true for those who hope to replace that leader. It is wise to track them closely, too, and know in advance what they stand for and how likely they are to succeed.

Another very important goal, especially in the days of the Cold War, was to assess and hopefully recruit Soviet and other Communists, either directly or using those close to them, who were known as access agents. We tried above all to recruit KGB and GRU officers and cipher communicators, or those Soviets who had access to such prime targets. In practice, however, it was so difficult to recruit Soviets during the Cold War that we went after whoever looked likely. Some of those least likely to defect were, in fact, eventual defectors who carefully hid their opposition to the Soviet regime; they had had to do so in order to survive.

Because secret agents are the principal assets of espionage operations, their recruitment must be followed up by competent field and headquarters' management and exploitation of these human resources. Other assets are also vital, such as competent case officers, adequate funds and equipment, effective cover, secure communications, efficient targeting (i.e. requirements and directives), and so on. The difference between the product of a well-run agent and one who is poorly managed is enormous, but the best espionage manager cannot make a star out of a lousy agent.

One of the great exhilarations of espionage is when a person you've been developing for recruitment looks at you and says, 'Yes, I'll be your agent.' It's even better if he or she also says, 'The cause we both believe in is worth the risk.' If that statement is convincing, you know you haven't just rented the person. His or her motivation is ideology, not money, and such agents are pure gold. What impels them comes from the mind, the heart and the soul, not just the purse. Agents strongly motivated by a great cause are likely to be guided by Shakespeare's famous line: 'Cowards die many times before their deaths;/The valiant never taste of death but once' (*Julius Caesar*, Act II, Scene 2). I always wanted to be one of the valiant, but it was not to be. In any case, someone who fears nothing is probably a fanatic – which a good case officer cannot afford to be, although his agents may be.

Like audio operations – the bugging of buildings, cars, phones, and so on (see chapter 10) – the recruitment of agents must be carefully thought out ahead of time. Some recruitment attempts are made after a long period of assessing and developing the prospective agent, without his or her knowing it is happening. Other recruitments take a short time because there is a hurry, or maybe the chemistry between the recruiter and his agent is unusually good. In the best of all worlds the case officer knows his prospective agent so well that he has no doubt that the answer will be 'Yes'.

However, there's always a risk of being turned down by the

best of prospects. Even the most successful recruiters sometimes get a negative response. Threats of violence or blackmail are sometimes used in recruitment attempts, but they rarely work. Even if they seem to work, the agent often falls away when it's safe to do so. Cold pitches, where the recruiter and his target don't know each other, are equally dicey and often don't work. Our case officers have had things thrown at them, or been beaten up, while trying cold pitches. Others have had notable successes.

One CIA officer named Don was about to leave for home at the end of an overseas tour when the station officer in charge of Communist Party operations asked him to do a cold pitch before he went. Don agreed to do so. The station had its eye on a Communist Party courier, a man who headed a labour union and made regular trips to the USSR, and it was thought that he might be willing to collaborate with the CIA if the right approach were made. Don was to go to the courier's home, pretend no knowledge of the local language and claim to be a member of the US embassy section dealing with labour affairs. The ploy was a routine espionage trick to suck a person into a clandestine relationship. Don was to suggest that much of the perspective of the labour section had been supplied by sources either from the extreme left or the extreme right, but what was needed was insight from a moderate, and he had been led to believe that the courier was such a man. Would he write a few papers for us on specified topics, for which he would of course receive payment.

Don went to the neighbourhood where the courier lived. The target was at home, and Don made the pitch. The man thought for a while and then indicated that he would have to think about it; Don should come back the following week. When Don arrived, the man regretfully declined the opportunity. Don left. A couple of weeks later, our people left a note on the floor of the target's office, which read, in English, 'Your last report was not up to snuff. If your next report is no better, we will be dropping your salary somewhat.' A few days later, an embassy officer dropped by the CIA unit with a note for Don which had been received in the mail. It was from the courier, saying, 'I give up! Don't send me any more notes! Where can we meet?' A rewarding and durable relationship began that simply.

The KGB had its share of failed attempts using cold pitches and blackmail. Not long after the Cold War began in earnest, an

Allied military attaché in Moscow was a bit too aggressive in his efforts to line up sources on the Red Army. The KGB decided to use blackmail to turn him into a KGB agent. They assigned a KGB 'swallow' the job of entrapment, her task being to lure the attaché into bed under conditions controlled by the KGB. She was very successful. Not long afterwards, a Chekist called the attaché and made an appointment to meet him in a hotel room. Several KGB officials showed up, eager to share the prize. They sat him down and showed him the photographs. 'These pictures will ruin your career,' they said, 'and your marriage. But if you will work for us, we will destroy them. However, if you won't play, we will send them anonymously to your ambassador.' The victim looked the photographs over very carefully and then replied, 'Terrific shots of me and that girl! How very kind of you. I'll take six of these, four of those, and ten of this superb shot – enlarged, if you please. By the way, I hope she doesn't get a dose. I have a very bad case of syphilis.' They left him alone after that.

Years later, a French military attaché was similarly trapped, but his way out was to commit suicide. The KGB learned from these two events: when one of their own officers was treated to a similar blackmail attempt, he laughed and asked for copies of 'those wonderful shots'.

Agents themselves come in all shapes and sizes, all ages, genders and nationalities. They play one or more of various roles. There are straight espionage agents, who collect and report intelligence information. There are support agents, who help operations by supplying such services as surveillance, safe-house renting and staffing, clearing or filling dead drops, acting as live or telephone cutouts, and checking for surveillance – maybe from an apartment, or watching to see if your car is followed. Children have also been used to support operations. For example, a male or female case officer under surveillance may elect to take his or her unwitting children to a park, where, while they play, the officer discreetly loads or unloads a dead drop. Pigeons and dogs, cars, aircraft and trains have been used to carry secret messages, sometimes without the knowledge of their owners or handlers.

There are penetration agents – now often called 'moles'; covert action agents; double agents and triple agents. There are even piston agents, who go back and forth depending on which service pays more – until they're caught at it, which most eventually are. There are fabricators, who make up their reports and who are often called paper mills. Stay-behind and sleeper agents may wait twenty years or more to be activated. There are agents who believe they are working for a different service or country than is the case, victims of what are known as false-flag recruitments. An example would be the recruitment of a devoted Communist by a CIA case officer pretending to be a KGB case officer. The agent is led to believe that he is helping the KGB because that is the only way to recruit a devout Communist. His information might be invaluable: details of the capabilities and intentions of his country's Communist Party, its links to other such parties elsewhere, their support for terrorism, etc. The KGB has used these methods, as does its successor, the SVR. And so did we.

Fully fledged and controlled agents of all types are normally acquired in what is sometimes called 'the recruitment cycle', which is usually set in motion because a sponsor wants certain protected information. For example, suppose that in 1996 CIA headquarters at Langley was asked by the Intelligence community (IC) to find out what the Rwandan Patriotic Front's armed forces would do next. In such cases, open sources are tapped first – the UN, NATO, friendly African and European intelligence services, our embassies and military attachés, etc. – but let's say without success because the Front does not wish its military intentions known to outsiders. The IC then turns to the CIA. Langley sends a message to selected field stations directing them to address the question. This is known as the sponsor's 'requirement'. For example, our representative in neighbouring Burundi has an agent who can probably help by tapping the right source. The chief in Burundi assigns the case to the field case officer who handles that particular agent. The case officer briefs the agent, who starts by spotting the best person(s) for the job. The agent must then find a way of meeting the prospect under circumstances that do not appear suspicious or contrived. When he does, the agent then begins to assess the prospect's access and character. If the prospect looks promising, the agent may be asked to arrange a meeting between prospect and case officer (who will probably use an operational alias). If the case officer agrees with the agent's assessment, the next stage is developing the prospect until a recruitment attempt is both warranted by his or her access to what we want to know, and is likely to be accepted. In this case, the prospect is an old schoolfriend and cousin of a very senior officer in the Rwandan Patriotic Front's armed forces. He can, and does, often travel to Rwanda, so he has access and is assessed as being likely to accept recruitment. Designing the recruitment pitch – e.g. who does it, where and when, using what cover, what approach, with what arguments and what inducements – is the next task, followed by getting Langley's approval. The final step is making the recruitment pitch, which may be made by the agent, a CIA case officer, or some other asset. Sometimes an agent or a case officer is brought in from a third country – often introduced as 'the boss' – just to make the pitch.

When it comes to the actual recruitment pitch, the prospect should be comfortable with his recruiter and vice versa. Ideally, the outcome should be almost a certainty if the prospect has been assessed and developed properly. Motivation and inducements are critical: examples are ideology, anger, revenge, disdain, ethnicity, false flag, fear, entrapment, money, friendship, or (rarely) just plain excitement. Forcible recruitment by the use of coercion, blackmail or physical threats can also work, depending on the character of the prospective agent and the nature of the threat. Most case officers, however, prefer to work with prospects who are strongly motivated by ideology. Such people are usually driven by forces, often including political hatred or revenge, that are far stronger and more reliable than motives such as money, thrills, fear or coercion.

Regarding the cold pitch, few really work, because out of the blue you're asking an acquaintance or even a stranger to work against his own country at great personal risk. The shock often kills the offer and, therefore, cold pitches are used very sparingly. One cold pitch that didn't work resounded through the CIA corridors for years, causing far more laughter than tears. A youngish CIA case officer – who went on to greater things – made a cold pitch to a Soviet intelligence officer in a German beer hall. The Soviet, who was suspected of being approachable, was in fact anything but. He was so infuriated by the pitch that he threw his mug full of beer into the CIA officer's face and stalked out of the place. The same officer was beaten up, decades later when he was very senior, by another Soviet to whom he made a cold pitch.

Successful recruitment is followed by the next phases – training, managing and exploiting the agent, and evaluating his information and reporting it. The average agent needs to be trained in what to report or what action to take; when, how, and where to meet his or her case officer or handler (who may well be a cutout); how to communicate without physical meetings by using such techniques as dead drops, live drops, brush contacts, safety and danger signals, accommodation phones and addresses, radio contact procedures, secret writing systems, concealment devices and methods, disguises, and so on. He must be trained in how and when to report the information he acquires or the actions he takes; how to detect surveillance and use it against the surveillants; and, if appropriate, how to be a surveillant. In wartime, the list may also include training in parachuting from various types of aircraft; using explosives and small arms; and identifying weapons, troops, supplies, transport facilities, and other military or civilian war assets.

Adequate training can be a long, exhausting and risky process, especially if the agent has a full-time job and a family, and may at any time come under hostile surveillance. Secure places – such as safe-houses, preferably in third countries to which the agent can travel – have to be acquired and set aside for the training sessions. The agent and the case officer normally arrive separately, taking routes designed to make it hard to follow them. Sometimes specialists must be brought in to brief or debrief the agent on matters beyond the case officer's knowledge. For example, if the agent is a Chinese nuclear engineer recruited to uncover North Korean nuclear secrets, he will need to be briefed in detail on what is known and what remains to be discovered. Later, when his mission is accomplished, he may need to be debriefed by a specialist who must be brought to the safe-house surreptitiously.

Returning briefly to my Rwanda/Burundi example, let's say the agent accepts the pitch and is willing to travel up to Kigali – the capital of Rwanda – as often as may be necessary to meet his friend and cousin in the armed forces. The agent will need training in how to elicit information without raising suspicions, on what intelligence is needed and how to recognise it, and on how to communicate with and report back securely to his handler. If time permits, fairly complete training will be given to the agent, preferably in a carefully chosen safe-house, where his visits can pass unnoticed, or can be explained.

In this case there is no time as the requirement is urgent. We bank on his natural common sense and his close ties to his cousin, the ultimate target. This works more often than one might think. Our Tutsi agent makes several visits to Kigali, returning each time to Bujumbura – capital of Burundi – with increasingly valuable information. Finally, during an alcoholic evening, he elicits from his cousin the short- and long-term plans of the Rwandan Patriotic Front. Our agent thereupon volunteers to start an RPF office in Bujumbura – to be their man in Burundi. The RPF accepts the offer and *voilà*, a nice little espionage operation is off to a good start.

This example is typical of the basic world in which field case officers in the CS operate. These officers are judged by their ability to operate successfully while living their cover. Base and station chiefs are also judged on the same grounds as their subordinates, as well as their ability to manage human and physical assets, and to follow directives from home. For everyone in the business, emphasis is placed on language skills and on such obvious character traits as honesty, courage, integrity, common sense, good judgment, loyalty, stability, patience, thoroughness, the ability to 'think on one's feet', flexibility, intuition, curiosity, self-discipline, memory, imagination and perseverance – just about all the traits, in short, that one hopes for in an exemplary employee of any serious organisation. Very few people combine all of these traits, although a surprising number harbour many of them. In an imperfect world, that's usually enough.

Many things can go wrong when you're running agents. A good agent may, for example, suddenly become at risk of being compromised through no fault of his own. Once I recruited an agent whom I'll call Karl. He was an officer of a hostile intelligence service and he became a mole working for the CIA. The other side's traitor was our side's hero. Karl was by far the best agent I ever recruited and ran – the sort you dream about. He was intelligent, energetic, imaginative and motivated by ideology, and his job gave him access to a vast amount of very important and sensitive information that we badly needed. He brought me photocopies on undeveloped film of thousands of sensitive documents from deep inside his organisation. As a result, we were able to piece together the names and the secret work (much of it against us) of many hundreds of his service's agents and informants. The product from this brave man was so good that a specially reinforced vault room was set aside at headquarters for people to work on his 'take' and to store his documents especially securely.

Not only was Karl the best agent I ever recruited, but the process of recruiting him was incredibly swift. We met at a private party – he was a neighbour of our host, who was a diplomatic colleague – and we talked for an hour or so, the chemistry being perfect. He already knew who I was and luckily he trusted me from the start. To my surprise, he quickly made his dislike of the regime he worked for obvious. It turned out that he had been hoping for some time to meet a CIA officer in whom he could confide his anger and his commitment against the regime. His motivation was that by helping the United States to understand what was really going on, he could help hasten the day when his regime could be changed for the better and start to promote the good of his nation. Immediately, he gave me documentary information that his regime would not have allowed out, and his bona fides were impeccable from the start.

After the initial period of getting to know each other and settling on how to communicate securely, we sorted out what Karl would report on and in what order of priority. From then on I met Karl clandestinely in various European countries. At one meeting, as can happen in the best operations, things went a bit awry. We were to meet at a European seaside resort, where he was to take an ocean-view room in a particular hotel on the waterfront. It had a park in front, and I sat in the park and watched the hotel. Karl was to wave to me from inside his room, standing back from the open window so that only I could see him. That way I would be able to count the floors and windows and figure out which room he had rented. Then I could make my way to it at night.

The trouble was that after a long and rough all-night flight from New York, I was very tired and fell asleep on the bench. I woke up at one point and vaguely saw a man waving in a window, but he didn't look like Karl so I was reluctant even to lift a finger in response. Sleep got the better of me again, and by the time I was fully awake the window was closed.

Our first alternative meeting-place was to be in my hotel room, so I placed a note with the name and room number in our previously agreed-upon dead drop. Karl recovered the note, burned it and came to my hotel at midnight. He knocked on the door

several times, he later told me, but there was no reply. He wondered if I'd contracted sleeping sickness during one of my African
tours of duty. In fact, he wasn't knocking on the door of my room.
Unknown to us, the hotel had recently added a new wing and had
given the rooms there the same number series as the old building,
which still existed. Back I went to the dead drop and left another
message. Finally, we got together in his room for what turned out
to be a marathon meeting that went on non-stop for over thirty
hours. The 'take' from that meeting was spectacular.

For a brief while, we thought Karl might have been doubled by
his service – not doubled by his own doing, but as a result of a
blunder on the part of my successor, his new CIA case officer.
The officer lost a film cassette with reams of Karl's 'take', which,
he speculated, had fallen into a gutter while he was getting into or
out of his car, and perhaps rolled down a storm sewer. But his
search of the area was unsuccessful and nothing turned up.
Given the low-rent area he had lost it in, the chances were good
that it had indeed rolled down the sewer, or been squashed by a
car, or swept up by street cleaners, but the agent's life, like his
'take', was so valuable that we had to know for certain.

There was, in this unique case, only one way to find out:
someone had to go into Karl's country to meet him without
diplomatic immunity. If Karl were doubled, his handlers would
not be able to resist the chance of grabbing a CS operations officer *in flagrante*, especially one with a long record of operating
against them. They would try to turn the CIA man against the
US, or – if he refused – they would take him to their interrogation
centre for a 'working over'.

I volunteered to be the bait, although I was no longer Karl's
case officer. The professional risk was really quite low; in fact, so
low that it was warranted as the means to determine for certain
that this very valuable agent was still our man. The chance of the
film having been found and given undamaged to his service was
remote. Then, too, if they had caught him, he would have tried to
warn us using a code inside his messages to us, but he hadn't.
Also, his service would almost certainly have felt it necessary to
amend or even slowly decrease the flow of information to us. Yet
Karl's product had not lost its quality or quantity since the roll of
film was lost. The risk was even more diminished since we had an
exchange in mind if I were caught. I was told that we had in our

hands an agent whom the other side badly wanted to get back. All things considered, the enterprise looked well worth the risk.

By mail, through an accommodation address and in secret writing, we scheduled a brush contact followed by a clandestine meeting with Karl in his own country. We gave him the location of a safety signal, a chalk mark I was to make on a particular wall if I was clean. If he was clean and ready to meet, he was to make a different mark on a different wall. We would then meet in the city's cathedral. I would sit in the tenth pew from the front, on the right of the middle aisle, at ten in the evening (after the last service), on a given day. The cathedral would be almost empty by then. He would sit near me – not less than two metres away, and not more than four – in the same pew, and he was to be in a light disguise. I would get up and leave right away, having taped, under my pew bench, a match folder from the inn where I had rented a room. The number of my room would be written, in a simple code, inside the match folder. Karl was to exit the pew by sliding along it and, passing where I had sat, discreetly recovering the match folder. Then he was to come to my room exactly twenty hours later.

I planned to stay in a largish country inn in the hills well outside the city, where men from the city took their 'secretaries' on assignations, so the staff were discreet and didn't care who was in which room. I would be there in my cover role as a tourist from a neutral non-aligned country. If the coast was clear, Karl would simply walk into my unlocked room, and we would have all night to talk. He would hand over his unprocessed film, perhaps twenty cassettes with thirty-six frames on each one: 720 documents in all, most of which were of great value to Uncle Sam. These new films would be coated with a substance that prevented their being developed unless you knew how to dissolve out the coating. It was a pity that hadn't been the case with the lost films.

In the event that Karl didn't make the quasi-brush contact in the cathedral, our alternative plan was a brush contact on a certain unlit street corner an hour later, at precisely eleven o'clock. I was to drop the match folder an instant before we crossed paths, each of us walking towards the corner from opposite directions. He would pick up the folder immediately after he turned the corner. I would then continue up the street, not turning the corner.

The evening before the meeting, I checked into a hotel in an adjoining West European country. After dinner, I took a very long, hot bath to get rid of the tension that accompanies even a slight risk. Murphy's Law operates overtime in espionage, so anything was possible. However, I slept well enough and drove off early the next morning, crossing the border in the afternoon without incident. My forged documents passed inspection by the border guards, which was a great relief.

The big test, however, was still to come. If Karl was doubled, I would be grabbed during our actual meeting in the inn so that proof would be obtained that Karl was being run by a CIA officer. The fact that I would be in alias as a 'neutral' would be no help since Karl would be forced to testify to my real identity. In addition, he had previously reported that his service's files contained visa photos of me in my cover role as an American diplomat. There would be no excuse, and no appeal. The smallness of the risk became larger in my mind as the time approached.

I drove to the country inn, hired a room without apparently arousing curiosity, explored the inn and its surroundings, had what might conceivably be my last dinner and set off for the cathedral. It wasn't practical to wear a disguise – the reception desk faced the main door of the inn and the receptionist would certainly have reported to the police if one of the foreign guests had gone out in a disguise, and to put on a disguise in a car at night was impossible – so I wore a dark duffel coat over slacks and a turtle-neck sweater and tried to look as innocent as possible when I made my chalk mark, checked Karl's mark out and entered the cathedral. I had the duffel coat's hood up, hiding my face on either side.

I sat in the tenth pew from the front, right side of the centre aisle, as the cathedral's huge clock chimed out the hour. The bell boomed eleven times, and I waited. Nobody came to sit near me, although a man I didn't recognise sat at the very far end of the same pew, over thirty feet away. I barely glanced at him, thinking that Karl would either have sat closer to me if the coast was clear, or not come at all if he thought he was being watched. I left the cathedral after waiting the agreed half hour, which was spent hoping in vain that he would come.

The alternative brush contact at the street corner went as planned. At eleven o'clock I passed the corner, continuing along the street I was on. Karl, too well disguised – the man who had been in the tenth pew – turned the corner seconds after I had passed it. He picked up the match folder where I had dropped it – maybe three feet from the corner – and continued back up the street I was on, going in the opposite direction. We quickly put a lot of distance between us.

Karl got a room at the same inn and came to my room on time. We gave each other a bear-hug, I turned on the radio plus a special noise-maker to add to the ambient noise, and we began our meeting. I could feel the tension rising in my body as I listened for the banging on the door that could be the end for me. I was able to hide my anxiety from Karl because he was in a great mood, but it wasn't easy. He had brought two-dozen film cassettes, and he spent over two hours excitedly describing their contents and what they meant. It was a huge haul of sensitive and valuable intelligence, and of course I made much of it, congratulating him several times. As our meeting continued into the small hours without incident, I began to relax. Finally, after he had left my room at dawn, I was able to sleep. But it wasn't until I got back across the border that I felt safe again.

All agents deserve good tradecraft, and very good agents deserve the very best in tradecraft, especially when they are meeting their case officers or handlers face-to-face. Until the rise of electronic communications made it less necessary, one of the most fascinating and vital elements of agent meetings was the brush contact, where case officer and agent make eye contact or pass messages or small packages very quickly and hopefully unobserved. The planning, setting up and successful execution of brush contacts are demanding and exciting. I used brush contacts extensively with agents, including Karl, often as the preliminary to a face-to-face meeting. Each face-to-face meeting site must be picked with great attention to the security it offers. Conversation must be possible without it being overheard or recorded. It must be impossible for an outsider to photograph the occupants of the site. A good safe-house, a secure safe apartment, or a suitable hotel room discreetly booked at the last minute, are usually good enough. Under perfect conditions the suspect agent – hence any hostile service he may be reporting to – should not know the location of the meeting site until just before he gets there. A brush contact beforehand, to establish when and where such a meeting will be, is therefore necessary.

In one case, I had scheduled a brush contact ahead of time because I planned to meet the agent in a hotel room which I had just rented in a new identity. The time of the meeting would be given to the agent only hours beforehand, the precise location only at the last minute. That would give any hostile effort – including one that the agent himself might mount – minimum time to arrange such things as audio surveillance or a trap.

Brush contacts must occur in such a way that even if the agent or his case officer is under surveillance, anyone (even a surveillant) observing the contact will not see anything that links one person to the other. Brush contacts which don't involve actual brief physical contact are even safer. They are structured so that agent and case officer visit the same spot with a minimal time gap in between. They are not in the same spot at exactly the same time, just a few seconds apart. There is minimal time for a possible surveillant to intercept the message, and the brush contact leaves no evidence that either person has contacted the other – unless, by bad luck, it is spotted by the opposition. One example of a brush contact is when a case officer and his or her agent, timing their arrivals perfectly, meet on a stairway – one going up and the other going down. They exchange film for instructions, perhaps, as they pass each other. If the stairway is enclosed so that nobody can see in from outside, and deserted (maybe because it's late at night), the brush contact can be safe and take less than a second.

In one case I used the men's room of a corner restaurant during the middle of the afternoon when there were few customers there. I locked myself in a toilet stall and taped a message behind the water tank. Twenty seconds after I left the restaurant and turned down one street, the agent (in disguise) entered it from the other street and locked himself in the same stall so that he could retrieve the message undetected. We were not on the same street at the same time, let alone in the restaurant together.

Setting up and conducting successful brush contacts was, to me, one of the most interesting aspects of the work.

10

Audio Operations

After recruiting agents, the planning and executing of audio operations was for me, and many others, the other most exciting part of espionage. One way to learn what made Soviet and other Communist officials tick personally, and what they were up to officially or unofficially, was to enter their buildings secretly and implant microphones so that we could listen to them. Bugging their code rooms was a high priority, but just about the most difficult target imaginable: once established, their code rooms were extraordinarily well protected. I suppose what appealed to me most about breaking and entering was the boyish notion that being a skilled cat burglar in a good cause was fun, as well·as being useful. The physical risks – which certainly exist – usually seemed quite acceptable.

Audio operations are, however, not only almost always a gamble but not often all that cost-effective. They involve considerable risks of various types, as well as great expense before, during and after actual installation. If detected, they can be played back against you without your knowing it. Even if successful, the end product often doesn't justify the risks one has to take and the costs in time and money, because breaking and entering without the fact of entry being detected consumes a lot of highly skilled manpower. Full-time translators listening to endless chatter in hopes of a pearl are also very expensive, and a pearl is only received now and then. A defector-in-place inside the opponent's camp is much more effective and efficient, but at least as difficult to acquire.

Whether an operation was successful or not, I found breaking and entering into hostile buildings for Uncle Sam with the intent of bugging them to be a fascinating challenge. In good audio operations, everything has to be carefully planned down to the last detail right from the outset. The main idea is to implant the device without the victims being aware that it has been done. The risks are calculated beforehand, and everything practical is done to minimise them. The casing of a building, or a complex of buildings, and their occupants is one of the most important prior requisites no matter how much operational information your agents have provided. This was where patience developed hunting rabbits as a boy made me comfortable sitting motionless for hours observing a target from a concealed spot.

Murphy's Law, however, can always show its head, because a successful entry and exit is only the beginning. A job well done – with the bug or bugs well hidden, with nobody hurt and the entire operation conducted without the other side being aware of it – is wonderful, but is by no means the end of the story. Much can still go wrong, even if you have bugged one of the most rewarding places of all – the enemy's code room, which gives you an electronic look at both the plain text of its messages and the same text encoded.

The reward for a good audio operation is enormous: the other side unknowingly talking to you through your hidden microphones or video cameras and telling you what he or she is up to. The risk however is severe. The other side doesn't want you listening in and is willing to stop you with lethal force. Since we usually use staff officers to make covert entries, this is one of the areas where the physical risks are greatest. The use of agents to install bugs is normally limited to those few experienced, trusted agents with very special skills not available among ordinary staff officers.

Audio operations involve almost all aspects of espionage. Before deciding to make an audio installation, we must be sure that it is worth it and that we can't get the desired information any other way. Also, that when we do get it, we will be able to afford the time and expense of establishing a secure and discreet listening post, and of recording, transcribing and translating the product. The final result must therefore first be deemed to be worth the effort.

Once we decide to try to enter a target building, we must case it. This requires photographs from all angles, architectural drawings, and reports from people who know the building and hopefully from its occupants too. It includes the collection of operational information such as how carefully the target is guarded by day and by night, what are the best approach and escape routes, and how we can get in and out undetected. We have to know, or surmise, what every room is used for and who works in it, so that we can best assess where in the building the bugs should be located. Usually, it is practical to enter a well-guarded hostile building only when it is being renovated and the occupants haven't yet fully moved in. All possible assets must be used ahead of time to determine if it is a trap, if we are being set up. Recent defectors, double agents and any other likely sources must be questioned.

When we face risky entry into a hostile space, the need for technical and professional excellence is vital. The technicians assigned to the task must be first rate, and it takes only one idiot to foul up an operation. The case officers who protect the technicians, either inside the building or deployed around it as watchers, must be the best available – experienced men and women who are unafraid.

Audio/video operations are inherently costly and have a high failure rate. There is also the very real danger that, if the people we bug discover the installation, they can leave the bugs alone and use them to feed us with disinformation. Prior assessment of the substantial manpower effort and financial cost of an audio/video installation must be balanced against expected results. Even then, one well-placed traitor in the DO and the work is wasted and lives may be lost.

I had no idea of all this, of course, when I conducted my first audio operation. At about the age of ten, I listened in on one of my mother's phone conversations with my father. She was at home, while he was in his London office. She reminded him of a dinner party they were giving and asked, 'We'll be eight at dinner on Saturday, Don. Anything special you'd like?' He answered, tongue in cheek I now realise, 'How about pancakes?' He was devoted to pancakes, which he called flapjacks and which he had learned to make while mining in New Mexico. My mother laughed: 'We can't have pancakes for a formal dinner. What will the cook think? What about beef Wellington?' That suited him fine. I was ashamed of having eavesdropped on my parents, but I had learned two things, and my parents didn't know I had learned them. Firstly, I knew what the adults were to have for their main course on Saturday – Sue and I usually had a simpler menu – and secondly, that meals had to be planned ahead of time; they didn't just appear from the kitchen. I had simply never thought about it. In that early case my operation was very cheap and the product was good.

All told, I organised and personally conducted at least fifteen attempts to install clandestine audio penetration devices in hostile buildings – some in the Far East, some in Africa and some in Europe. Some were successful, others were not. The purpose was usually to listen in on the private or official conversations of priority targets – people we wished to recruit – in order to learn what made them tick (i.e. gaining operational information). My targets were invariably Soviets, Soviet satellites or Chinese Communists. Their access to sensitive information and their personal vulnerabilities were, of course, of prime importance to our attempts to recruit them. In other cases, which were far more difficult, we tried to penetrate the code rooms of hostile organisations, and to pick up and decipher their communications.

Almost to a man, our audio technicians were not only experts at their various jobs but they had guts. I never knew one to refuse a mission, even the lock-and-key man described below. He was scared to death, but he went on two very dangerous operations. Most of the technicians would go into the most hostile buildings, where to be caught meant capture and death after a brutal interrogation. They trusted the competence of people like me, the case officers who planned the entries and accompanied the technicians into the target installations to protect them.

The stories that follow are typical of the work done by surreptitious entry teams. I present these tales as a generic digression because audio and video penetrations of opposition premises really are in a class alone – and it is arguably more effective and certainly more secure to describe them generically rather than by location and date, which are still too dangerous to reveal. I have included some failures because they frequently had their amusing sides.

For example, during one attempt to bug a hostile embassy in an Asian country, our people managed to insert a sleeping potion into the bowl of noodle soup that was delivered to the night-watchman every evening by a local restaurant. The sleeping potion had been made up by the technicians in Washington with advice from the medical staff, and was 'guaranteed to work'. The watchman drank the soup, but instead of going to sleep he became much more active than usual. He telephoned for a call girl and spent the night playing with her while the entry team watched in dismay. The operation couldn't go forward that night. When headquarters was questioned, they came back with an irritatingly weak reply: 'Regrets, but the technicians and the medical staff can only assume that the local people react differently to the sleeping potion than do Americans.' One of the case officers then got a sleeping potion from a local drug store, and this time everything went well.

In another case in Asia, I had approval from headquarters to break into the embassy of an Eastern European country. The embassy was being completely renovated, and we were going take advantage of that to put in audio devices. The target was worth the risks and effort: the ambassador was a former top Communist Party official and a member of the Central Committee, and therefore technically in line for Politburo membership. He was reported to be out of favour with the Party general secretary, which explained why he had been sent overseas as an ambassador. He had, however, a large, high-level constituency in the Central Committee and throughout the regional Party organisations. He also had excellent contacts among top Soviet political and military leaders, including close personal friendship with the Soviet ambassador, who was also a key man in his own top Party structure. There was, of course, a possibility that the target would eventually return to his country and be rehabilitated, and our aim was to learn enough about him to decide whether to try to recruit him in place, or enable him to defect while he was still in the doghouse.

The 'take' should have been good, not only for the personal information we would receive about the ambassador, his staff, and his Soviet and other Communist friends – for example, such information could lead to the discovery of malcontents ready to escape the system – but it was also expected to produce intelligence on the entire Soviet Bloc. Through a support agent we prepared a listening post in a rented house nearby and arranged for translators to work on the resulting tapes. We worked up our entry plan and got ready for the operation.

During the same period as this operation, the station was being inspected by a senior member of the Inspector General (IG) Staff. As a result, the chief of station was itchy about the operation and was threatening to abort it. I got around that by inviting the IG visitor to come along with us when we made the first entry and did part of the work inside the target. He had never been on an audio operation before, so he was delighted to join us. We briefed him carefully on the need to maintain absolute silence, because there was a night-watchman in the gate-house of the compound. Every two hours, the night-watchman took his guard dog and inspected the embassy. One of our people was stationed where he could keep an eye on the gatehouse and be ready to radio us if the night-watchman started to make an unscheduled inspection. If so, we would quietly leave the compound until the danger was past, leaving behind a spray that would inhibit the dog's scenting us.

On the way into the garden of the target, however, the IG man grabbed the coping on the wall we were scaling and a large piece of it fell off, landing on the ground with a loud thud. He had grabbed the top of the wall just the way we had warned him not to. 'Oh my God, I'm so sorry,' he whispered. I just shook my head. We all froze and waited. No windows were suddenly illuminated or thrown open. No doors creaked open. No one shouted to ask anyone else what had happened. Nobody, neither the night-watchman nor the neighbours, seemed to have noticed. We went on in, after replacing the heavy coping with some difficulty. Phase One of the installation was a success: we managed to evade the watchman and his dog by getting the first part of the job done between his inspections.

The IG was very embarrassed. He made up for it by singing the praises of the operation to the COS, who changed his mind and let us finish the installation the following night. We did so without incident. Now we were ready to hook up and start the tape-recorders. The COS got his own back, however, by having a fit of caution and refusing to let us hook up the wires. I assume that some future COS got the operation going again. If not, the microphones may still be hidden in the walls and the wires still buried beneath the lawn, their 'business' ends still lying coiled up and sealed under the compound wall. Either way, I had left the station by then and had no need to know what happened afterwards.

In another case of an Iron Curtain embassy in Asia that was being renovated, we had the original architectural plans and we obtained the renovation plans from an apolitical subcontractor with a love for money. We cased the place for days using photography and surveillants, and quite soon a pattern became obvious. Just before the workmen and their Iron Curtain 'guards' quit for the day, a night-watchman became active. He had a very aggressive German Shepherd dog, which was kept outside, chained to the gate, during daylight hours, but was let loose at dusk and patrolled the grounds all night. The watchman usually stayed in his little house by the gate all night, coming out only if he heard the dog making a fuss.

The project was going to be a fairly big job, and the technicians estimated that they would need to enter the building for three nights in a row. That meant we needed two things: a sleeping dog and very bad weather. Luckily, a fierce typhoon was predicted shortly, so we waited for it. In the meantime, we fed the dog undoctored hamburger, dropping it over the wall after dark. The dog got used to his nightly snack and waited for us at the same spot each night. Twice we test fed him some hamburger that had a sleeping powder from headquarters mixed in it. We looked over the wall several times, using trees as cover. The drug put him out for six or so hours. He looked a bit groggy for a while afterwards, but he was not harmed in any way.

The typhoon was due to hit town early in the evening, so at dark we fed the dog some doctored hamburger. Soon afterwards, he disappeared, and it was time to start our entry. Although it was over thirty years ago, I can still see that embassy, darkly forbidding and enormous, looming above the wall of the compound – and the blackened faces of the others in the entry team as they huddled against the wall, trying to keep the worst of the rain from running inside their clothes as they waited for the signal to go over the wall. The wind had really picked up now and the trees were thrashing wildly about. The noise was tremendous, which was just what we wanted. The typhoon was strong enough to keep people off the streets and make a deafening racket inside the building.

I went over the wall to see if I could find the dog and make sure that he was asleep. I had a can of a Mace-type powder in a small plastic dispenser in case he attacked me, but he didn't show up. He certainly should have detected and found me if he'd been awake. I never did find him and was thankful that he stayed out of our way. He had probably found a dry spot to sleep off the drug.

Everything seemed OK, so I decided we'd go ahead. I went back over the wall to get the entry team. We were all wet and cold, and more than ready to get on with it, so I called the lookouts on the handie-talkies (radio transceivers with which one could communicate at fairly short range). We had two of them watching the street as well as the night-watchman's cottage. They gave us an okay, so over we went.

The actual entry was not entirely flawless. In a couple of minutes, we were at the front door, and the lock-and-key technician began his efforts to open it. We waited for fifteen, twenty minutes before I finally got sick of it. Two of us then went around the building, checking. We got a window open and went in. The look on that lock-and-key man's face when we opened the front door was marvellous. He actually fell in, like a scene from a comedy, with total surprise on his face. His keys spilled out on to the hall floor.

We escorted the four technicians to the second (and top) floor. We knew from the plans we had obtained which rooms would be used for what purposes. The first target was the ambassador's office. We knew where all the pipes and wires were, so that the technicians could put the bugs where they would be shielded from metal detectors. The technicians set up their toys and went to work. They did a beautiful job. By 3.15 a.m. they had installed the bugs and closed up and repainted the wall. They had an uncanny ability to match paint by artificial light so that there was no trace. We cleaned up, checked and double-checked, and started out, almost an hour ahead of schedule. Our exit actually began at 3.45 a.m. I left the study last. The others went in single file ahead of me, down the stairs and along the main corridor towards the front door. The storm was making a hell of a noise,

Just inside Germany, October 1944. John Mowinckel (left) and I had gone to the area around Aachen to do some line crossing.

This photograph was taken in March 1945 as we were preparing for the airborne assault across the Rhine at Wessel. Captain Vinciguerra, our commanding officer, is at the left foreground; Lieutenant Hall, his deputy, is beside him. The four men behind them are, left to right: Sergeant Wenzel Profant, Sergeant Lee Jungen, Lieutenant A. Grima Johnson, and myself.

1949, when I graduated from Princeton and joined the CIA.

Secessionist Katanga welcomes the USA, Elisabethville, 1960.

Moise Tshombe, leader of the Katanga, on his way to the Stadium to give a speech, 1960.

Independence Day, Usumbura, Burundi, July 1962.
Mwami Mwambutsa IV (in white, centre) reviews the troops.

Our house in Usumbura, 1962.

With Ann and the children in Dakar, Senegal, 1966.
From left to right: Mark, David F., Chris, Peter and Katherine.

The Central Intelligence Agency

AWARDS THIS

CERTIFICATE OF RETIREMENT

TO

David W. Doyle

In recognition and appreciation of more than 27 years of faithful service to the United States Government.

Washington, D. C., 31 July 1975

DIRECTOR OF CENTRAL INTELLIGENCE

My Certificate of Retirement from the CIA.

The United States of America

To all who shall see these presents, greeting:

This is to certify that the Director of Central Intelligence has awarded the

Intelligence Commendation Medal

To

DAVID W. DOYLE

for especially commendable service

Given under my hand in the City of Washington, D.C.

31 July 1975

Director of Central Intelligence

My certificate on receipt of the Intelligence Commendation Medal.

In retirement in Honolulu, April 1992, after the publication
of my novel.

with rain pouring down and the wind still howling. We felt our way rather than use torches, and the lightning flashes helped.

The chief audio technician was leading the parade. As he reached the front door and shone his flashlight on the lock, he saw it slowly turning. He correctly assumed that the night-watchman was at the front door, unlocking it. Quickly he warned us, and we backed up and slipped into a side room off the main corridor. From there we scooted through three connecting rooms, making no noise because we only had socks on – our shoes had been stashed in a closet by the front door. Through an almost shut door, I could see the night-watchman and his dog start down the main corridor in our direction. He was in no hurry. Apparently, he was checking the building because of the storm, unaware that anyone was inside. The same storm that brought him along saved us. The noise was so incredible and the wind was so strong, even inside the building, that the dog was unable to scent us. We hadn't yet cleaned up the muddy water on the floor inside the front door, but apparently the night-watchman had missed that. His own muddy boots and dripping clothes had covered our traces.

After the night-watchman and his dog passed the door to the first room, all seven of us skated back through the three connecting rooms and came out into the main corridor. We peeked out and saw them start up the stairs. This gave us a little time, and we rescued our shoes, rushed out of the door and left. The night-watchman never knew we'd been in there, because he and the dog never showed up during the next two nights. Had he caught us, we would have had to use B-3 tear gas on him and his dog, but of course the operation would then have had to be abandoned. As it turned out, the operation was a success.

Not long after, we planned an entry into a Soviet installation in the Far East. The building was used as office space and living quarters by several KGB officers. We had cased this target for weeks and planned to bug their phones and offices since they were actively working to recruit US personnel. The entry was to begin after dark on a night when we knew from a sensitive source that the target – a large house set in a garden – would unusually be deserted for several hours. The entry team consisted of two audio technicians, a lock-and-key expert, two case officers and myself as team leader. We assembled in a temporarily rented safe-house next door to the target. All six of us were dressed in dark sweatshirts and jeans, with dark gym shoes. We painted our hands and faces matte black, and waited for the KGB officers to leave.

When they had gone, we started the entry. The heftiest and toughest case officer, a former US marine, went over the garden wall first and stationed himself inside the street door of the garden. He had a sandbag with him, a long, thin affair like a large sausage. His orders were to swat anyone who came in on the head and make it look like a robbery by relieving them of a wallet and any other valuables. Then he was to warn those of us inside the house to abort the mission.

As soon as his voice came over the radio with the code word that all was OK – in this case the word was 'joy' in the local language, repeated three times in quick succession – the rest of us started over the wall. The lock-and-key man assigned to us for this mission had seemed unusually jumpy while we waited, but I didn't pay much attention to it. Sometimes the most courageous people show nerves before the action begins, and my experience had always been that our technicians were cool and competent once we got going. But it turned out that we had a very scared man with us. He came along, but he was too scared to do his job properly. He had six large bags of keys hanging from a heavy belt around his waist. He tripped going over the wall and fell into the Soviet garden with a horrendous crash that sounded like a car accident: his bulky body hitting the lawn sounded like the collision of two cars, and his keys sounded like several large glass windows breaking. What seemed like a thousand keys of all shapes and sizes spilled out over the lawn, mercifully in total darkness. Worse yet, he cursed out loud, in English. We froze.

Windows went up in two neighbouring houses, and we could hear people asking each other where the crash had been. After a while, windows closed and the neighbours went back to sleep, or whatever else they had been doing.

We picked up the keys and handed them to the lock-and-key man, who placed them back in his bags as quietly as he could. The grass and leaves that went in with them probably helped to deaden the sound. This seemed to go on for ever, but finally we were sure that we had picked up all the keys off the lawn. We moved across the lawn to the house one by one, slowly and as silently as possible. We got the lock-and-key man to the front door, and the four of us stood guard for him.

We waited, watching the garden and the neighbours' windows. We waited, watching the lock-and-key man. We waited some more, wondering. Then I noticed what he was doing: he was taking out one key at a time and trying it in the door lock. He then put that key into a bag and picked out another key from a different sack, but he never got below the first few layers of keys in each sack. I whispered to him that he could never try more than a few keys that way. He shook his head and carried on. It still hadn't occurred to me that we had a scared guy on our hands, instead of the usual brave, competent technician.

I walked around the house looking for a way in, but the other door was locked and had steel bars in its glassed area. All the windows were locked and barred. I went back to the front door to find the same mad scene going on, but now the technician's hands were shaking so much that he had trouble getting the keys into the lock. We had to abort the entry. At the wall dividing the gardens of the target and our safe-house, we had the lock-and-key man untie his sacks one by one. Then two of us handed them over the wall to the rest of the team, who had already gone back into the safe-house garden. We helped the lock-and-key man over the wall, this time without incident. Once inside the safe-house, he got himself together and apologised, but he was unable to explain why he hadn't picked the lock, or why he had devised the six sacks' system that clearly wasn't a winner. Instead, we had to wait for a replacement lock-and-key man to arrive.

While we waited in the cold grounds of the target house, one of our technicians started to whisper a tale about a pipe-pusher. I had to ask him what a pipe-pusher was. He laughed and explained that plumbers use it to push a pipe along beneath the surface. I am repeating his story here because, although amusing, it illustrates the kind of thing that can go wrong. The plan was to install a bug in the Soviet ambassador's residence and to use wires rather than radio transmission, which it was feared the Soviets would quickly detect. This was before we used other technology to get audio transmissions out of target buildings. The wires were to be run out under the garden to the house next door, which the station had rented through a support agent recruited just for this operation. To carry and safeguard the wires, a pipe had to be inserted underground below the ambassador's lawn. After the pipe was installed, a surreptitious night entry would be made to install the bug and hook up the wires.

The specialists came out to insert the pipe, bringing with them a pipe-pusher. They dug a large hole in the garden of the rented house next door and fed lengths of pipe into the pipe-pusher, which forced the pipe (the first section's front end was a sharply pointed cone) through the ground at a depth of about three feet. The pipe, already wired, was pushed under the wall between the two houses, and (still underground) across the ambassador's lawn. The pipe would be stopped when it hit the in-ground basement wall of the target house.

However, despite prior assurances from the specialists, the pipe either had a mind of its own or it hit something that deflected it upwards. The next thing we saw through our peephole in the fence was the sad and unsettling sight of the Soviet ambassador and the KGB *rezident* standing beside the pipe, which had surfaced in the middle of the lawn and was waving gently in the breeze. The two men turned and started across the lawn towards the rented house. Our crew evacuated at flank speed, abandoning the errant pipe-pusher.

Not long afterwards, the technicians at headquarters sent their latest invention out to the field to demonstrate it for us. They were very proud of this achievement, we were told, and the demonstration took place on a street in a US military area in the Far East. A couple of other case officers and I watched and listened from an open third-floor window while the technicians set up their gear behind us. It was a parabolic microphone with which one could listen in on conversations up to 100 yards away, and was the size of a hand-held telescope, mounted on a tripod. They adjusted it and pointed the microphone down at the street, where two technicians were talking to each other. The distance to the two men was about 200 feet, well within the microphone's supposed range. We listened carefully and heard nothing. The technician fiddled with the microphone, and we still heard nothing. The two technicians in the street came closer, and there were still no results. The test broke up with us laughing and the technicians with red faces all around. That was the last I heard of parabolic microphones until eventually one that worked was developed.

11

Posted to Africa

In May 1960, I was offered an opportunity to go to the Belgian Congo, which was about to become independent on the 1st of July. I had heard about Africa all my life from my parents and their friends, and our house was full of African art and other objects, and photographs of events and people in the Congo. I therefore jumped at the chance; it would be – and indeed was – great fun to work in small stations in Africa, where I could do minimum management and paperwork and concentrate on running operations.

Ann and I, now with four children, left the Far East on the last day of June. On leave in Washington before going to the Congo, we read and heard daily reports of violence in the newly independent Congo. Black on white cannibalism was reported to be rampant. There were also many reports of the Congolese raping Caucasian women. One foreign service officer back from Leopoldville (soon to be re-named Kinshasa, the capital of the new state, which was its original name when my parents had lived in the Congo) told us that rape had become a social event without stigma. These stories turned out to be greatly exaggerated; there were only a few verified cases of each. However, Ann didn't relish taking four small children to the Congo to risk being eaten, so I departed alone for Leopoldville in late July 1960.

My mission was to take over in the Katanga, where one officer and one communicator had been sent in a hurry because the CIA had had nobody there before July 1960. The job was to gather intelligence on the area and its major players, and to recruit appropriate espionage agents. I would be starting CIA operations there virtually from scratch.

The Pan American DC-7 flight taking me to the Congo for the first time stopped at the old Accra airport in Ghana. When we landed, the chief stewardess invited the flight's most important passenger to the VIP lounge: Mrs Julie Timberlake, who was making her initial trip to Leopoldville to join her husband, Ambassador Claire Timberlake, at our new embassy in the former Belgian colony. Claire had asked that I escort and assist her in any way I could on the flight. In fact, she was a vivacious, outgoing lady of Latin American parentage, a wonderful personality who needed neither an escort nor assistance. There were a group of Argentinian UN soldiers on the flight, and she entertained them with stories and songs from Argentina.

Once on the ground in Accra, Julie Timberlake and I were shown to a small table in the VIP lounge by a silent Ghanaian waiter. We sat there for some time chatting, and she asked for a drink. I called over the waiter, and he pointed to an unopened bottle of Scotch whisky that was standing in the middle of the table.

'Oh, I thought that belonged to somebody,' I said. 'Is it for us?'

The waiter grinned somewhat mysteriously and nodded. He went back to the bar and watched. I poured each of us a drink, Scotch and warm water – this was before ice became *de rigueur* in former British West Africa – and we sipped our drinks and talked about what the Congo might be like. The newly liberated nation was in turmoil, with fighting in various provinces, murders of Congolese and Europeans all too frequent, and even cannibalism. I asked her, since she had diplomatic immunity, to carry a .38 revolver through customs in Leopoldville, and she agreed. The revolver was destined for the defence of the office in Leopoldville. It was highly unlikely that the US ambassador's wife would be searched for weapons or anything else, and so it turned out when we got there.

After we had sat talking in the VIP lounge at Accra for a few minutes, a Ghanaian gentleman came to the table and asked if he could join us. We waved him to a chair, and he sat with us sipping a Scotch until it was time for the aircraft to leave. He was charming: a tall and slender older man with grey hair and a perfect carriage. He asked us for news of 'the outside world'. We all talked for an hour, covering many different subjects. He was remarkably well informed about such disparate things as the plight of the Baltic states that the USSR had swallowed up in the Second World War, the desperate situation in the Congo, Nasser's view from Cairo, the future of the King of Morocco, the value of Britain's House of Lords, the future of the Lion of Judah and the Shah of Iran, and even the latest American football scores. His questions about the United Nations, Cuba, Franco's Spain and the movement for a European Common Market were incisive and well phrased. No matter how much he knew, he wanted to acquire more knowledge.

His discussion of the march of former African colonies towards freedom displayed a sense of understanding, tolerance and balance that later turned out to be rare in the Congo. Our hour with him was a thoroughly warming, truly instructive experience. When our flight was called, he left the table with much handshaking and thanks to us for the drinks. We were sad to see him go. After he had left, the waiter come over to clean the table.

'Who was that gentleman?' we asked.

'The Lord Chief Justice of Ghana [Sir Arku Korsah],' he replied. 'He comes out here almost every evening, whenever an international flight comes through. He buys a bottle, puts it on the table, and watches to see who sits there. If he finds them potentially interesting, he joins them, makes friends and brushes up on the latest news.'

'He's a remarkable man,' I commented.

'Yes, quite remarkable,' said the waiter, laughing happily. 'He's my uncle. Brains run in the family.'

My three posts in Africa, and my extensive travels throughout the continent, took place during the period which saw the end of colonialism and the beginning of independence. De-colonisation was handled differently in every country. Some countries became independent without at first having serious problems (e.g. Ghana, Ivory Coast, Sierra Leone and Burundi). In others, colonial favouritism of one tribe led to strife; in the case of Nigeria, furious ethnic rivalry ignited, which led to civil war. In the Congo, law and order broke down right away, in one way or another.

In August 1960, the Congolese masses were simply trying to survive as well as to understand the drastic changes already wrought by one month of independence; the expected improvement in life had failed to appear. There was massive unemployment and personal danger. Their leaders, some of humble origin like Congo Prime Minister Patrice Lumumba, and some of royal descent like secessionist Katanga President Moise-Kapenda Tshombe, were rivals locked in a fierce struggle to acquire and expand power. The struggle was often rooted in old tribal or personal hatreds, mixed in with greed and family feuds, plus of course East-West politics.

One of the many dilemmas was whether to rely on white advisors – and, if so, whether from East or West – or to make do without them. Many Congolese leaders could not forgive the Belgian colonialists for having treated them as '*macaques*' (monkeys), an epithet I sometimes heard them use in the period 1960–1, even after independence. That appellation was so abrasive that Lumumba publicly rebuked the King of Belgium at the independence ceremony, shouting: 'We are no longer your *macaques*!' Other Congolese – like President Tshombe – had been reasonably well treated by the Belgians and had no real quarrel with them.

The Congolese soldiers, who were mostly from the old Force Publique, were armed with live ammunition and were ill-disciplined, illiterate, often arrogant and dangerous to everyone. Their officers, mostly former NCOs, rarely appeared to take control of road blocks or breakdowns in law and order.

The Belgians had gone almost overnight from wielding colonial power to being an unco-ordinated bunch of bitter, demoralised and often panicky whites. They had reason to beware, for the Congolese soldiers had a penchant for beating up whites, even UN troops. In August 1960, ten US and Canadian airmen were brutally beaten in Stanleyville, and Lumumba ignored it. Other African leaders warned him to disarm the unruly soldiers and stop the disorders, but he didn't.

The CIA's role in the newly independent and chaotic Congo was to discover who the real shakers and movers were, what made them tick and what they planned to do. We were also there to identify and counter any and all Communist (Soviet, satellite, or Chinese) efforts to subvert the country and its leaders.

I spent the first three weeks in Leopoldville helping Larry Devlin, our representative there, by handling a few agents and prospective agents. I was also preparing to go on down to the Katanga. I was living with two other CS officers, Mike and Gene, in a small furnished house in town. Mike, an Arab specialist, was on loan from a station in northern Africa and was anxious to get the Congo mess over and go back to his station. Gene was a Far Eastern specialist and he too was out of his usual element. But both men were truly fearless professionals, who were out there day and night recruiting agents and running them under conditions of dangerous public disorder that would have had others fleeing for their lives.

The three of us discussed the problem of Lumumba at length. At that time none of us had any real concept of what he stood for. He was simply an unstable former postal clerk with great political charisma, who was leaning towards the Communist bloc. In Cold War terms, he represented the other side; the fact that he was first and foremost an African nationalist who was using East-West rivalry to advance his cause was played down by the Belgians, who greatly feared him. Lumumba had indeed brought in a dozen or so IL-14 aircraft with full duplicate Soviet crews to transport his troops against the Katanga and Kasai secessions. Czech officers had led a bloody attack which had dislodged 'Emperor' Kalondji from the Kasai, while a second Soviet airlift of Congolese troops to the Katanga appeared likely. Soviet Premier Nikita Khrushchev had sent Lumumba a personal gift of an executive aircraft.

Among African leaders, only President Sekou Touré of Guinea applauded Lumumba's use of Soviet aircraft, military personnel and weapons. The others opted to support UN efforts to restore peace and order, but of course a military victory would more than offset adverse world opinion.

On the ground, it looked as if Lumumba was about to shift the Congo into the Soviet camp. President Kasavubu had yet to move against him, but he finally did so on 5 September 1960 by sacking him and promising that he would one day die for his 'unpatriotic' actions.

Mike and I soon became close friends. We were not aware

that President Eisenhower had hinted that the CIA should have
Lumumba assassinated, but we felt certain that the only way to
prevent the Congo from falling into Communist hands was for
Lumumba somehow to leave the scene before he could consoli-
date his grip on power. Murder, a favourite KGB political
activity, was in the air in the Congo, as the Soviets were not
above knocking off some of Lumumba's many enemies.

Mike and I were both expert shots with military experience,
and we agreed that Lumumba could be shot at long range with
the proper equipment. We suggested to Larry Devlin that we
would, if necessary, be willing to do just that. We made the suggestion together, only half seriously, hoping that Larry would
reject the idea – which, as a devout Catholic, he did most stren-
uously, to our great relief. In fact, if Larry had approved the
idea, neither Mike nor I could have actually killed a defenceless
man. I relate this story knowing full well that some will read
more into it than there was, but it does honestly illustrate what
Larry has always claimed: that the murder of Lumumba was a
concept he strongly opposed on ethical grounds.

Many of Leopoldville's urban dwellers were country people
looking for work, or former servants of Belgian households
whose employers had fled, or undisciplined Congolese soldiers
prone to beating and looting. So many ordinary people were
pitifully poor, dressed in ragged clothes and living in shanty
towns, that the widespread belief that after independence things
would quickly change for the better was gone. Although it was
obvious that the transition to good times would not be fast or
easy for them, nobody could foresee just how badly it would go
under President Mobutu, who took power in a coup in 1965.
Since then, exports, agricultural products, personal security,
GNP and per capita income have all fallen. Foreign planters and
other entrepreneurs were ordered out of the country, and their
banana, rubber and coffee plantations and other enterprises
reverted to the jungle. Congolese business people were strangled
by corruption, and white-collar workers by inflation. Mobutu
and his top assistants, by enriching themselves, saw to it that
their people remained among the poorest in Africa for thirty-
two years. Would Lumumba have done better? Much of the
world thinks so, but of course we will never know. Had he followed the Soviet pattern, the Congolese would probably have

had minimal food every day, but no bright future. Now they have neither.

One prospective agent I handled was a European of great courage, who was also very streetwise. 'Paul' had been born and raised in the Congo and spoke Swahili, Lingala and various other African languages and dialects. He lived in a spacious, ramshackle rented apartment in a low-rise building near the city centre. His living room looked out on to a central courtyard, which had a huge shady tree and some lovely flowering bushes. The courtyard was alive with birdsong during the day, but it was still and dark at night except for a few very dimly lit windows. Many of the tenants had fled after independence when violence against Europeans was widespread, so many of the apartments were uninhabited.

I always visited Paul's apartment after dark, when the chance of being seen was limited, approaching it through a long, unlit tunnel from the street. The tunnel, which ran under the front of the building, was both a blessing and a problem. The good side was that, once I was sure that I was not under surveillance, I could enter the tunnel and wait for several minutes, out of sight from the street, to make doubly sure that I was not being followed. The bad side was that I could see nothing in the tunnel because the inner courtyard was so dark, yet I was backlit from the street where a distant light on a pole provided a faint, but visible glow. I was, therefore, an easy target in a city already experiencing virtual anarchy. I normally avoided carrying a revolver, but when I visited Paul a defensive weapon was necessary. I carried my preferred one – a palm-size plastic tear-gas dispenser made by our technicians, which, if squeezed, accurately shot a thin stream of gas out about twelve feet. Luckily, I never had to use it in the tunnel. Now it seems funny, but at the time the trips through the tunnel were even tenser than walking the streets to get there in the first place.

The first time I visited him, Paul amused himself in a way that almost got him a dose of my tear gas. As soon as I entered his apartment and closed his front door, which he had left unlocked for my benefit, he switched on the lights. There he was, sitting in an over-stuffed armchair, drawing a bead on my heart with an antique, loaded crossbow. There was a long silence, during which I stood still with the tear-gas dispenser in my hand ready to go and the arrow pointed unwaveringly at my heart. I figured that if his fingers squeezed the trigger of the crossbow, I would have enough time to step sideways and dust him with the gas, but I didn't initiate an attack because what he was doing seemed rather improbable in light of his previous contacts with us in Leopoldville. After what seemed an eternity he laughed, lowered the crossbow and announced that I had earned my spurs: I hadn't flinched. We became good friends and stayed so until he died some twenty years later.

One night I was driving through town with him on our way to a meeting he had set up with the ruler of a Congo province. Leopoldville was divided into unofficial, rapidly changing sectors controlled by armed factions of various feuding political parties. Each faction staked out its territory with roadblocks tended by unruly soldiers or untrained but fully armed men. Each night we had to negotiate several roadblocks in order to go anywhere, and their locations and owners changed frequently, as did their mercurial moods. This night we got through the first roadblock without serious incident, but the dozen or so 'soldiers' at the second roadblock cocked their rifles and motioned us to get out of Paul's rickety old car.

'Into the ditch,' the men said in Lingala. 'Lie down on your bellies.' Paul translated for me in whispers. Neither of us was adequately armed to take on a dozen men with guns, no matter how poorly trained they were. We lay down and waited. After a while Paul asked the soldiers what they planned to do.

'You were allowed to pass by the last roadblock,' said the leader, 'and they didn't shoot you. As they are our enemies, you must be our enemies too, so we will shoot you.' His men murmured agreement.

'They plan to kill us,' Paul said unemotionally.

I was wondering if it was worth trying to get up, gas them and make a break for it when Paul started talking. Soon, the soldiers began to laugh. Finally, they were roaring with laughter. He asked a question, listened to the reply and grabbed me by the elbow, saying, 'Up and out of here, we can go.'

Back in the car, driving towards the next roadblock, I asked what had happened. 'I started telling them funny stories in their own language,' he said. 'Native stories. The people here love a good story, and they love good story-tellers, so the leader said that we could go because nobody would dream of killing a good story-teller and his friend.'

'Did they ask a price?'

'Yes. They want me to come back every night and amuse them. I promised I would, but of course I won't.'

Paul was so good at his work that he became a very valuable, principal agent. He eventually made the CIA his career, was decorated for valour and died in the service.

One evening Larry Devlin, his wife and I were invited to dine with Ambassador Timberlake and his wife, Julie. There was a curfew from nightfall to dawn, and violators without passes were liable to be shot on the spot. Even those with passes were almost always fined – 'fines' which went into the soldiers' pockets, of course. Some of them had not been paid since independence.

While we were still drinking a pre-dinner cocktail, one of the CIA communicators telephoned to say that there was an Immediate cable in for me. Being a temporary visitor en route to the Katanga, I had no pass, so Timberlake loaned me his. I drove to the embassy, read the cable and started back towards the Ambassador's residence. I was soon stopped by a Congolese soldier with a rifle, who asked in rubbery but understandable French, 'Your name?'

I had to tell him what was printed on the pass in case he could read, so I replied, 'Ambassador Timberlake.'

'Where is your pass?'

I showed it to him, upside down.

'Aha,' said the soldier, pretending to read it. 'I've not been paid since June. The fine tonight is three hundred francs, but for ambassadors it is five hundred.' He rattled the bolt of his rifle suggestively, so I paid the fine.

Back at the Timberlakes, I returned the pass to the Ambassador and told him what had happened. 'Serves you right, David,' Timberlake laughed, 'for impersonating me.'

12

The Katanga

A few days later I left for the Katanga, the south-eastern province of the Congo. I arrived in Elisabethville (now Lubumbashi), the capital of the Katanga province, in early September 1960 and stayed there until April 1961. The Katanga had seceded from the Congo on 11 July 1960, after the newly independent Congo had become a scene of mutinies, tribal fighting and sporadic attacks against whites. Moise-Kapenda Tshombe had seized the opportunity to declare the Katanga to be completely independent of the Congo. His decision was widely condemned, not only by Lumumba and his central government, but by the United Nations, the US and its major allies, the USSR and all its allies, and by most of the Third World. Opinion and official action varied in the West, with Belgium, France and the United Kingdom reacting ambiguously as they weighed the pros and cons of letting the Katanga go free. They did, however, endorse UN Security Council resolutions calling for the return of the Katanga to the fold, but they insisted that the resolutions not be enforceable by arms. It would be many months before the UN was manoeuvred into putting down the secession by force.

The importance of the Katanga to the Congo government in Leopoldville cannot be overstated. Loss of the province was a matter of vital concern because the Katanga had most of the mineral resources and capital of the Congo. Tshombe had broken away from the Congo at a critical time when Katanga's mineral wealth was vitally needed. About eighty per cent of the Congo's $3 billion or so annual exports were produced in the Katanga. As president of the breakaway province, Tshombe had the backing of the most formidable enterprise in the Congo: UMHK (Union Minière du Haut Katanga), which alone accounted for almost half of all the Congo's exports.

Tshombe's secession was wildly applauded by many Belgian officials who remained directly on the government payroll, or were hired as advisors, and by most Belgian and other foreign settlers and businessmen. Secession was highly favoured not only by virtually all the Europeans in the Katanga but by a large number of Katangans. Both groups had traditionally been hostile to what they called 'parasitic intervention' by the central government bureaucracy of Leopoldville.

Secession had temporarily spared the Katanga from the worst of the disorders that were still tormenting the rest of the Congo – and from the perceived danger that Lumumba would deliver the entire country into the eager hands of the Soviets. But loss of the Congo's wealthiest province was anathema not only to Leopoldville and much of Africa but to the rest of the world. Overnight Tshombe became the most unpopular and reviled black leader in Africa, and was regarded as a traitor to African nationalism by many African leaders. Tshombe's few supporters in Africa included South Africa and some of the Congo's neighbours: the white government and settlers of Rhodesia, and a very conservative African priest, President Abbé Youlou, of the French Congo (known then as Congo/Brazzaville). Even then, Youlou never officially recognised the Katanga secession. In the former colonial powers – Britain, France and Belgium – there was popular support for Tshombe's secession, as indeed there was in the US when people began to realise what an unstable leader Lumumba was, but all four governments officially supported the UN's effort to bring the Congo back together. Tshombe was defiant and refused to end the secession

On 10 July 1960, serious trouble had broken out in the Katanga itself. Six unarmed and inoffensive whites riding in a civilian automobile were stopped at an Elisabethville railway crossing by a nervous or drunk (or both), Congolese soldier with a submachine-gun. For some reason, he shot and killed them all. A Belgian priest had witnessed the incident from his nearby cloisters and told me later how senseless it was. One of the victims was a young Belgian who lived among the Africans and was much loved by them. Nobody was safe from such random violence. Panic, disorder and lawlessness spread rapidly. Dozens of other whites were murdered in the bush, or raped, beaten, robbed or just scared half to death. There were stories that ranged from the greatest of human courage (black and white) to the worst of man's depravities. There were Africans who took revenge on Europeans, as well as their tribal opponents, in horribly vicious and brutal ways, and Africans who gave their lives for Europeans they hardly knew. There were Europeans who killed Africans simply because they were afraid, and those who risked their lives to save beleaguered Africans simply because they were God's children.

Of the 23,000 or so Belgians who lived in and around Elisabethville in July 1960, all but about 500 had fled to Northern Rhodesia. The fire engine from the town of Kolwezi reportedly ended up in N'Dola, Northern Rhodesia, its Belgian crew complaining that they had had to escape 'because Kolwezi was in flames'! A Rhodesian border guard of Indian origin told me in disgust that the fleeing Belgians had been relieved of six tons of small arms as they crossed into Northern Rhodesia. Six tons, he snorted, was enough for them to have put down the various outbreaks of mutiny and violence throughout the Congo. There were some acts of courage during the exodus, but mostly it was an undignified and unnecessarily panicky retreat. The disgusted border guard also told me that the only death during the exodus was suffered by a young white Rhodesian driving north to see if he could help in Elisabethville. His car was struck head on by a frantic Belgian speeding on the wrong side of the road.

One of the heroes of early July 1960 was Major Guy Weber of the Belgian army, who stood firm and kept his troops in order, but he was the exception rather than the rule. Weber later became Tshombe's military advisor and was thenceforth reviled by the many opponents of Tshombe's secession.

The Katanga was still in an uproar when I got there in

September, although by then disorder and violence in Elisabethville itself were sporadic. Most of the fighting was small scale and took place out in the bush between the newly formed Katangan Gendarmerie and Baluba tribesmen, who were the traditional enemies of Tshombe's Lunda tribe and its allies. The Gendarmerie, which was once part of the Congo's Force Publique, was at first led by Belgian officers and senior non-commissioned officers (non-coms), but when Belgium pulled out its officers and non-coms, Tshombe replaced them with a very mixed bag of foreign mercenaries of various levels of skill, will and integrity. The Balubas were against secession, but few of them could actively fight it. They received virtually no protection from far-off Leopoldville and were given short shrift by Elisabethville, which used its Gendarmerie against them. Many Balubas in the bush, who were either unarmed or armed with 'poopoos' – old smooth-bore muskets – were killed or wounded by the Gendarmerie, or were driven into a huge refugee camp established in Elisabethville. By the end of 1961, that camp was overflowing with some 35,000 refugees.

There were occasional fights between Tshombe's forces and elements of the Congolese National Army under orders from Leopoldville, but they did nothing to end secession or to disturb the relative calm returning to Elisabethville.

The CIA had sent its first representative into the confusion of the Katanga unprepared and with no operational assets. The late John Anderton, a bright and dedicated senior officer, was about to go on vacation after an arduous Far Eastern tour when word came that he was to go out to be acting chief in Elisabethville. He was not at all pleased at having his vacation postponed; in fact, he was highly irritated by the unfairness and inconvenience of the situation. When I finally arrived to replace him, he explained what had happened: at a Georgetown cocktail party, President Eisenhower had taken the Director of Central Intelligence, Allen Dulles, aside and asked if he had a man in Elisabethville. Dulles had replied that he had of course foreseen events and already had a man there. In reality, the DCI had nobody there, so the next day there was a frantic search for someone suitable, who was also a French speaker, and John was told to 'volunteer'.

I did not replace him until a month later, by which time John had written some thirty messages to headquarters, roughly one for each day he was there. All but a couple of them asked when his replacement was arriving so that he could go home. I inherited those thirty odd messages, the sum total of our Elisabethville records: there were no agents and no operational files. In fact, there was no space to store such files even if they had existed. We had one drawer in a four-drawer consular safe that would have taken an amateur safecracker thirty seconds to open.

My existence in the consulate was technically an oddity as I was still under the cover of the Department of Defense yet serving in a US Foreign Service post that had no military presence. US Consul Bill Canup and I kept quiet about my irregular status, and he discreetly arranged for the communicator ('Frenchy') and I to occupy a ramshackle bungalow next door to the consulate. The absentee owners, a Belgian couple named Questiaux, had left for Belgium. Early each morning I was awoken by Katangan policemen climbing up a huge avocado tree in the garden. We didn't mind their picking the fruit since cops trespassing in the garden was something of a guarantee against the many robbers and murderers who lurked about town.

In early September, the virtually empty town was slowly filling up again with returning foreign businessmen and officials – mostly Belgians – and with the first of hundreds of mercenaries recruited for the Katangan Gendarmerie. The UN now had armed troops in the province, and an uneasy truce was in effect between them and the Gendarmerie. Some of the Belgians who had fled and were now crawling back into town were volubly ashamed of having run away; they were also frantically pro-Tshombe. Tempers were short, people took strong positions on post-colonialism, soldiers were poorly disciplined, fights were common and murders frequent. The future was completely uncertain, both for the Africans and for foreigners. There was tension everywhere as the pro-Katanga people feuded more and more aggressively with those opposing secession – especially the growing UN presence and our small consular staff. Violence occurred regularly, at first just between individuals, but as time went on Katangan soldiers faced UN troops with weapons, and with both sides ready to fire.

All this made it fascinating to be the CIA representative there: every day was a new challenge, a new adventure, as the Katangan government struggled to protect itself, and the Congo government in Leopoldville and its UN and other supporters sought to get the province back.

There was certainly no shortage of foreign influences making themselves felt in Elisabethville. The UN, which had come into the Congo in July as a police action to restore order, made some initially fruitless efforts to have Tshombe dismantle the Gendarmerie, get rid of its mostly European mercenaries and return everything to the Congo. These efforts were cheered by most black African leaders, who increasingly portrayed Tshombe as an evil, greedy Uncle Tom – a self-seeking stooge of the European neo-colonialists. Tshombe and his supporters responded by asking why the anti-Communist West wanted the Katanga to be swallowed up by a disorderly Congo that might well go into the Communist camp? Was not the Katanga the only province of the Congo that was humming along as usual, economically vibrant and with a sound future?

Speaking selfishly, the Katangans were right, but what they were up to was undoing the rest of the Congo and its thirteen million or so people. It was feared by many leaders that the Katanga secession would encourage other secessions, such as that of the Kasai province under self-styled Emperor Leopold Kalondji. The Kasai secession had, in fact, been quickly and bloodily put down by Lumumba's forces, led by Communist Czech officers, but that event had only served to stiffen Katangan resolve to stay out of the clutches of the central government.

An independent Katanga – properly run – could survive without significant foreign help, but the Congo was not viable by itself and needed either the wealth of the Katanga or massive foreign aid.

To those few of us in the Katanga who tried to be objective, the dilemma was very real. The Belgian Congo had been a thriving nation before independence; the Belgian colonialists had ruled with an iron hand, but in exchange for enforced acquiescence they had provided the natives with social and medical services and economic opportunity. Progress was being made each year, by Congolese as well as by whites. All that was now in serious jeopardy in the rest of the Congo. The Katanga would probably continue to prosper if it remained independent, but the rest of the Congo seemed likely to remain in disorder and

penury for a long time. A prosperous, independent Katanga
might well act as a stabilising influence throughout the area, but
the political battle lines were drawn and the world was not going
to let the Katanga 'steal' most of the Congo's wealth. Without the
support, or at least the acceptance, of most of the world's leaders,
Tshombe was facing increasing difficulties as opposition to his
secession mounted. If his secession eventually collapsed in dis-
array, the damage to the Katanga would merely add to that of the
rest of the Congo.

The book solution for us in the US consulate was to accept
Washington's hostility to the secession and so try to help end it.
Yet I had a nagging feeling that Tshombe deserved better than to
be called an upstart Uncle Tom. The obvious solution, it seemed
to me, would be for Leopoldville to invite him back into the
union on such terms that would make him one of the Congo's
top leaders and keep the Katanga economy from being looted.
The trick was to discover what really made the man tick, and
what would convince him to accept some form of central government authority.

I decided that a good source of information on Tshombe
would be one of the leading members of his government. This
man had a secretary in whom he often confided, a single
European woman in her late thirties with no known weaknesses
other than her obvious lack of a mate. An agent I was developing
towards recruitment was an uninhibited, lusty European, who
was also single and who had a knack with women. His task was
to woo and win the secretary's favours in bed and to get her to
talk about Tshombe's real character and plans.

A week later I met my prospective agent and got a negative
report. 'I wasn't able to go through with it,' he said, regretfully.

'Why not? What happened?' I asked.

'Oh, she came out with me every night. We dined and then
went to her place for a nightcap."

'Well?'

'David,' he said, 'I did my best for you. But have you ever tried
to stuff a marshmallow into a piggy bank?' I've often wondered
if he invented that line on the spot, or borrowed it from some
previous experience.

Meanwhile, I got to know Tshombe personally and sometimes visited him in his 'palace' across the street from Dr

Questiaux's house. I found Tshombe bright and personable, and he was friendly towards me despite our official opposition to his secession. I used discreetly to attend his public speeches in town to watch him in action among the crowds. I could understand very little Lunda, but he was certainly a charismatic speaker with a large stock of jokes that had the crowd roaring with laughter. He was probably no more corrupt and greedy than his Congolese opponents, and it seemed to me entirely possible that he might overcome his detractors and eventually take charge of a unified Congo. That was an unpopular view in 1960–1, but it came true three years later when he became Prime Minister of the Congo, albeit rather briefly. Lew Hoffacker, who became Consul after Bill Canup (who was almost paralysed by fear that Tshombe would have him killed), knew Tshombe better than I, and at a time of more tension between the UN and the US on one side and the Katangans and their foreign supporters on the other. Lew found Tshombe defiant, often deceitful, and quite determined to keep the Katanga out of the chaos of the Congo; he was equally determined not to share Katanga's wealth with the Congo.

Tshombe was also a realist in that he believed in keeping European advisors in the Katanga – indeed, in the entire Congo – until it could fly on its own. One day we were talking in his office, when he glanced out of the window and then motioned me to look too. Across the street (in the Questiaux garden) a native woman was trying to figure out how to get water from a hose faucet. She was obviously baffled. Tshombe said to me, 'Look at her, she's the reason we need Belgian advisors here. When she knows how it works, they can go home.' His tone was defensive, reflecting his dilemma. He wanted the Belgian advice and assistance to which he and the Katanga were accustomed – and with which they were comfortable – but the price was dis-approval on the part of most influential world leaders. He didn't seem to understand at first that he ignored them at his peril.

He must have known that the Belgians were willing to stay and work out of self-interest. Their rather shrill 'loyalty' to seces-sionist Katanga included fraternisation between whites and blacks for the first time. The whites felt welcome and their jobs were well paid, so they seemed to have a future. They were there to help themselves as much as to help the Katanga, and while

most of them patted the Katangans encouragingly on the head,
they did not really befriend them. Neither in the Congo, nor
later in Rwanda and Burundi, did one see the close personal
friendships that existed between educated blacks and whites
which were common in French and Portuguese Africa. For
example, black priests in the Belgian Congo were often openly
treated by their white colleagues as savages with a veneer of civil-
isation.

I felt that despite his reputation, Tshombe was not really
solidly in the Belgian camp. The Belgians (and some other foreign advisors) had indeed played a critically important role for
him in 1960–1, helping to keep the Katanga running. They had
also kept order among his Katangan Gendarmerie in the early
post-independence days of inter-tribal fighting among the
troops. Tshombe often let it be quietly known among foreigners
that he trusted white officers and NCOs more than his own soldiers. That was part of his rationale for bringing in mercenaries
after Belgium withdrew its army personnel. But the Belgian advisors were really a temporary convenience which he was able to
use to his advantage – until Foreign Minister Paul-Henri Spaak
returned to office and stiffened the Belgian government's resolve
to side with the UN. At that point, Tshombe began looking for
other solutions.

First he had a short flirtation with a rather fanatical French
colonel named Trinquier, who wanted to bring thousands of
'*pieds-noirs*' (Algerian-born French people being forced out of
Algeria) into the Katanga as settlers. He proposed that Tshombe
provide thousands of hectares of farm land for these settlers, and
there was even talk of merging the Trinquier settlers with
increased white settlers in the Rhodesias from such areas as South
Africa. Such a white enclave was touted as an attractive alternative
for those Katangans and their European supporters who believed
that almost anything was better than submission to the
Communists, especially since there seemed a chance that the
Congo disaster would be repeated in other sub-Sahara nations. A
West-oriented pro-white belt of states all the way south to South
Africa seemed to the white extremists in the Katanga and the
Rhodesias to be a very attractive goal. The bulk of the interested
world, of course, saw this as blatant neo-colonialism and lumped
Tshombe in with the extremists. No compromise was to be

tolerated. Britain, Belgium and France (which was anxious to solve its *pieds noirs* problem) were out-shouted if not out-gunned.

Tshombe's greed for wealth and power was no less than that of the leaders in Leopoldville, and he was essentially a Lunda first and a Congolese by historical accident: after all, the boundaries of the Belgian Congo were a European invention that had brought under one name hundreds of tribes with no traditional loyalties beyond their ethnic borders, and no common language. Swahili was a trade language and French was used by the educated, while the great mass of people spoke only their own languages or dialects.

Then there was the screaming rhetoric of the USSR, its satellites, and China, who claimed that the West, led by the 'imperialist' US, was secretly trying to establish neo-colonialism. Tshombe and his ilk were their 'running dogs'. The Communist propaganda worked, and it was therefore impossible for a 'good' Westerner to accept Tshombe and his secession.

Tshombe was a natural leader. He had been born into a royal line of the Lunda tribe, which had once ruled a very large empire that had included parts of the Kasai, Angola and Rhodesia as well as most of the Katanga. His father was a wealthy Congolese businessman, who owned a hotel, several plantations and shops. He had been educated through junior high school by American Methodist missionaries and had then been sent to visit Europe as a young man, an unusual treat for a Congolese at the time. Tshombe inherited the family businesses and presided over the African Chamber of Commerce in Elisabethville and the Lunda tribal organisation. He married a daughter of Paramount Chief Mwata Yamvo of the Lunda tribe, and co-founded Conakat (with Bayeke tribal chieftain Godefroid Munongo, who as Katanga interior minister was one of Lumumba's murderers). Conakat was an association of political parties which called for the Congo to become a federation of autonomous states. Tshombe had had no quarrel with the Belgian colonisers and, as we have seen, after independence it was natural for him to make full use of Belgian advisors. Conakat included the Union Katangaise, a party dominated by Belgian settlers who favoured Katangan autonomy if not complete independence. Tshombe was a pro-Western leader of relatively significant stature in Congolese terms (in 1960, the entire population of the Congo – fifteen million people – had only fifteen university graduates).

The United Nations, which because of Cold War concerns quickly became the principal player on the scene, called for the immediate return of the Katanga to the Congo. UN Secretary-General Dag Hammarskjold skilfully manoeuvred so that the West, not the Communists, could most influence UN decisions in New York and UN activities on the ground. As a result, the Soviets were furious that the UN was acting against Communist interests. They howled bloody murder, but were unable to make any headway after Lumumba was removed from the premiership in late 1960. Britain and France supported a UN military presence in the Congo to restore law and order, but not one that would force Tshombe back into the fold by force of arms. The United States officially backed Hammarskjold's policies and was therefore opposed to Tshombe's secession. That made the position of our consulate in Elisabethville difficult: we were against the main goal of the state we were living in.

In February 1961, the UN came out with a stronger resolution enabling its growing military forces in the Congo to cope better with civil unrest and the problem of Tshombe's growing number of mercenary soldiers. The UN sent in Moroccan, Indian, Swedish and Irish troops to the Katanga to restore order and try to influence Tshombe to return to the Congo fold. (Later on, shortly after I left, the UN troops were used to force the Katanga back into the Congo.)

The Belgian, French and British government positions were initially ambiguous, although they did not officially or overtly support the Katanga secession. The Soviets were doing their best to turn things their way, but they had no presence in the Katanga. Many of the former Belgian colonial officials, and most – if not all – of the Belgian and other foreign settlers and businessmen, and the first media representatives on the spot (who were mostly from other African areas such as the Rhodesias), were openly pro-Tshombe and his secession. South Africa, also unofficially on Tshombe's side, sent trade commissioners to Elisabethville to open relations and negotiate trade arrangements.

Given the various viewpoints on the ground, the US consulate and its staff were treated with hostility by most Katangan officials as well as by the majority of foreign residents. Consul Bill

Canup's refrain that the US had fought a great civil war against its own southern secession was treated with scorn. Too many in the Katanga either feared that Lumumba would sell out the Congo to the Soviets and the Chicoms (Chinese Communists), or that a Lumumbist Congo would loot the Katanga and ruin it if the province was taken back. Given Lumumba's rhetoric, they had a point, but it was overwhelmed by world opinion against Tshombe.

In the Congo of 1960–1, our prime CIA mission was clear: to stop Soviet and Chinese Communist efforts to move in and oust the United Nations and its non-Communist supporters. The biggest perceived danger was Lumumba, who had a large following, so he was the West's enemy number one and the darling of the Communist world and its allies. His detractors did their best to get rid of him and, as I relate below, on 17 January 1961 they succeeded in killing him.

Although President Eisenhower and President-elect John Kennedy apparently wanted Lumumba removed from power and had discreetly made that clear to the CIA, their wishes produced nothing more than some fruitless efforts by headquarters that were quietly blocked by Larry Devlin. As I have already recorded, Devlin, a personal friend whose strong religious ethics and courage I admire, took the view that it was immoral to kill a leader who might side with the Communists but who was clearly not trying to start a Third World War.

A thousand miles to the south-east, in the secessionist Katanga, there would be no Soviets, satellites or Chinese Communists as long as the pro-Western Tshombe was running things. My orders in Elisabethville were simply to recruit a stable of agents who could keep us informed – among both the Katangan government and its white supporters, and the main tribal opposition, the Balubas. I set out to conduct the standard recruitment cycle: to spot people who looked like good agent prospects, to contact and assess them, and to develop and recruit those who would make good agents. The task was not easy. The US consulate had been there for forty years, but mainly because of the US private sector's mining interests in the region. In July 1960, the consulate had had to switch gears and become, in effect, a political listening and diplomatic action post – an extension of our embassy in Leopoldville. The consular officers had to

start from scratch, trying to work with a newly formed government of people they hardly knew: inexperienced Katangan
government officials and their Belgian advisors. About the only
cause they had in common with the US was anti-Communism;
otherwise the consulate and the independent Katangans were, in
effect, enemies.

By the time I got there, there were very few Belgians still in
Elisabethville, so at first there was a critical shortage of people
whom I would normally have relied upon to learn what made
people like Tshombe and his principal followers tick. The
Belgian officials who remained in town were already suspicious
of, if not openly hostile to, US intentions and were not inclined to
confide in its representatives. Even though some of the commercial and other non-official residents were friendly, they were
equally hostile towards us because it didn't suit the majority of
the whites to have the Katanga brought back into the Congo. I
was particularly unpopular when word got around that I had
advised an American citizen not to join the Katangan
Gendarmerie as a mercenary. The pay was good – $1,000 a
month, if memory serves – but, as I knew from my army experience, he would have lost his citizenship if he had sworn allegiance
to a foreign head of state. The man was furious and accused me
of inventing that regulation, but I was able to convince him that
not only was it established US law, but that I had been the victim
of it myself. He went off growling, and I never saw him again.

One of the most memorable things about the Katanga was
the vehemence of the rains, perhaps due to its altitude: for example, Elisabethville is at some 4,000 feet. Huge thunder clouds
rode in from the east coast of Africa hundreds of miles away –
produced by the monsoons of the Indian Ocean – and the rain
would pour down so hard that it splashed up to five or six feet,
forming a white mist that made it impossible to see more than a
foot or so ahead. Driving a car was out of the question. You
simply had to stop and wait until the thunder had passed.
Walking was better, but an umbrella offered no protection
because the splash drenched you from the bottom up. A raincoat
ensured that your head and neck, as well as your lower legs and
feet, got wet, while the rest of you was quickly soaked by your
own perspiration.

The distances in the Katanga seemed vaster than in the United

States because so little of the country was inhabited. You could travel for hundreds of miles in the bush and see nobody, nor any works of man, just miles and miles of scrub, huge anthills (sometimes fifty feet high) and red earth. The British good humouredly called it MMBA – miles and miles of bloody Africa, but to the Katangese it was the cradle of life.

Cannibalism had once existed in the Congo, and in 1960, as I've mentioned, there were reports that it was still being practised. Because of these reports, it was widely believed by Europeans to have been revived after having been virtually extinguished during colonial times. However, during my years in Africa I never witnessed it and received only one verified report of cannibalism in the Congo: the gruesome deaths of a dozen Italian airmen at the hands of rebels in the Kivu in 1962.

However, Jos, my cook/house servant in the Katanga, was a Mulunda, from a tribe in which cannibalism had been reported several times by the Belgian colonial authorities. Jos, so he claimed, was a reformed cannibal, a very nice guy with a charming smile. He did have light fingers, but whenever he stole something, all I had to do was ask him if he knew where it was and the next day, by magic, he 'found' it. One evening, I invited two American religious missionaries to dinner. Upon learning that Jos claimed to have been a 'practising' cannibal, they made the mistake of teasing him about it. Jos, who had a very straightforward way of protesting against any taunts, went into the kitchen, got a large carving knife and came back into the dining room. He said nothing. He just stood there staring at the two missionaries. He made no move to serve dinner, and I made no move to force him to do so. I felt that they had gone too far and that he had the right to express his anger. They blushed, said not a word and left shortly afterwards, still hungry.

White mercenaries (known as *Les Affreux*, the dreadful ones) were everywhere, shooting off their mouths, drinking and squabbling, and sometimes shooting up UN units. President Tshombe was flying high and had turned against the United States, and the UN was increasing its armed presence. Then Lumumba came on to the scene. After having been deposed as Premier of the Congo, on 17 January 1961 he was flown to Elisabethville and handed over to the secessionist government of the Katanga province. He arrived in a DC-4 plane which was scheduled to land in the Kasai province, but the airport there had waved the aircraft off. The pilot then flew to Elisabethville, where he circled while Tshombe and his government decided what to do. They agreed to let the plane land and, accordingly, Lumumba, in chains and badly beaten, arrived in Elisabethville accompanied by an international hue and cry.

I was so frustrated by the intrusion of his presence into an already complicated, delicate and at times frenetic situation, in which I had insufficient assets to cover events, that I cabled Leopoldville: 'THANKS FOR PATRICE. HAD WE KNOWN HE WAS COMING WE'D HAVE BAKED A SNAKE.' A copy went to headquarters, and the communicator feared that I would be fired as a result. However, Ed Welles, then chief of the Africa Division branch that handled the Congo, sent me a cartoon of two Texans baking a snake – the first sign that I wasn't going to be fired. I learned later that the cable had appealed to CIA Director Allen Dulles's sense of humour, which certainly saved my skin.

Lumumba was put to death in Elisabethville almost immediately, but the murder was a very well-kept secret of which I was not aware for some time. Weeks later, it was announced that he had been killed while trying to escape from a hut, deep in the bush, in which he had been imprisoned. A few days after that, at a reception given by the US Consul, I talked with Interior Minister Munongo and Finance Minister Kibwe, two of the toughest nuts in Tshombe's cabinet, who wanted to know what I thought of the 'news'. It was a good time to find out how much imagination they had. I asked them, 'Why didn't you simply announce that he really had escaped? That would have paralysed Stanleyville, and they would have waited years for him to show up.' From the looks of consternation on their faces, they obviously hadn't thought of it.

Lumumba's murder was the death knell of the Katanga secession. Internationally, Tshombe and his two principal ministers, Munongo and Kibwe, were now billed as cold-blooded murderers. The UN Security Council reacted by approving the forcible arrest and expulsion of foreign advisors and mercenaries. The scene was set for two rounds of bloody fighting that eventually ended the Katanga secession.

Years later, that snake cable enabled me to demonstrate that I was unaware of Lumumba's murder until long after it had happened – and therefore that I was not implicated in any way. I was required to testify to a congressional committee about my knowledge of – and suspected role in – the assassination, and I was allowed to set the time and place of the meeting. My identification was also to be kept secret. I picked a quiet Washington restaurant for the meeting, after the dinner hour.

The committee's chief counsel arrived on time, and we had a drink together. He displayed a fair knowledge of the events surrounding the assassination, and I was able to demonstrate that I had had nothing to do with the assassination. The first part of my 'defence' was that right after Lumumba's arrival in the Katanga, I had sent that cheeky cable to Leopoldville, with a copy to Langley. My second line of 'defence' was that two years later, while I was serving in Usumbura, the capital of Burundi, I had acquired an informant who had said that he had been in the room when Lumumba was executed. It had been done by two Katangan cabinet members right after Lumumba's arrival in January. My source described the murder in detail, and I wrote it up in a lengthy report to headquarters. No busy officer would have wasted that much time, I pointed out, if he already knew how, by whom and when Lumumba was killed. The chief counsel said that that sounded right and agreed to dig up the cable and the dispatch. That was the last I heard of the matter.

As we shook hands and parted outside the restaurant, the chief counsel thanked me and, with a knowing smile, said, 'Goodnight, Colonel Hasey.' Seeking to parade his knowledge, he had decided that he was interviewing Jack Hasey, who in fact hadn't been posted to Elisabethville until more than two years after I had left. I said nothing, but started laughing once I got in my car. It was a real honour to be mistaken for Jack Hasey, who was one of only two United States citizens inducted into the Companions of the Order of Liberation by General Charles de Gaulle. In June 1996, at the age of seventy-nine, he had also been made an Officer of the Legion of Honour by President Jacques Chirac. Hasey, a charming man and a true professional, served all over the world in the CIA from 1949 to 1974.

Not long after the Lumumba incident, three Fouga Magisters (French jet fighters) were secretly flown in by US commercial aircraft and crew, in direct violation of US policy, to join

Tshombe's forces. During a routine airport check-up, I chanced on them being unloaded from a US civilian KC97 pipeline cargo aircraft at night. When I chatted with the US air crew, they were mere delivery men, with no idea of the situation their cargo was about to make more tense – the aircraft were obviously there to shoot down UN planes. The three Fougas were actually training aircraft, but they were armed and perfectly able to destroy UN piston driven transports. The UN was furious, and it was suspected that this was a CIA operation to help secretly build a stable, pro-Western Katanga in case the rest of the Congo were to fall under Communist domination. If it was, nobody had told me anything about it – which makes CIA involvement highly unlikely.

The embassy in Leopoldville and the consulate in Elisabethville had SSB (single sideband) radio transceivers, and Bill Canup frequently used his set to communicate in the clear with Ambassador Timberlake. One day I happened to be walking along a street which housed one element of the Katangan Gendarmerie when, loud and clear over a speaker, came Canup's voice, followed by Timberlake's. The Belgians had rigged up a listening post for the Gendarmerie, but had forgotten to make sure that they didn't play the results on a loudspeaker – especially with open windows. I told Canup right away, of course, and when he at first had difficulty believing that the Belgians would do such a thing, I quoted to him what he and Timberlake had just said. After that, no more classified information was passed over the SSB.

Bronson Tweedy, then chief of the DO's Africa Division, came to visit the Katanga, an occasion that was both useful professionally and a pleasure socially. His father and mine had been classmates in Princeton, and we were good friends. We talked most of the time, but one evening we toured Elisabethville. Around 11 p.m., we noticed a glow in the sky, which was coming from the vicinity of the railway station, and so we drove towards it. Further investigation led us to a building on the roof of which a Belgian officer was standing, spraying something with a hose. He shouted to us that part of an ammunition train was on fire and that the cargo was about to explode. People in the neighbouring houses were at risk. There were other hoses available, and he urged us to help him. I asked Bronson if he was willing to stay and help, or if that was a silly way for the Africa Division chief to risk his life. Bronson, to his lasting credit, laughed and said that we should help. We did, and the fire was soon under control.

Louis Armstrong, the King of Jazz, and his band, with the well-known singer Thelma Middleton, arrived in Elisabethville for a stay of several days. Their trip was sponsored by the USIA, and I put on my other hat to help Canup and his small staff. The visit was a great success. Armstrong was a wonderfully good-natured man with a great sense of fun. Tshombe had an equally good sense of humour and had long been an Armstrong admirer, so they took to each other like brothers.

Thelma Middleton however had a different nature from Armstrong's. She was rather waspish, seldom smiled and didn't seem to be enjoying herself. One evening Canup asked me to pick her up from her hotel and drive her to a reception being given by Tshombe, which I wasn't planning to attend. I could just do it if she were prompt, because I had an agent meeting shortly afterwards. She kept me waiting for over thirty minutes, and when I drove like mad, trying to make up the lost time, she did nothing but complain. Fortunately, she got to the reception on time, and my agent waited long enough so that we could meet. To give Thelma her due, she never complained about me to either Bill Canup or Louis Armstrong.

The visit did a lot to ease the tension between the consulate and Tshombe, and prospects looked brighter between the US and the secessionist Katanga. Ambassador Timberlake was about to visit, to discuss some form of reassociation between the Katanga and the central government in Leopoldville, and Tshombe and his cabinet indicated that Timberlake would be welcome. Then things flew apart.

A very senior State Department official, Loy Henderson, was visiting Africa, looking at existing embassies and acquiring new embassy buildings where we had none. He was in Leopoldville and his next stop was supposed to be Tananarive, in Madagascar. He travelled in an official US aircraft and invited Timberlake to go with him as far as Elisabethville. Henderson had no plan to spend any time in Elisabethville, but things went wrong. As Henderson and his entourage drove out to the airport, an African riding a bicycle (for the first time in his life) lost control and burst out of the bush in front of one of the cars in the cortege – a car in which Frank Carlucci (who later became Secretary of State for Defense) was riding. The African was killed and, in the resulting melée, Carlucci was stabbed. Henderson brusquely took charge and ordered Timberlake to stay in Leopoldville and calm things down. Timberlake could delay his visit to the Katanga for a few days, said Henderson. Although Timberlake protested, Henderson, who was either unaware or unwilling to take into account what was at stake, was adamant.

Meanwhile, we were ignorant of all this in Elisabethville. No message came in from Leopoldville and, when we went out to the airport to greet Timberlake, we waited in the hot sun, wondering why the flight was late. Tshombe and his entire cabinet were there too, with the Katangan Gendarmerie band. The sun sizzled, feet were shifted and watches were gazed at, until finally – at least an hour late – the flight arrived. It wasn't the plush C-47 but a much larger aircraft, and the first man out was not Timberlake, but Henderson.

The scene now took on a surreal quality. The band played the only American tune it knew, 'Marching through Georgia', and when Henderson stopped on the way down from the aircraft doorway to the tarmac, there was a look of disgust on his face. He was a southerner, I assume. He resumed his descent, and Tshombe came forward to greet him. I was standing next to Canup, who tried to introduce them to each other, but Henderson ignored Tshombe and said to Canup, 'Timberlake isn't coming today. There was an accident on the way to the airport. An African was killed, but luckily none of us were killed. Carlucci was stabbed, but he'll get over it. I told Timberlake to stay there and sort things out.' The implication was that an African life was less important than an American one.

What Henderson didn't know was that Tshombe spoke fluent English. He got the message all right, but he was a polite man and invited Henderson to tour Elisabethville with him. Henderson looked at his watch and snapped, 'I can give you twenty minutes, that's all.' The tour in fact lasted an hour, and Henderson was less than gracious about it at the time (although Consul Lew Hoffacker, who replaced Bill Canup in November 1961, remembers Henderson later saying that Tshombe had impressed him quite favourably).

By the time Timberlake showed up a day or so later, the tide had turned thanks largely to Henderson's *faux pas*. Tshombe's Belgian advisors worked on Timberlake, pushing the point that Henderson had insulted all Africans. The relatively minor nature of this event was indicative of how unlikely reassociation was, and of how little remaining faith Tshombe had in the US to help rather than harm his cause. Timberlake and the US were roasted at a meeting with the Katangese and their Belgian advisors, and we were the enemy again.

An amusing sequel took place while Timberlake was in Elisabethville. Out at the airport the air attaché's plush C-47 was sitting on the tarmac. The airport building was occupied by UN forces, while the Katangan Gendarmerie held the other side of the airport. A Swedish UN officer went to the pilot of the C-47 and said that he was sorry, but the colonel would have to get out of his aircraft and take cover. The two sides were about to open fire on each other – not an unusual event in those days. The air attaché refused. He had signed for the aircraft, was responsible for it and he would stay in it. The Swedish officer understood at once. The C-47 was an expensive piece of equipment, and so the 'war' was postponed until Timberlake and the C-47 left Elisabethville.

One result of Henderson's *faux pas* was an orchestrated 'attack' on our consulate. I was visiting friends on the following Sunday when the communicator called to say that I'd better come over because the consulate was being bombarded – not by shells, but by ripe avocados. Newsmen staying at the Hotel Leo II had called – just as 'the attack' began – to ask how it was going, so they had clearly been forewarned. Most of them were pro-Tshombe anyway and were prepared to blow any small incident into a major anti-US news story. The communicator held the phone out so that they could hear the crash of the avocados on the tin roof, which sounded like heavy artillery, and he invited them to come over to see for themselves what kind of attack it was, but they were reluctant to risk their skins, so the publicity that Tshombe's propagandists hoped for never came about. I got to the consulate just as the attackers were leaving. They consisted of about two hundred young African boys in their pre-teens, led by several white priests – probably Belgians – in their cassocks. The communicator was duly commended for his cool reaction to the newsmen when they called him.

For the rest of my time in the Katanga, the consulate was left undisturbed. Shortly after I left, however, tensions rose again, and the consulate's windows were smashed and Lew Hoffacker was placed under house arrest for a while. The Katanga secession eventually was put down by force. Round One started in a bizarre way: UN Representative Conor Cruise O'Brien, without specific authority from Secretary-General Hammarskjold, and against the latter's stated policy, had UN troops try to round up the foreign mercenaries, arrest Tshombe and his ministers, and install a pro-Leopoldville provincial government. They succeeded in evicting a few mercenaries from the Katanga, but hostility against the UN grew much stronger and Katangan units fought bloody battles with UN troops.

Ironically, as I have already noted, one unforeseen long-term result of the eventually successful UN effort to force the Katanga back into the Congo was the thirty-two-year rule of Mobutu (a Force Publique sergeant when I first met him), during which much of the wealth of the Congo (Katanga included) seeped into his pockets. International funds earmarked to help the Congo/Zaire were abducted and further lined Mobutu's treasure chest. His total take reportedly came to the equivalent of between $3 and $5 billion.

Despite the difficulties, in the eight months I was in the Katanga our tiny CIA representation – one intelligence officer and one communicator – went from having very little intelligence and no assets, to having built up a fair knowledge of the key players and a sound basis for future operations. I was able to recruit some agents and informants whom I turned over to my successor, the very energetic, effective and courageous Dave Whipple. When Dave arrived, we still had no safe storage and were using the same drawer of the consular safe, so all our operations had to be stored in our heads. It was a good, but not an easy, exercise in brainwork.

Looking back now, I wonder if my half-serious thought at the time was valid: why not let the Communists have the Congo (and Rwanda and Burundi)? They would have broken their teeth on it. Just as the average native of those areas cannot easily accumulate wealth and become a capitalist (because of the extended family system), so too the average person is not adaptable to the disciplines of Communism. I tried more than once to help

Africans in the Congo and later Burundi to start small businesses, but they failed because the extended family soaked up whatever income was produced. As to Communist cell meetings, the extended family means that a cell member might – for family reasons – come to a secret meeting with one or more relatives tagging along. In addition, secrets are hard to keep in Africa – perhaps harder than in Washington. A Congo saying is, '*En Afrique tout fini par se savoir*' ('In Africa everything eventually becomes known'). There's a definite charm and great value to the extended family way of life, but in black Africa it does not readily lend itself to foreign ways.

13

A New Posting to Burundi

Towards the end of my time in the Katanga, news came that for the first time a CIA representative was to be sent to Burundi. I applied to be the first one and was accepted right away. In July 1961, Ann and I with our five children arrived in Usumbura (now Bujumbura). The job included covering Rwanda, which was then in the last throes of its first twentieth-century civil war pitting Hutu against Tutsi.

I had prepared for the task of opening up in Burundi before going there by taking a CIA training course in one-time pad ciphers and in photography, including the development of negatives and the printing of film. The photo training was very useful, but it didn't cover the practical problem of maintaining the right developer and fixer temperatures in the tropics without air conditioning. I had to learn by trial and error how to cool the fluids with ice and still not ruin the film. I learned how to prepare and seal pouches, and how to do the myriad other things usually done by secretaries or intelligence assistants. Finally, I had a refresher course on hand weapons and was issued with a .38 detective special for personal protection (which I never fired in Africa except to keep in practice).

For the first six months after I arrived in Usumbura, Rwanda and Burundi were still governed by Belgium under the oversight of a UN trusteeship (which dated back to a League of Nations mandate of 1922). At the end of 1961, there was six months of autonomy, during which the Burundi government handled all matters except for foreign and military affairs, which Belgium continued to handle. Finally, complete independence was announced for 1 July 1962.

We had no official orders in Burundi other than to get things going. The CIA had never had a presence there and the US consulate was brand new, so our mission was to get established, learn who made things go, and start establishing a stable of agents who would provide intelligence not overtly available. We decided to open windows into the opposition, pretty much leaving the government to the consulate, although the political officer, Ambassador-to-be Julius Walker, and I worked closely together and became good friends. This also happened with the US military attaché, Colonel Alex Alexander.

As usual CIA goals were compatible with and complemented those of the State Department chief of mission and his staff, but our methods were not the same. In addition to covering the local scene, they were as interested as we were in trying to find out what the Communist representatives were up to, although there were, in fact, no Soviet, satellite or Chicom diplomatic presences there during my two years in the post. However, we knew that they would inevitably come, so we prepared for them by recruiting people most likely to know them, or to work for them in some way.

I had two notable failures right from the start: firstly, I failed to flag the fact that the left-leaning Uprona party was going to win the 1961 general election. The fact that the Belgian government officials in place and our own consulate were also taken by surprise was no consolation. Secondly, not long afterwards, Prime Minister Louis Rwagasore was assassinated by a group that included a prominent politician I was developing as a potential agent. As I had been there for only a couple of months, Langley forgave me.

After that things went pretty well, and our assets produced a good picture of what was going on and what might happen. I had at least one Hutu agent in Burundi (long since murdered by the Tutsi) who took to espionage like a mongoose to a snake. He was fascinated by the subject, was quick to learn and act, was determined to do a perfect job, and needed very little training and no encouragement.

It was a fascinating two years spent in one of the most beautiful areas of the world – Burundi and Rwanda were often called the Switzerland of Africa. The irony was that all that beauty did nothing to stop the ethnic hatred, and the barbarity which that hatred provoked. Five hundred years of social, economic and political rivalry on a feudal scale – and post-feudal mutual fear – is hard to assuage.

Rwanda and Burundi are small countries, about 10,000 square miles, with some six million souls in each. This means that there are 600 people per crowded square mile – although there were 'only' 300 per square mile when I left there in 1963. The two countries are populated by Hutu (between 85 and 90 per cent), Tutsi (10 to 12 per cent), and Congo-Nile Crest pygmies, the Twa (about 1 per cent).

Tutsis are Nilotic in origin. The more adventurous migrated slowly south with their long-horned cattle and their spears from the area of Ethiopia and southern Sudan, drifting into Rwanda and Burundi some 500 years ago. The majority, the Hutu, are of Bantu origin and came from what is now the Congo. They were in Rwanda before the Tutsi arrived, but they were soon dominated by the Tutsi, and it was common for the Tutsi overlords to occupy the tops of the hills while the feudalised Hutu lived at lower levels.

The Hutu traditionally viewed the Tutsi as cunning, vicious and deceitful, and they feared and hated them while at the same time obeying them. The Tutsi tended to despise the Hutu as being of an inferior race, useful only as cultivators or herdsmen. The two ethnic groups were more often than not at odds with each other. The Tutsi usually outwitted or outfought the Hutu, usually with the help of the Twa, whom the Tutsi used as warriors and court jesters. Wealth was mostly counted by the numbers of goats and/or long-horned cattle a person owned, and it was rare for a Hutu to have many animals.

The arrival of European colonialists in 1895 slowly put a lid on tribal fighting, although murder, rape and mutual harassment persisted. Both countries were part of German East Africa until the end of the First World War, after which (from 1922) they were administered by Belgium as a League of Nations mandate. They were then under the trusteeship of the UN and were finally granted independence in 1962. Rulers of Rwanda and Burundi – each was called a Mwami – reigned under German and then Belgian supervision. However, Belgian trust in the Tutsis (especially those of Rwanda) slowly eroded because they saw the Tutsi leaders as being particularly devious and cruel.

The Mwami of Rwanda was overthrown by a Hutu revolution in 1960. The accompanying bloodbath saw the Hutu killing thousands of Tutsis and driving some 60,000 out of the country. That revolt was initially cheered, if not backed, by the Catholic church and some of the Belgian trusteeship administrators. Later, as questions were asked in the UN, and UN observers arrived to look things over, the killing virtually stopped.

I lived there for a couple of years in the early 1960s and visited again several times over the next ten years, but little changed. The departure of most of the Europeans had simply made it open season. The killing began again in Burundi in the mid-1960s, this time with a massacre of Hutu by the Tutsi. A few years later, the Tutsi soldiery murdered almost all their Hutu comrades-in-arms one night, while the Tutsi students at the College du Saint Esprit executed most of their Hutu counter-parts. Hutu politicians were executed in great numbers, and eventually the life of any literate Hutu was in danger. In both Rwanda and Burundi, political feuds, mixed with family vendet-tas and profound ethnic hatreds, erupted time and again before the latest Rwandan catastrophe in the 1990s.

The problem is so old, so complex and so unresponsive to common sense as we know it that some must sincerely doubt that there is anything practical to be done by the rest of the world but to let the fighting take its course. Logic would seem to call for the Organisation of African Unity to march in and make peace, but that would be as fruitless, no doubt, as expecting the Organisation of American States to solve the problems of Haiti or Nicaragua.

The sadness is that all this killing in Rwanda, eastern Congo and Burundi is taking place in one of the world's most beautiful regions, along the western arm of the Great Rift Valley. A land of perpetual spring, with breathtaking vistas of upland lakes, green hills, cool mountains, active and dormant volcanoes, and the rain forests of the Congo-Nile Crest, it is for the moment, sadly, the genocidal capital of Africa.

Wives of officers in the less comfortable overseas posts often suffer more than their husbands, who at least have their work to distract them. The afternoon we arrived in Usumbura, with five small children, Ann walked out on to the balcony of our hotel room and disturbed two huge vultures who had been perching on the balcony railing. They flew off squawking, with a rustle of dry feathers. A couple of bird lice had been left behind, and they scampered around frantically looking for their vultures. My wife looked at the copious, smelly vulture droppings on our balcony, the baked brown soccer field across the unpaved road, and the forbidding mountains shimmering in the heat, and said nothing, but shook her head slightly. A silent tear came from each eye and slid down her cheeks. Thankfully, within a week we moved into a house, and she set out to enjoy the place as much as possible.

CIA representation comes in a variety of sizes, and a large station may have its people under several different covers – usually either diplomatic, military, or commercial. Its various segments may operate against different goals or targets, and so have personnel with different skills. Small stations, on the other hand, may contain only three people – the chief, his intelligence assistant (IA) and a communicator. Usumbura was that small in 1961. We covered Rwanda as well as Burundi, and paid attention to the eastern Congo, which was also in turmoil because rebels against Leopoldville held much of the area.

One of the problems of opening the Burundi office was that we had no files. No cards with names and basic biographical information existed, not even on top government and other political leaders. Requests to headquarters for name traces – asking what they knew about someone – produced nothing. Since there was at first no official Communist presence, our goals and directives were nonexistent and had to be made up as we went along. Also, the budget had yet to be devised, justified and approved by headquarters.

Whereas in the Katanga John Anderton had left me a few files and name cards, and the consulate had been open for decades, in Usumbura we had nothing. Even the US consulate was newly established, and everything had to be started from scratch. This made it more fun and certainly more interesting than following a well-worn track.

When you open a peacetime espionage operations office under these circumstances, you get a really good look at the guts of this unique profession. The first officer on the scene usually arrives before his IA. He must therefore know how everything in a station gets done. For example, how to type intelligence reports and in what format; how to prepare, seal, do the contents manifest and send a classified pouch to headquarters; how to prepare cable traffic for the communicator to send; how to get rid of classified trash, and how to develop and print film. He must deal effectively with US Foreign Service colleagues and with US military attachés. He must know what information to give his embassy colleagues – usually only information which he gathers openly – and he must decide what to transmit in classified communications to headquarters and elsewhere. This is not only information from established agents, but also from prospective agents. He must of course know how to spot, meet, develop, recruit and manage agents as covert agents are the lifeblood of human espionage. Reports based on their information must give the consumer a clear feel for these sources' level of access and degree of reliability, while protecting them by disguising their source descriptions. He must also know how to deal with questions of housing, vehicles, security, liaison, counter-espionage, covert action, physical threats, local politics, the handling of the occasional hostile US Foreign Service officer, and so on. Unlike life in a large station, there is nobody to turn to for instant advice.

Ambassadors and other Foreign Service chiefs of missions – i.e. ministers running legations, or consuls and consuls-general running consular posts isolated from embassies – are a very special matter to CIA representatives. They must be 'recruited', as it were: won over so that they will help rather than hinder. Mostly it is an easy job, since the chief of mission also wants to get along with, or 'recruit', his local CIA representative. However, some are not easy. I had two ambassadors whose mothers got them the job. One was the son of a very well-known public figure whose mother pulled political strings to get him a very nice embassy. But he didn't want the job, and he took to the bottle. He was drunk almost every morning from ten o'clock on. Now and then he'd stagger into my office, put up his feet, sigh and say, 'This is the only place in the embassy where anybody knows what they're doing.' This was, of course, nonsense. When he finally left the post after a couple of years, he still didn't know who half the members of the host country's cabinet were.

The other was an ambassador to an African country whose mother had contributed $40,000 to the political party in power to buy her son a third-rate embassy. He used to crow about the fact that his mother had made a really good investment – his annual salary was more than her 'down payment' – and he spent his time watching birds and plants grow.

However, most ambassadors and other US diplomatic and consular mission chiefs were very professional, solid citizens. The first chief of mission in Burundi, Consul Herbert Olds (later consul-general), was a most helpful and kindly man. He and his wife Mary did their best to make things easy for us. Our first meeting with Herb was embarrassing, but he took it in his stride. He came to the airport to meet the Sabena DC-7 flight we were on from Cairo to Usumbura, but he had to wait for about half an hour before we could leave the aircraft as we were searching for eight pairs of shoes. Our youngest son was then an infant in a crib, but the other four were between nine and two years old. They were active kids, who had spent part of the long flight talking to other young passengers. In the process, they had left their shoes all over the aircraft. Since most of the passengers were in transit to Elisabethville, the aircraft was still fairly full. Finally, thanks to other passengers, we collected the shoes, put them on wriggling feet, collected the baby and went down the steps to the tarmac. Herb was smiling patiently, not at all put out. He welcomed us warmly, which set the tone for our relationship. Our families quickly became friends.

One of my first memories of Burundi is that our third son, Dave – then aged two – disappeared shortly after we had moved into our house, which was up a mountain. While we were searching for him in the three-acre garden and its large banana patch, a huge Murundi appeared at the front door. Sitting in his enormous hand was Dave, smiling happily. The contrast between the colossal black man and the tiny blond white child was striking. It turned out that the Murundi was chief of police, and he lived half a mile or so farther up the mountain. He asked, 'Is this yours?' When we said that the child was indeed ours, he said that he had found him 'exploring' along the dirt road between our houses.

We thanked him profusely and, as he started to lower Dave to the ground, the little boy reached up and put his arms around the man's neck. They hugged briefly, and then Dave was lowered down. In their normal state, the people of Rwanda and Burundi love children, which makes it so hard to understand how they kill them so easily. When society breaks down to the point where people feel that little children are a threat because they will some day be old enough to kill, one wonders if the breakdown is ever going to be reversible.

The first communicator in Usumbura – 'Jerry' – was quite unforgettable. He was the hardest-working communicator I ever served with, which is saying something because, like our audio technicians, the communicators were generally outstandingly efficient and highly motivated.

One of the most endearing things I recall about Jerry was his ability to overcome his frequent late nights. He was a bachelor and he caroused with the best. On the mornings after his more eventful nights, he always came to work on time. We shared an office with the intelligence assistant, a fine young lady called 'Lila'. Jerry stopped himself from passing out from fatigue by sticking broken matchsticks in his eye sockets to keep his lids from closing. The result was effective, if not decorative. Those huge red eyes were forced open, and he managed to work his 'bug' – a noisy little side-saddle Morse key – with astonishing speed and skill. By late morning he had recovered and the matchsticks were removed. .

A few months after his arrival, Jerry suddenly developed a badly infected appendix, which required an immediate operation. There was no time to get him to the US military hospital in Frankfurt, so we arranged for him to be operated on at the local Belgian-staffed hospital. It was a rule that any staff person undergoing an anaesthetic in the presence of uncleared people had to be observed by a colleague. The reason was that if the patient talked while 'under', we would at least know if he or she had revealed anything sensitive. The observer might even be able to obscure the patient's revelations by shouting something, or singing the 'Star Spangled Banner'. On this occasion, I went as observer.

Things went smoothly enough in the hands of three very capable people – a very experienced surgeon, a young anaesthetist doing his military service, and a very prim, middle-aged nun. Jerry slept soundly and said nothing while under the anaesthetic. However, the two doctors were not so demure. They joked and told lurid stories the whole time. They were very impressed with Jerry's genital equipment, and they teased the nurse unmercifully while she shaved his crotch area and applied an antiseptic lotion. They instructed her three times (twice more than necessary) to lift up Jerry's plumbing again and swab it with the lotion. During that operation, I learned a little about surgery and much about the conduct of surgical teams, as well as gaining a new friend for life – the young Belgian anaesthetist, Tony Stockman. Our families still get together after all these years.

Burundi was in transition in 1961. Civil war in Rwanda, to the north, had ended in a Hutu victory but there was still sporadic violence. Many European settlers were leaving, fearing for their lives. The only remaining person with good technical ability in the building trade left in Usumbura was a European named Paul. He was a man who feared nothing, and he was just what I needed to help get some audio devices into various Communist embassies that would soon be purchased and customised for their new occupants. I developed a good rapport with Paul, a wiry, fit, little man, and he began to open up about himself and his activities. He had once trained as a ballet dancer, and his regular workouts included many of the dance routines he had been taught. When he showed me some of them, he was as quick as a mongoose.

One day he went hunting Cape buffalo – one of the meanest, most dangerous of the big game – down at Nyanza Lac on Lake Tanganyika. He got a good shot at a large male, but only wounded the animal, which made it very irritated and it came charging at him full bore. He lined up his sights for a chest shot and pulled the trigger, but nothing happened. There was no time to reload, nor any nearby tree to climb. Paul threw down his useless rifle and, for what seemed like an hour, he danced with that enraged buffalo. He waited until it was almost on him, then pirouetted away and took up another position a few yards off. The animal would charge again, and the same scene occurred dozens of times. Finally, the buffalo got sick of it and left.

'Paul,' I said, 'don't do that again. You're unique here – a national treasure – and there's some work I'd like you to do for me, so don't commit suicide, at least not until it's over.'

He laughed and agreed to be careful. We arranged to go hunting for crocodiles the next night, a sport which he regularly enjoyed. I had a small motor boat, and we agreed to use that. I invited two colleagues from the US embassy to join us so that people at the yacht club wouldn't see me alone with the electrician and assume I was developing him. One of the embassy colleagues was a southerner, a newcomer to the embassy staff, who claimed to have been hunting game – especially alligators – all his life. The other was a former marine, whom I knew was an experienced hunter and a very good shot. We met after dinner, and I ran the boat across the north end of Lake Tanganyika to the mouth of the Ruzizi River that feeds into it. That was where we expected to find the most crocodiles. The moon was out as we slowed down near the bushes and reeds at the river mouth. I let the boat drift. We searched the water with a powerful flashlight and, sure enough, a large crocodile was just visible in the spotlight, its eyes gleaming. It was a fairly easy shot at about fifty yards. Paul and the marine were on the side of the boat facing the crocodile, so they quietly sighted their rifles. Protocol had it that the newcomer – and I as host – would sit still until they got their shots off, but before they could shoot, the newcomer got excited and pulled his trigger without sighting. His rifle went off with a flash and bang, just behind Paul's head. How the bullet missed him, I'll never know. The back of his neck and his cheek were singed by the muzzle blast. The crocodile decided things were dicey and left.

There was a long silence. The newcomer muttered something about letting it get away from him, while Paul spat in the water. The marine took the rifle out of the newcomer's hands. I cranked up the engine and ran the boat back to the yacht club dock, where we invited the newcomer to get out. We went back to the hunting area, but saw no more crocodiles that night. The next day, Paul joshed me about the incident. 'I thought you were concerned about my life? If so, why did you bring along that assassin?' he said. Fortunately, he was a good sport and forgave me.

My first visit to Kigali, capital of Rwanda, was by chartered

Cessna 310. Ambassador Georges Carlier, Belgian delegate to the UN Trusteeship Council, was visiting Burundi and came along for the ride. The pilot had to swoop low over the town to alert the airport office that we were arriving. There was no office at the airport, only an empty hut. Then he had to sweep low over the unpaved airstrip in order to warn some small boys to get their goats off the grassy 'runway'. We paid a visit to Colonel Logiest, the resident (governor) of Rwanda, who was an erudite man with no apparent racial bias, although his South African wife used to call the natives '*kaffirs*' (an Arabic word meaning 'unbeliever', used as a racial insult in South Africa). Logiest's deputy, Robert Regnier, and his wife Jackie were also there, and we were shown some of the little baskets that the Tutsi girls wove. Logiest and Regnier gave us a briefing on the situation in Rwanda: it was relatively peaceful after the recent massacres of the Tutsi and, with luck, Rwanda would hold together and prosper.

After that first visit, I drove to Kigali quite frequently since Rwanda was part of my territory. The road had been paved from Usumbura for the first twenty-five miles up the escarpment, and there was one kilometre of paved road in downtown Kigali. It was interesting to stop along the way at Catholic mission stations. The priests were always glad to talk about events in their parishes, especially if the visitor brought along a supply of whisky.

I made it a practice to pick up hitchhikers, since one must look for agents under every bush. In a small village in the northern part of Burundi, my car was flagged down by a young man. He turned out to be younger than I had thought before he got into the car, and was about sixteen years of age. We started off and I asked him where he wanted to go. His reply was a bit surprising: '*N'importe, Monsieur. Je veux que voyager . . .*' The boy just wanted to travel, anywhere. I'd never met anyone in Africa (or anywhere else) who just wanted to be driven, so I questioned him as we drove to Kigali, which we reached a couple of hours later. He was a bright boy, who was bored in his village and wanted to see the world. It was a commendable ambition, but it didn't fit into my plans.

'I will be staying here overnight, maybe longer.' I told him. 'I may not even go back through your village.'

'That's all right, *Monsieur*,' he said. 'I'll go wherever and whenever you do. I love riding in your car. Where are we spending the night?'

'I'm sorry,' I replied, 'some of what I do is rather private. I cannot have you along.'

'That's all right,' he answered. 'I won't listen or look.'

Having espionage business to attend to, I had to get rid of this youngster who wouldn't take 'No' for an answer. I told him to wait the next day at the corner where I'd let him off, and I might come by. He smiled appreciatively and waved as I drove off. I avoided that corner and drove off into the bush without him. But there the enterprising young rascal was, at the fifth kilometre stone out of town, standing in the middle of road and waving for me to stop. Reluctantly, I drove on.

Not long before Burundi and Rwanda became independent, David Halberstam came to visit Burundi. He was then a young and eager *New York Times* reporter on his first African assignment – very sharp, but with little experience in Africa. He had spent a good deal of time covering the early civil rights struggles in the southern US, but I believe he had spent only a couple of weeks in the Katanga, where he had witnessed some bloody firefights, before coming to Burundi, which was brand-new ground for him. We met in the US embassy, and he explained that he wanted to learn all he could about Burundi. This was unusual because most of the journalists who visited Burundi tried to hide their ignorance. David's intelligence, enthusiasm and honesty about his lack of local knowledge were appealing, and I liked him instantly. I invited him to our house, where we spent hours discussing the political situation in Burundi. I told him what I knew from overt sources, and gave him some information from covert sources whose descriptions had to be disguised. I never mentioned being with the CIA, nor did he ask. If he guessed it, or if someone in the embassy had spilled the beans – which sometimes happened – he didn't mention it. Anyway we got along well, and David learned the complicated Burundi ethnopolitical scene very quickly.

We took time off one day and went hunting together, along with the British journalist Gavin Young, whom I had known briefly in the Katanga. There were two amusing incidents while we were together. On one occasion David, Gavin and I drove up country to meet the commander of a Belgian parachute battalion. Belgian troops were rumoured to be taking sides against the Tutsis – the former ruling minority. Rwanda was then experiencing its first bout of ethnic cleansing, which went on from 1959 to 1961. The Hutu, backed by the Roman Catholic church, had killed many hundreds of Tutsis and driven thousands more into refuge in Uganda. It was a precursor of the even greater ethnic disasters of 1995–7.

The Belgian commander was distant with us, but did agree to be interviewed. He was trembling all over as he vigorously denied the reports of his troops' anti-Tutsi bias. Driving back to Usumbura, both journalists wondered aloud if the Belgian was lying because he had acted as if he were very nervous. After leaving David and Gavin in town, I discreetly checked with a friend at the Belgian parachute headquarters. 'Oh,' replied my friend. 'We all call him "Shakey" because he always trembles. It's an affliction he's had all his life.' I relayed this to David and Gavin.

David wanted a scoop, of course, and I could think of none at the time. A call to Léon Ndenzako, Mwami Mwambutsa IV's chief of protocol, worked wonders: right away Léon came up with what he called a scoop. A very old man, he said, had witnessed the murder of a white horseman – a soldier – many years ago, but had never been interviewed about it. Would we care to talk to him? It sounded interesting so we agreed, assuming that if the story was a bore, at least the time with Léon would be well spent. The next day we drove to a hut near Rumonge, a village on Lake Tanganyika some fifty miles north of Ujiji, in Tanzania. Ujiji is the village where, in late 1871, Dr David Livingstone, the famous 'missing' British missionary, was 'found' by Henry Morton Stanley, the equally famous US journalist. The old man's hut was, in fact, a few hundred yards from the most northerly point to which Livingstone and Stanley walked after they met.

Léon, David and I squatted in the hut, where the old man sat surrounded by his relatives. He must have been eighty, but seemed to have retained all his mental faculties. He told his story in Kirundi, with the occasional sentence in French. Léon translated the Kirundi into French, which I then translated into English for David. The old Murundi described how in the late nineteenth century, when he was about ten years old, three strange apparitions were reported to be on the way to his village. One of them, a scared courier shouted, was part horse and part devil. The devil was followed by two men with white skins and white robes, sitting on horses. Only the devil had a weapon; the others were apparently unarmed. The elders of the village decided to ambush the invaders, who were surely up to no good. They hid in the bushes alongside the trail and, sure enough, the first to appear was the half-man half-devil. The villagers, who were scared to death, fired their arrows, and the devil was struck several times and fell to the ground, dead. When he fell, they suddenly saw that he was in fact a leather-clad man on a brown horse.

At that moment I realised what the old man had seen. I had just read a biography of Cardinal Lavigerie, the French Roman Catholic missionary who had founded the White Fathers. In the book, a late nineteenth-century murder was mentioned, which had happened beside Lake Tanganyika in Burundi. A Swiss Guard protecting two missionaries was killed, but no witnesses were cited in the biography other than the missionaries themselves. We were hearing what was probably the only living survivor's account of the unhappy incident. What about the two missionaries, we asked. They had fled up the mountain, the old man explained, and founded a mission station up there. It was still functioning there in 1963, when I left Burundi.

Léon was triumphant because he had produced a scoop for this nice young reporter. David very politely avoided telling him that he couldn't use the story. His editors would have 'spiked' it and probably wondered if he had caught cerebral malaria, or started smoking hemp. A seventy-year-old Central African murder was hardly news, except to a dedicated historian.

After David left Burundi and went on to great success as a journalist and author, our brief friendship lapsed. On my part it was for fear of 'tainting' him. I had done the same thing after making friends with Stewart Alsop in the Katanga. Even back in the 1960s, CIA officers were not allowed to recruit several categories of US citizens, including journalists. Discreet continued contact with one could have invited perceptions that the relationship was more than mere friendship. My embassy colleagues, for example, almost always suspected that everyone I knew was an agent.

Some weeks prior to the scheduled 1 July 1962 independence of Burundi, I asked one of my agents, a Hutu who was very close to the common people, what '*Uhuru*' (the Swahili word for freedom or independence) really meant to the masses of Burundi and Rwanda. Independence, he told me, was a totally strange concept. Before 1922 when the Belgians took over, both countries were German colonies, administered as part of Tanganyika. By 1962, very few Burundi could remember the days before the first armed German troops had begun to colonise the country seventy years before. Those who could remember were aware only that their lives back then had been as feudal subjects of various warring Tutsi factions.

Uhuru, Burundi's politicians told the people before independence, was what the Europeans had: freedom. Now, they would have it too. Burundi would be governed fairly by Burundi politicians, and the people fully expected the new government to provide a better life. Wags joked that the truly unsophisticated masses were being led to believe that *Uhuru* would come in a trunk or a packing case, like those goodies that arrived in aeroplanes from Europe. They looked forward to going out to the airport from then on, as the Europeans had done, and selecting what they wanted from the cargo holds.

In fact, after independence, no planes arrived filled with free products. Instead, a small inside group of African politicians began to enrich themselves. The politicians soon fell out, and factional or ethnic violence took place on a large scale. The lives of the masses, far from being improved, began a descent into misery and fear.

As part of the Burundi independence festivities, the Mwami held a reception at his palace for the still small foreign diplomatic corps. About a dozen of us were invited. The Mwami welcomed us as we stood in a row in his large living room. He then asked a guest I hadn't noticed before to come forward. A very small man stepped out from the shadows of a curtain. The Mwami told the group, 'This is the Indian high commissioner to Uganda. There is no Indian embassy here yet, so he drove from Kampala – more than a thousand kilometres – just to attend my reception and our other independence ceremonies. I invited him to come as my special guest because of my respect for Prime Minister Nehru.'

The Mwami then asked the high commissioner to say a few

words to us. The Indian was a tiny, impish man with a twinkle. He beamed at the line of diplomats and inclined his head benignly. When the nodding and bowing had ceased, he cleared his throat importantly: 'His Majesty has very kindly given us this moment together before the festivities so that I can tell you a truly wonderful story.' He spoke in English, knowing no French. The king understood English and looked pleased.

'As you know, both Rwanda and Burundi are throbbing with the thrill of independence,' the Indian went on. 'I drove here through Rwanda as well as through a hundred miles of Burundi's beautiful countryside. To my amazement and great pleasure the name of our Prime Minister Nehru was on every tongue. As soon as the people saw the Indian flag on my car, they shouted our beloved Prime Minister's name . . . Nehru, Nehru!'

I looked at the Mwami and could almost read his thoughts: 'Nehru? Our bush people don't know about Nehru. I'd better listen to this.' Then he began to smile.

The Indian had stopped, giving the Mwami and us a solemn stare. 'I was so moved that I sent a telegram to Prime Minister Nehru the moment I got here. I told him how much he is loved in Africa. He will be thrilled.'

By now everyone in the room who understood English realised what had happened. The people were shouting '*Uhuru*', independence or freedom, and the Indian had mistaken it for Nehru. There was subdued consternation. I stole a quick look at our US mission chief, who was shaking with muffled laughter, like many of those in the group. The Mwami was doubled over, a diplomatic coughing fit covering his laughter. Finally he was able to stand upright, but he was still grinning broadly, his tummy heaving with smothered gasps.

The Indian surveyed the group with intense pleasure. His story had been a great hit. Clearly, he perceived the red faces as showing honest emotion, the streaming eyes as shared happiness, the grins and laughter as open enjoyment of how Nehru was so widely loved in Africa. Nobody was mean enough to tell him the truth: that far from identifying his car as Indian, they were probably wondering if this large, beflagged limousine was the vehicle bringing them their *Uhuru*.

Mwami Mwambutsa IV was a unique character, a man in his sixties with a boyish streak a mile wide. He loved to do the twist, which he did with showmanlike skill and grace. He also loved to tease people. After his country became independent, he used to tease the first Belgian Ambassador to Burundi, Edouard Henniquiau, a former colonel of the Congo Force Publique. Belgium was at that time suffering substantial clashes between its Flemish-speaking and its Walloon (French-speaking) activists. Fights were common and some killings had occurred. In the second half of 1962, the ancient kingdom of Burundi, by contrast, was quiet despite potential hostility between the Tutsi and the Hutu. Whenever the Mwami spotted the Belgian Ambassador, he would do a few twist steps and shout: '*Alors, Henniquiau, comment vont les guerres tribales chez toi*?' ('How go the tribal wars in your country, Henniquiau?') The Belgian never failed to look embarrassed, which of course is exactly what the Mwami wanted.

The Mwami owned an Edsel automobile, the only one in town. One day in October 1961, he was driving himself through town and had an accident, which demolished a Belgian woman's Volkswagen and badly wounded his Edsel. Fortunately, neither he nor the woman was hurt. He walked across the street to our consulate and asked to use the phone to call the palace and get another car.

After his call, he mentioned the Cuban Missile Crisis, which was taking place at the time. With a straight face, he offered the United States two war canoes fully equipped with fighting men. The *quid pro quo*, it turned out as he expanded on his symbolic offer of support, was for the US to lend him a battalion of marines to guard the palace and his other residencies. When we explained to him that it would not be practical for many reasons, he nodded and smiled his usual good-natured smile. He had tried, and it hadn't worked, but at least he'd had a bit of fun.

One day a Murundi came to see me with a sad tale. He had been a very senior official in the Front Commun government, but was now out of work. He wondered if the consulate could help him in any way. As it happened, I was planning to give my African spear collection to the Smithsonian Institute. The curator of African art was an acquaintance who had long sought to have my parents' very extensive African collection transferred from the Princeton University Art Museum, where it had been donated by my mother in memory of my father, to the

Smithsonian. I wrote to the curator offering the spears and asking him if he wanted a knowledgeable Murundi to collect artefacts for the museum. Back came a rather modest cheque – if memory serves it was $500 – and a signal to go ahead.

I added some money from my own pocket and recruited him for the job. He turned out to be just the man. He combed the twin countries at length, raking through rubbish heaps, and turned up dozens of artefacts, some of which pre-dated the German occupation of Burundi and Rwanda. We packaged them up and sent them off to Washington. Looking back, his fall from power turned into a real coup for the US national Museum of Natural History.

A good source of information – an informant, not actually an agent – was a European coffee planter, whose plantation was on the shore of Lake Kivu, in the Congo. He and his wife told me that their cook was in trouble because he had joined the wrong political party, which had lost the first round of the local civil war. The winners were threatening to kill him. He was illiterate, the planter told me, but he was an astoundingly good cook and had a real gift for preparing food. He also had a photographic memory and could remember hundreds of Russian, French, Spanish, Italian and other recipes. Without being able to calculate on paper, he could extrapolate the proportionate amount of ingredients to feed any given number of guests. I was already aware that illiterate people usually have extraordinary memories and can do sophisticated mental arithmetic, so what they told me sounded logical. I had eaten at their house, and the food was certainly delicious. Would I like him as a second cook, they asked.

'Certainly, if it saves his life.' I replied. 'For a time, anyway, until he's out of danger.'

They brought him out of the Congo to Burundi a week later. They had been chased part way down from the mountains and had just got away with their lives.

Dominique was short, square, very black, and with a charming smile and manner. He owned one torn T-shirt, one pair of ragged shorts and a belt; no shoes, no hat, no coat and no blanket. We clothed him, but all we had for him to live in was an enormous packing case that had contained our effects when we had moved to Burundi. It turned out to be the largest dwelling he had ever known, and he was pleased enough with it.

Dominique lived up to his billing. He cooked so well that we took him on permanently. We outfitted him with a white uniform jacket (over his shorts) for formal occasions, but he wouldn't wear shoes, not for anyone. His cooking was so spectacular that we made no fuss about the shoes. I doubt he could have worn them, anyway, for his feet were covered with huge calluses, typical damage after a lifetime without shoes. Dominique soon became a fixture at our house, and because we now had two cooks, we were able to have guests to dinner virtually every night, even on the spur of the moment. That flexibility enabled me to develop more potential agents than would otherwise have been practical.

One day, we were visited by a CIA staff physician, who came to see how we were faring in Central Africa. He looked my family over and decided that we were healthy, but that Dominique might have some infectious disease. The doctor volunteered to have a sick call for all our helpers: two cooks, one washboy (who did the washing by hand) and two gardeners. We announced the sick call for the next day and told our helpers that they could bring their wives, children and whomever else lived with them. Over fifty women and children, dependants of our five helpers, showed up. They lined up on the lawn, each helper in front of his family group. The doctor then went slowly down the line, observing, taking pulses and temperatures, asking questions, even giving out a few pills. Sadly, he discovered that one of the gardeners, a young man, had an advanced case of cancer of the spine. Another child was terminally ill and died not long afterwards. Everybody else was pronounced healthy, except for the washboy, the father of the sick child, who was fiercely uptight. The doctor decided that he needed tranquillizers and gave him one. The poor man slept for three days, never having taken a pill before in his entire life. When he eventually came back to work, he was still woozy. Fortunately, Dominique was healthy after all and could continue cooking for us. So he did, and he lived peacefully in his packing case until we left the country.

On one occasion, I responded to a call for help from the newly arrived US Ambassador in Kigali. As there was still no CIA representation in Kigali in 1962, I handled Rwanda from Burundi. The Ambassador wanted a single sideband radio transceiver installed. I drove up with one of the station communicators – we now had two of them as Burundi was on the CIA map! – who set to work right away. I sat down to chat about Rwanda with the Ambassador on the lanai of his residence. There was so little to do in Kigali (it only had a population of 5,000 then) that, the Ambassador told me, he knew every bird in town. I looked startled, but he actually meant real birds – not ladies. He was an avid bird watcher and had recorded every feathered critter he saw.

Half an hour into our discussion, there was a thunderous crash in the garden. The ambassador and I raced around the corner of the house and saw the communicator standing unhurt, staring at the remains of the residence's brick chimney. Bricks were all over the lawn and a cloud of cement dust was hanging in the air.

'What on earth happened?' asked the Ambassador, visibly very upset. 'Thank God you're all right.'

'I'm lucky, sir,' said the communicator. 'I was walking past and lightning hit the chimney.'

'Lightning? But the sky is totally clear. How can it have been lightning?'

'That's the way it is out here, sir,' responded the communicator. 'It comes from nowhere.'

As the mystified Ambassador turned away, grumbling about the mess, the communicator winked at me and pulled from behind his back the coiled antenna cable, with which he had inadvertently toppled the entire top of the chimney.

On the road back to Usumbura, we came upon a Volkswagen beside the road with a Belgian standing beside it and two bare brown legs underneath it. We stopped to ask if we could help. The Belgian thanked us and said that it wasn't necessary because he was accompanied by the best amateur mechanic in Rwanda. He motioned to the bare legs, which were squirming as their owner worked his way out from underneath, and when the 'mechanic' stood up and introduced himself, he turned out to be President Gregoire Kayibanda, who announced that he had fixed the car. We stood around talking for a while and then drove on. That was the only time I met Kayibanda, and I was impressed by his straightforwardness and his common touch.

Further down the road we saw a few bodies strewn about here and there, and wondered what had happened as the fighting had temporarily ceased. Back in Usumbura the mystery was solved: a Belgian friend had driven down the same road an hour before us. Some Hutus had decided to knock off some neighbouring Tutsis, and had speared a Tutsi right in front of the Belgian's car. The Hutu had then waved a friendly greeting to the Belgian, as if nothing had happened.

At the time, I was assessing and developing Philippe, a senior Burundi politician, preparatory to recruiting him. One evening, he and his wife, a large woman with a jolly laugh, came over for dinner. She sat on the best couch while we had drinks, and both Philippe and his wife told some very funny tales of political infighting. Ann and I watched in dismay as a pool of liquid slowly formed and spread on the stone floor under where Philippe's wife was sitting. She was apparently able to control herself at dinner because there was no liquid under her chair, but when she sat on the couch again after dinner, drinking a nightcap, the pool got larger and larger. After they left, I mentioned her weak bladder to our cook, M'Pishi, who laughed and told me what had really happened. Apparently, she didn't like ice – it was too cold for her – so she had kept slipping her ice cubes under the couch, where they had melted and formed this large pool of water. She had said nothing to us about disliking ice, M'Pishi said, for fear of embarrassing us. That was one more lesson learnt, not automatically to believe one's own eyes.

Among the dangers that accompany the espionage profession is one also well known to postmen – dogs. Unknown to me, an agent prospect of mine in Burundi owned an attack-trained German Shepherd. One day, I had to visit his house on an operational emergency. Fortunately, the house was far from any other houses and could be approached discreetly. It was a Sunday, and I planned to join my family at the beach after meeting him and sending an appropriate cable to headquarters. I was therefore dressed only in a pair of swimming trunks and sandals. My car keys were in my hand, and I had no weapon of any kind. As I walked into the man's garden and up on to his lanai, the dog came from nowhere – silently – and, running at me, jumped for my throat. I saw him only as he left the ground, so there was only time to raise my forearm. He bit that to the bone. On the way down, he took a chunk of flesh out of my side and then he turned for another charge. My right arm was already useless and I only had one more to offer him. After that, my only option was to curl up in a ball and hope for the best. At that moment, my prospective agent came out of his house and called off the dog. I couldn't see a local doctor, since he would have asked questions and perhaps told the police, thus endangering my contact. The agent-to-be patched me up as best he could, and we discussed the possibility that the dog might have rabies. He didn't think so, but there was no way, without having its brain sectioned, that he could tell if the dog had been infected.

I therefore cabled headquarters to ask about rabies, which was endemic in much of tropical Africa. The answer came back that if the dog lived for ten days, he did not have rabies when he bit me. If the bites were on most areas of my body, I had ten days before treatment must start. If, however, the dog had bitten a mucous membrane, I should start treatment within three days. The treatment was very long and painful, and there was a new strain of rabies in the area that didn't always respond to the standard Pasteur treatment. I recalled that a British physician from a rabies unit in a tropical medical research institute in Africa had told me of a Gambian stevedore – a very muscular man – who had died in spasms that had actually broken his own bones. I decided to wait the ten days, which seemed a very long time, and which was made especially difficult by my friend. I saw him daily to enquire about his dog. Sometimes he would hide the dog and tease me unmercifully by starting off saying that he had bad news for me; then he would go off on a tangent, usually about a subject of operational interest which I couldn't interrupt, and finally he would laugh and say something like, 'My dog has caught a cold from biting you, David, but don't worry, he's all right.' Fortunately, the dog survived and prospered. So did my friend, but that's another story.

One day in Burundi I learned that an American missionary wanted to sell his car, a rough-country vehicle which I needed. I also wanted to enquire about a Soviet neighbour of his, a UN official whose mission was to watch and ensure that the coming national elections were honest and fair. My goal was to get a handle on what made the Soviet tick, and what he might be doing to further the goals of the USSR, under cover of his UN job. Was he disaffected with the USSR or his job, etc.?

I drove to the mission station and, without haggling, bought the car. Unfortunately, the missionary had never met the Soviet or heard anything about his character, but he did have a unique tale on quite a different subject. Many years before, he had bought a pygmy – a Twa, a member of the tribe who inhabit the Congo-Nile crest living mostly in the high forests of eastern Congo, western Uganda, and the Congo-Nile divide in Rwanda and Burundi – to release him from slavery. The missionary had tried to set the pygmy free, but the Twa, who was by now used to being a kept man, refused to leave and had stayed with the American for many years. Now the missionary wanted to retire to the Midwest and, as slavery was now illegal in Burundi, he couldn't take him with him because he had no papers. As he said, 'They would arrest us at the airport, and I'd be sent to prison for trying to smuggle out an illegal slave. I can't sell him, or even appeal to the courts, and since I still own him, I would be sent to prison. I also can't abandon him because he refuses to be abandoned. So why don't you buy him, as a private purchase? You can then have him taken out in the diplomatic bag.'

I said that that would be impossible. It would not only be illegal, but the diplomatic bags going to and from Burundi were far too small, even for a pygmy. However, the missionary was determined. Would I at least meet the Twa and see if anything came to mind? I agreed to do so, and the pygmy was brought out for inspection. He was indeed very small, maybe four and a half feet tall, and he was so skinny that he probably only weighed about ninety pounds. He had dark brown, curly hair and the most profoundly sad eyes I had ever seen.

When I was introduced to the Twa, he stared at the ground. My presence was clearly a threat. Every line in his body, every motion, every expression on his face demonstrated a mixture of depression, fear and determination. He looked dejected by his lot, yet devoted to his American owner. I wondered just what it meant to him to be introduced to a *Mzungu* (white foreigner) whom, he had been told, could get people out of the country. Perhaps he thought I was going to take him away from his owner, because that's what he feared most. When I questioned the Twa, he indeed refused to consider leaving his 'owner', even for a moment. 'No. He bought me. I belong to him and he can't just throw me away,' he said, and he meant it. There was nothing more I could do. I left, wondering who in fact owned who. Each man was enslaved to the other, whether by law or by habit seemed immaterial. For all I know that missionary is still living there, with his 'slave', unable to go home.

A Bantu lament of the colonial period goes like this: 'Before the European missionaries came, we taught our young that if they were stood upon the skin of a leopard, they would be struck down if they lied. Now, the missionaries tell them to ignore us, that their God will forgive them their lies if they apologise nicely. Discipline and respect are gone.' The Tutsis had traditionally invoked mythical leopards and had used cruel steel claws in night-time attacks to strike fear into the Hutus, but the Tutsis were not themselves bound by the terrifying custom. Use of the leopard threat was only one example of Hutu-Tutsi hatreds, which ran very deep.

Since independence, the hatred had become worse and the willingness to kill had skyrocketed. The first Rwanda bloodbath of the twentieth century had started in 1959 and was winding down by 1961, although things were still bad enough and thousands of Tutsis had been killed. The leading Hutu during that bloodbath was Gregoire Kayibanda (mentioned earlier), a Catholic seminarian who had been persuaded to give up his priestly ambitions and run for President. He did so and won, with the tacit help of the Catholic church. The civil war temporarily settled down to harassment and sporadic killings of the remaining Tutsis, who were now a smaller minority and utterly cowed, but who were awaiting their turn. The Hutus and Tutsis of Burundi, spared for the moment, eyed each other warily in 1963. For the moment they had what passed for a mixed government in which Hutu interests were relatively well protected.

A group of US Protestant missionaries in Rwanda called for help from the US embassy in Burundi, but because there was still no US representation there, two of us – Julius Walker and I – drove up from Usumbura. We found a typical situation. Since 1955, the Protestant missionaries had backed the Tutsis and were now perceived by their neighbours and by the government in Kigali as being anti-government and anti-Hutu. It doesn't pay to be perceived as taking sides in a civil war if you are unarmed and vulnerable. These Americans had their mission strung out along seven kilometres of mountain-ridge top and were being attacked nightly by Hutus from the villages on the adjoining hillsides – with clubs and spears then, no modern arms, but people were being killed and maimed. The missionaries quite rightly feared that the situation would get worse. Like most Americans in trouble overseas, they appealed to the US embassy for help. All embassies have to respond, if possible, to such appeals.

Julius, a former marine who was the political officer, and I were both Second World War veterans and had kept up our small arms skills. On this occasion we took side arms, just in case. As soon as we arrived in late afternoon, we were asked to listen to the threats from the Hutu village. Sure enough, we could hear loud shouts coming from the Hutus across the steep valley and could see them brandishing clubs, machetes and spears.

It was still daylight, and no attacks were expected until well after dark. The head missionary invited us to dine with his family. We were starving, having eaten only a sandwich each that morning, and we were delighted to see the lady of the house put what looked like a beautiful meat loaf on the table. Unfortunately, the 'roast', as she called it, was made of ground lentils. We felt that calling the dish a meat loaf was an unnecessary deception. They also didn't drink, but they served a dark fruit juice which was referred to as 'our wine'.

The Americans asked us to patrol their mission all night long. When we asked why, we were told that at night their African communicants – who were all Tutsis – were being attacked by Hutu men from the next village, who were Catholics. The attacks were sporadic and of short duration, but they were increasing in frequency and ferocity. Then came the clincher, a bombshell which infuriated us. 'We missionaries are not allowed to kill', we were told, 'because it's against our ethical code. But you can kill the attackers for us.'

'That's just as unethical on your part,' we replied, 'as if you killed yourselves. Anyway, we have no intention of killing, just making some scary noises. We'll patrol tonight and talk again in the morning.'

Julius and I walked the single dirt path until well past midnight, trying to stay awake as we'd been up since 4 a.m. and on the road since 5. At about 2 a.m. all was quiet, so we sat down on a rock. I had a small bottle of whisky, which we passed back and forth, and we both felt cold, uncomfortable and dog tired.

Julius suddenly said, 'You know, I think it's funny, ironic really, that a couple of Second World War vets are out here patrolling to protect a bunch of conscientious objectors.' I was stunned and told him that I would never have come had I known that. He agreed, and a little later we decided to go to bed and slept undisturbed. The missionaries woke us early and told us rather angrily that, while we had been asleep, the village had been raided and several people had been quite badly beaten. The attack had been several hundred metres from our hut, so we had heard nothing.

We told the missionaries that their position was untenable. They were perceived as siding with the wrong side, and their four-mile-long ridge be impossible even for a company of marines to defend. The attacks would indeed get worse and worse, and would persist until the missionaries left or at least were seen as no longer taking sides. We were very firm about this: we would not kill for them. In fact, we would not stay; we were going back that very day. They could come with us in convoy, abandoning their beleaguered mission station – which we officially and strongly recommended – or they could stay up there without us and take their chances. At least they should send their children and elderly with us.

They refused, and we left, taking two very old and quite harmless Tutsi communicants with us, the parents of a Tutsi employee at our embassy in Burundi. Burundi was still essentially in Tutsi hands and so they would be safe there.

Julius recollects our crossing the border: 'The two old people had a few possessions with them, including a sack of beans weighing about twenty pounds. We put them in the back of our van, and when we got to the frontier between Rwanda and Burundi, the Rwandan soldiers stopped us and wanted to know who the old people were. Dave, whose French was impeccable, handled it. He said, "They are just some people we are taking to Usumbura."

'"Who are they?" the soldiers persisted. "Do you have permission to take them?"

'"Yes. We have permission from the governor." [We had no such thing.]

'"Well, where is your permission?"

'"We don't have any papers. The governor just said we could take them."

'"How do we know?" they asked.

'"All you have to do is telephone him," Dave replied. That

stopped them. I'm not certain they knew what a telephone was, but if they did, they darned well didn't have one there. With that, Dave told the driver to go and off we went. The Rwandans had two .30 calibre machine-guns pointed right down the road we had to travel. We drove about a half mile towards Burundi, for a good three minutes with those two machine-guns aimed right at us, and we didn't know if they might be fired at any minute. Fortunately, they weren't, and the guard post disappeared when we went around the next hill.

'Back in Usumbura, our successful effort to save these two old people was rewarded by huge smiles and a flowery speech of thanks from a very grateful embassy employee.'

The attacks on the rest of the missionaries persisted and indeed got worse. They again called for help and were told that we would only supply an escort for an evacuation convoy. They stayed and were eventually expelled by an angry central government.

On 1 July 1962, I drove alone to Rwanda to be present at their independence celebrations. As I reached the border, a single Rwandan soldier stopped me and asked who I was. I handed him my passport upside down, and he looked at it, pretending to read it but without turning it the right side up. Not willing to admit that he was illiterate, he asked me what my job was. Since he had no way of knowing, and because I didn't want to be late for the ceremonies, I told him that I was the Belgian Ambassador. He grinned widely and waved me on, shouting, 'Welcome to Rwanda. You're the fifth Belgian Ambassador to arrive today!' He probably didn't even know what an Ambassador was.

A visa was available for my next trip to Rwanda, but it was issued by the Belgian embassy in Usumbura. There being as yet no Rwandan visa stamp, the Belgian official simply wrote the visa by hand in green ink. There was so little traffic into and out of Rwanda at that time that my 4 September 1962 visa was No. 7.

On 13 October 1961, the Prime Minister of Burundi was assassinated. It happened on my watch, and I knew both the victim and all his principal murderers. Looking back, I should have deduced what was going to happen, but I didn't. We had only been in the country a couple of months.

A prospective asset of mine, a conservative Burundi politician named Jason, was a friend and an informant, but not yet my agent. I was naturally interested in his potential as an agent since he had been Interior Minister in the previous (pro-Belgian) government. He had been offered a cabinet level position in the new government, headed by Prime Minister Louis Rwagasore, the Mwami's oldest son. Information I had elicited from him was useful, but I needed more product and more on his character before I could be convinced he was good agent material.

One evening, Jason came to my house unexpectedly after dark. He left his car down the street, which was unlit, and walked up the long driveway and through the front door, which we always left open until we turned in for the night. We shook hands. His large hand was warm and dry, as usual, and there was no sign at all of any stress in his features or his body language. He was carrying a very large, heavy package, which he put on a table by the door.

'A present for you, David. I want you to accept it, and keep it always.'

'Thank you, Jason.' I replied. 'What's in it?'

'Don't open it until I've gone,' he said, smiling calmly. 'In fact, wait a couple of days.'

'What's the mystery?' I asked.

He shook his head, saying, 'No mystery, really. Just a present to thank you for your friendship.'

He sat down, I poured some drinks, and we talked about his plans. He told me about the offer of the cabinet post, but, after several days of turning the offer over in his mind, he said that he had decided to reject it. He felt that he could not work with Rwagasore and 'those Communist revolutionaries; they're going to ruin the country'. He was, he said, convinced that Rwagasore secretly planned to oust his own father from the throne, to abolish the monarchy and become President-for-life.

Instead, Jason was going to form a resistance movement in the hills and fight until his side won, or until he and his men were all killed. He called his resistance movement a '*Maquis*', after the French resistance organisation of that name in the Second World War.

We argued the case for an hour or more. Jason was a very bright man of great presence and charm, but in this he lacked common sense and foresight. I tried to convince him that he would be far more effective, both for his side and for my government and its allies – he was already providing me with very sensitive inside information about the political scene – by being in the cabinet, especially as the cabinet post was a powerful one and he would have daily access to Rwagasore.

'Forming your *Maquis* might well be exciting and fun,' I said, 'but it takes you right out of the scene, perhaps permanently. All you can do is hope to win, but they have the army and the police on their side. If you lose, you lose everything. By contrast, in the cabinet, you'll at least be able to influence Louis and his people.'

Finally he agreed that my arguments were logical and that he would take the cabinet post. I congratulated him and asked him if he wanted to take his present back. He could always give it to me if he did eventually change his mind. Jason smiled, patted the package and told me to keep it as a token of his esteem.

He left the house repeating his agreement as he went out, and I was optimistic that he would stick to what he had promised. But when I opened the package two days later to see what his present was, I was dumbfounded. It was an elephant tusk, which I still have. This was far more than the 'token' he had mentioned. It was clear that Jason had in fact been saying goodbye in his own rather devious way. He had listened to me and had agreed to take the cabinet post, but this was a deception. I had failed to convince him and he just didn't want to tell me so. I later learned that, at about the same time, he had asked the Belgians if there might be some government post for him in Belgium.

Two days later, I learned on the radio that Prince Louis Rwagasore had been killed by assassins. The bumbling assassin and his very amateur co-conspirators were quickly identified as a young Greek named Jean Kageorgis, who was a seasoned hunter and was the actual hit man; Kageorgis's employer, another Greek named Michel Iatrou; and Joseph Biroli and his brother Jean Ntidendereza. The brothers were sons of an octogenarian chief called Baranyanka, who detested the Mwami's royal line. My friend Jason was also implicated.

I heard the story from several eye-witnesses. Apparently, Kageorgis shot the Prime Minister at a restaurant in Usumbura. Kageorgis had hidden in the restaurant gardens and watched Rwagasore parade into the restaurant like a medieval baron, his large figure dominating the place. The Prime Minister had led his group of young acolytes to their usual table on the covered terrace, facing the lake, while other diners, mostly Europeans, hushed their voices until he was seated and then tried to catch his eye for a nod of recognition if they could extract one. After all, he was the Prime Minister now, the Inheritor, technically the second most powerful man in the kingdom (in fact, the most powerful since the Mwami was loved but not much inclined to govern).

As the Prince sat facing out towards where Kageorgis was lying in wait, the assassin made his final preparations. He quietly chambered a round in his hunting rifle and sighted at the Prince – a hunter's shot, aimed at the breastbone with great care. As other diners recalled, the deafening bang of the rifle, the flash that seemed as bright as lightning and the smack of the heavy slug as it hit bone happened simultaneously. The Prince's upper body was torn almost in two, his flesh and blood spattered all over the terrace.

There was silence for a moment, except for the Prince's knife which spun on the wooden floor with a burring sound. Suddenly, the Prince's entourage reacted, diving for cover and screaming in panic and dismay. Other diners shouted, threw themselves to the floor, or ran into the main room. The French Ambassador sat quite still at his table, a large piece of the Prince's flesh splattered on his forehead. Blood dripped down his nose and on to his plate. Then he was sick.

Kageorgis was caught almost at once. He made off in a car that was easily identified. A witness – a Belgian warrant officer – stepped forward and described the car, and the search began. For some reason Kageorgis abandoned the car and hitch-hiked on the road that leads up a steep escarpment into the interior of Burundi. He thumbed a ride, and by astounding coincidence the driver who picked him up turned out to be the Mwami, the Prince's father, who was still unaware that his son had just been assassinated.

The police quickly put things together, and the assassin and his accomplices were arrested. They were immediately put on trial for murder, a capital crime in Burundi at that time. Unfortunately, I never had a chance to ask Jason why assassinating Louis Rwagasore was seen as an appropriate, or useful, way to start his resistance movement. But Herb Olds concurred with my request that I should attend the trial to observe the proceedings. I was personally interested because if Jason were to tell the court that he had my support and friendship, perhaps even my guidance, he would almost certainly have been given a reduced sentence. And I would almost certainly have been in serious trouble. My recent experience with Jason showed that he was not quite the man of honour I had thought, and there seemed to be a strong possibility that he would claim some US connection.

Sure enough, during the trial Jason was asked whether he had any contact with foreign diplomats, in particular frequent discreet contacts with a certain US citizen. Apparently someone who knew that Jason and I were good friends had reported this to the prosecution. Jason looked across the crowded courtroom to where I was sitting, trying to be inconspicuous, and caught my eye for a brief moment, enough to flash a goodbye. Then his eyes moved on, and he shook his head and denied that he had had any more contact with me than the normal occasional exchange of views between political figures and diplomats at receptions and other official functions.

Fortunately for me, the prosecution did not pursue the point. Jason went to his death without turning to the one possibility that he knew could have saved his life – trying to implicate me, and thus the US, as having been involved. Yet this was the very same man who had deceived me a short time before. Jason's execution was public and horribly gory. His denial of his friendship with me and of our discreet contacts was one of the most cold-bloodedly courageous acts I have personally witnessed in my career.

Our first offices in Usumbura were in a building belonging to a bank. One morning I was visiting the bank and noticed through a window that hundreds of Africans were racing past, heading uphill away from town. They were shouting to each other as they ran, and although some looked grim there was quite a bit of laughter. It looked as if Burundi might be entering a civil war, like its neighbour Rwanda. The banker explained, however, that far from being a civil war, we were witnessing a fairly routine event: the tax collectors had begun to raid the outdoor market, and these people were escaping the revenue officials.

The majority of the people of Burundi were still in native clothing, which ranged from dull to quite colourful. Young Tutsi girls wove beautifully decorated little baskets with tall conical lids, like the roofs of their huts. These baskets were similar to larger ones in which grain was stored. The weave was so tight that the baskets held water. The men made drums of all sizes out of wood and monkey skins, and the royal drummers of Burundi were famous for their costumes as well as their stunning percussion music. When they put on a show, you could literally hear their drumming for miles.

Most of the three million souls in Burundi were farmers, and I once asked an American missionary physician what their most common ailment was. 'Neuroses, anxiety and related illnesses,' he explained. He said that neuroses and anxiety run high among farming people, and speculated that it was particularly bad because of the constant underlying tension between the Hutus and the Tutsis. But at least nobody starved then. The crops came in on time, and the missionaries or the government fed those few in danger of starving. Medical services were primitive, but adequate and free. It was ethnic tension that was the clear enemy, destined to explode one day.

One of my agents, a small Hutu with the guts of a lion, became too well known as a dissident. 'Pierre' provided very useful information on the activities and plans of the underground opponents of the government. One day, I had driven up-country to meet him in a very out of the way place and was coming back to Usumbura when I heard on the car radio that the government was searching for him. Roadblocks were being established on all roads in and out of the capital, which meant that I'd have to negotiate one shortly. I was driving a car with diplomatic plates, which would normally have immunity from search, but when it was my turn to drive up to the roadblock, I was greeted by a very serious Tutsi sergeant, who said that he was going to search my car. I gave him my diplomatic passport, right side up, and he read every page. It had about one hundred pages in it, many of them glued in a concertina pattern, like those packs of postcards you open up. He knew what a diplomat was, but he also had his orders. I knew my rights and wasn't about to be searched. So we stared at each other. He looked down at his rifle and back at me, and I looked around to see who else was watching. Many people were. All traffic had stopped, and nobody was talking. Even those out of hearing range seemed to sense that we were at an impasse.

Luckily, I noticed that the car behind mine was being driven by Archbishop Ntuyahaga, a Tutsi with a reputation for fairness.

I walked back to his car and asked him to solve the matter before it became a diplomatic incident. He agreed, and we both walked over to the Tutsi sergeant. If the Archbishop looked in my car's trunk, I asked, and concurred that whatever they were searching for wasn't there, could we consider the incident closed? The sergeant was unhappy, but agreed to my suggestion. So he retreated, and I opened the trunk for the Archbishop, who looked in, saw a blanket that covered something quite bulky and motioned to me to close the trunk. 'There is nobody in there, sergeant,' he said.

I bade the Archbishop a good day, saluted the disappointed sergeant and drove on. Pierre was not in fact in the trunk. The Archbishop's reaction to what he must have thought was a dissident hidden under the blanket in the trunk was one more of the many mysteries of Africa. Pierre escaped on his own that time, and he survived a year or two longer before government assassins got him.

As I have already related, the only substantiated story of cannibalism I heard was when an Italian air-force cargo plane flying for the United Nations landed in the eastern Congo and its crew of a dozen or so were beaten and imprisoned by Lumumbist rebels. Eventually, they were chopped up and handed out to be eaten. A Belgian acquaintance of ours happened to be in town when the massacre took place. The first he heard of it was when one of the rebel leaders burst into the room in a clubhouse where he was playing bridge with three other Europeans, slapped a severed human hand on to the bridge table and asked them how they liked it. He then told them triumphantly what he and his colleagues had done. A human hand skilled enough to fly an aircraft was a meal to be proud of, he explained. In fact, all parts of the bodies of such talented men had been very well received by the rebel rank and file.

When the Belgian came through Usumbura a few weeks later, he was still rattled by what he had witnessed. I wrote up his story and sent it through diplomatic channels to Washington and Rome. A pathetic note came back from Rome asking us to stop sending in such reports because the document had made one embassy secretary physically sick.

Near the end of my time in Burundi I was offered – and accepted with great pleasure – the post of chief in Dakar,

Senegal. I was sad to leave the gorgeous weather and the mountainous beauty of Burundi and Rwanda, but it was a relief to get away from the explosive political and ethnic tensions that showed no signs of easing. There seemed to be no reason to expect that either Rwanda or Burundi would improve the lives of their citizens in the foreseeable future, nor that they would make a positive mark on African history.

Eventually they did become important, but for the wrong reasons: mass killing became common currency and began again with a vengeance in Rwanda in the 1990s. The masses in Burundi – eighty-five per cent of whom are Hutu – are all too well aware of the slaughter in Rwanda and don't want it to start up again in their country. But the masses have little influence and are no match for the armed forces and the politicians. The dilemma for both Hutu and Tutsi politicians and military leaders in Burundi is that if they do nothing, Burundi will probably eventually mirror the outcome in Rwanda. If the RPF victory up there lasts, the Tutsis will be strengthened in Burundi. Conversely, if the Hutus make a comeback in Rwanda, those in Burundi will feel heartened and the mass killing could well resume. Rwandan Hutus and their friends in eastern Zaire, Tanzania and Uganda might well feel impelled to intervene on behalf of the Hutus.

Against this backdrop, it is no wonder that the Tutsi and Hutu leaders in Bujumbura have trouble trying to work up a formula guaranteeing majority Hutu rights as well as minority Tutsi safety from Hutu massacres. The UN officials on the scene try to help the two sides negotiate rather than fight, but it is an uphill effort. Neither side is accustomed to negotiate, and neither side trusts the other one inch. And yet, taken out of this ghastly context, both Tutsi and Hutu can appear to be among the world's most charming, happiest and peaceful people.

14

Senegal

I took up my post in Dakar in the late summer of 1963 after some home leave. The family was temporarily lodged at the N'Gor Hotel, a fine French resort on a beautiful little sandy cove near Yof Airport, which was a heavenly place for an introduction to life in a former French colony. My deputy arrived the same week, and he was also lodged at the N'Gor with his wife and five children. We had to wait several weeks for adequate housing, and the fourteen of us quickly emptied the embassy's temporary lodging fund. We stayed in Senegal for more than three years, and the wonderful climate enabled Ann and the children to fully enjoy the ocean and the beaches.

Between 1963 and 1967 in Senegal, there were already Soviet, satellite and Chicom (including New China News Agency) presences. The principal CIA goal therefore was to recruit Communist personnel. Covering local and regional politics and events was the embassy's task, so we bugged Communist-occupied buildings, recruited their contacts and doubled their agents when possible. One such double provided leads which enabled us to find a Soviet bug in our own embassy. I tried to open liaison with the French SDECE, but de Gaulle was against it, and did open it with the Senegalese, who provided a lot on the Communists then trying to overthrow the government. We recruited and ran a number of very useful agents, who reported on what the Communists were up to in the area.

Unlike Usumbura, Dakar had everything in place and in good running order. It was a welcome change not to have to start from scratch. Much more time had to be devoted to office and embassy matters, but I was still able to develop, recruit and run agents as well as do the administrative work.

One of the many things that became apparent to me in Senegal was that KGB officers had become a great deal more sophisticated than when I had last observed them in the Far East. Most were no longer as crude, stolid and unaware of life in the West as they had been. They mixed more easily with the diplomatic crowd. That did nothing, however, to ease the difficulty of spotting who among them might defect, preferably in place. They were better clothed, more relaxed, brighter and younger looking, but they still tended to go about in pairs and to be suspicious of everyone. We were, however, beginning to see the first post-Stalin generation of KGB officers.

Almost as soon as we set foot in Dakar, the US Ambassador to Senegal asked for a list of all our agents. He explained that such a list would enable him to avoid appearing to be too close, in public and at receptions, to those people he met who were agents.

I replied that I couldn't oblige him because, among other things, he had to be able to plausibly deny all knowledge of what I did. 'Anyway,' I said, 'it's against our rules to identify agents to anyone unauthorised by Langley.'

'But one of your predecessors gave me his list,' he remonstrated and named the man who had done so.

'Did he, now!' I was horrified. 'But I still can't do it.'

'I shall get the Department to request the DCI to order you to give me your list,' he growled.

'Your request, which obviously reveals that we have espionage agents, must go through my communications channel, not yours, Mister Ambassador,' I replied. 'The DCI will see it immediately and he will refuse, I assure you.' The Ambassador, having tried and failed, dropped the request. He bore no grudge and we became friends.

The CIA technicians had managed to produce quite an effective method of personal protection, a powder called B-3 which was dispensed by squeezing a small plastic bottle. The powder squirted out some ten feet, and it could bring a gorilla to its knees in seconds. It was very, very effective, and if you had a bottle you never had to worry about being attacked. Or so the instructions said. One of our embassy officers in Dakar had to travel frequently and asked if we could provide him with a means for his wife – a very pretty lady – to defend herself while he was away. But it should not harm an assailant, just discourage one. I loaned her a bottle of B-3, telling her to be sure to squirt it in any direction except into the wind. I heard nothing more until the political officer came back from a trip. He was very upset to discover that his wife had squirted the B-3 at a potential assailant and had awakened some time later to find the supposed attacker – a delivery man – bending over her in sympathy. She slowly came to and realised that she had squirted the B-3 into the wind and gassed herself. She had done what I had done myself twenty years before in France!

Generally, the specialised equipment we received in the field was reliable and effective, like the B-3 powder bottle. Once in a while, however, things weren't so good, so we always tested the equipment when it arrived. An agent and I were preparing to enter a hostile embassy in West Africa and install an audio device. I asked for, and got, a brand new pair of miniaturised handie-talkies – radio transceivers with which one could communicate with an agent at fairly short range, not over fifty yards. This very short maximum transmission range, and the use of an open code with very few and very brief transmissions, would enable the agent and me to co-ordinate our actions with little fear of being listened in on. Or so I was assured by a dispatch in the pouch which brought us the radios.

In this case, we were planning an entry into a building that was being renovated. My agent was an African police official who was about to recruit the building guard, which he felt sure he could do. He would then transmit to me that I could bring the rest of the entry team – myself and one technician – up out of the ravine and over the back wall into the building.

Late one night, the agent and I went to a remote beach area and tried out our brand new equipment. By agreement, we tried it first with 100 yards between us. There was no response to my whispered 'Psst, psst.' Neither at fifty yards nor at twenty-five was there any response. I moved to a bush that I thought would be about fifteen yards from him and again went 'Psst, psst.' To my relief, he went 'Psst' in return. I responded, 'Good, reading you five by five.' The agent popped his head up from the other side of my bush and laughed, saying, 'That's because I'm so close you can hear me without this wretched gear.'

We tried the entry, using penlights to signal to each other. Our efforts failed: the night-watchman, who was supposed to take the night off, stayed in the building. Soon after, the technicians came up with some miniature handie-talkie sets that really worked.

Among the gadgets made by the technicians were various concealment devices. Some were extraordinarily good, while others were marginal. Either way, you could hide documents in them, or money, miniature cameras, and so forth. Once, bound for an operational meeting in Europe, I passed through London. I had called my sister, Sue, and invited her to an airport rendezvous. As I got to the customs officers, I realised I had made a mistake. My luggage was still in the aircraft's hold, onward bound to our final destination, while I was apparently arriving in the UK carrying only a briefcase. The customs officer asked me to open it, which I did, feeling certain that my secret was safe. To my horror, he reached for the supposedly secret hidden switches and, without hesitating, proceeded to unlatch the secret compartment.

It fell open, and there – in front of him, of a couple of his colleagues and some other passengers – was a classic spy kit: thousands of dollars in various foreign currencies, secret writing carbons, a gas pencil, a passport from another country, in another name, and so on. The other passengers crowded around trying to have a good look, although I tried to block their view with my body. The customs officer carefully scrutinised the contents of the open compartment, stared at me for a few moments, looked carefully at my diplomatic passport, then closed the case and let me go. He had presumably concluded that to detain or arrest a US diplomat in transit for espionage was not going to get him a medal.

My sister greeted me in the terminal with, 'My goodness, David, you look a bit pale!' I told her that I was tired, which was suddenly all too true.

After I returned to Langley, I asked the technicians how the British customs officer would have known precisely how to open the secret compartment. After all, it was, they had promised me when they issued it, a brand new design. They replied that they had simply forgotten to warn me that they had given a copy to the British and – of course – shown them how to use it.

My 'parish' in Dakar included coverage of Mauritania and the Gambia, which I visited periodically – nosing around in Nouakchott for potential agents willing to work against the Soviets and the Chinese Communists. The United States chargé d'affaires (temporary Ambassador) to Mauritania was a very bright, independent and experienced diplomat. He had a new go-cart and an ancient German shepherd, and he used to drive the go-cart at full speed around the compound with his dog following, getting his daily exercise. The French Ambassador also had a go-cart and a cheetah, which loved to lope along behind the speeding vehicle. The two men were good friends and often drove their go-carts to each other's embassy compound.

Late one afternoon, the French Ambassador came to the US compound in his go-cart, but this time he brought his pet cheetah along. The big cat liked people, but it had a different approach with dogs. Round and round the US embassy compound those two go-carts went, while the German Shepherd ran at flank speed, screaming in fear. Behind him the cheetah loped along, clearly enjoying the event. I watched in fascination as the scene continued for about five minutes. It was clear that the cheetah had no intention of catching up with the dog, which he obviously could have done. Eventually the dog was visibly exhausted, and the cheetah was called off. The scene was funny at first, an 'event' in Nouakchott which was such a desolate place. It went on too long, however, and I realised that this exercise in cruelty to animals was the result of boredom among diplomats trying to work in a non-capital. The real movers and shakers of Mauritania had remained in the desert, sending their less powerful relations to Nouakchott to represent them.

The President of the country called the US embassy, which was next door to the presidential palace, to ask that the go-carting be stopped. The President was having trouble getting his afternoon nap.

A directive came out from headquarters that made it very

clear that all case officers overseas were to report monthly on the exact hours of overtime they worked. Field case officers usually work two jobs (for one salary, by the way): their cover jobs and their CIA jobs. Often the cover job is the day shift, as it were, and the CIA work is done 'after work'. As chief, I was running my own agents as well as supervising the operations of the other personnel in an area covering many thousands of square miles. At the end of the first month I dutifully reported my exact hours over and above forty per week. The total was surprising, even to me. Even more surprising was a cheque I got in the pouch, payment of many hundreds of dollars for the overtime, plus a pathetic note asking me to ignore the directive henceforth. 'We don't have the money,' it said. 'Naturally, you'll understand.'

One always looked for agents whose espionage efforts were based on total commitment to the cause. Now and then such strong commitment can have strange effects. I had an African agent who was a physician and who was a totally committed anti-Communist. He was a very good source of all kinds of information, and our cover for meetings was that he was our family physician, which was true.

I fell ill with a fever that raised my temperature to a very dangerous 105 degrees, and Ann called him out on an emergency basis. He came over all right, but he also had some important information which he was eager to tell us. For a long time, she couldn't even get him to take my temperature. Meanwhile, although I knew he was there, the room was swirling around and I couldn't make any sense of what he was saying. Ann told me later what happened. She grabbed his arm and shouted that he must do something or I would die. He settled down and took my temperature. When he stared at the thermometer, it suddenly registered. 'My God,' he said. 'It's almost forty-one degrees Celsius [106 Fahrenheit].' He used ice-cold cloths and pumped me full of antibiotics, and the fever broke.

Another time, the same agent – who had a very good sense of humour – listened as I tried to describe another Caucasian to him. I wanted my agent to meet, assess and develop the Caucasian – a Communist bloc official – preparatory to an attempt on our part to recruit him.

'Brown eyes,' I started. 'Brown hair, ruddy complexion, largish nose, thick eyebrows . . .'

'Stop,' he said, putting up his hand. 'It's no good, David. All white men look alike.' He almost fell off his chair laughing.

The late Ambassador Mercer Cook, who took over the US embassy in Dakar from Ambassador Philip Kaiser, was a most courageous man. He could easily have passed for white, but in his late teens (in the 1920s, I believe) he made a conscious choice to stay with his ethnic group, black Americans. Back then it must have been a decision demanding a great deal of raw guts. In the mid-1960s, the President nominated him to be Ambassador to Senegal. It was a good choice, for Cook had translated the renowned poetry of Senegalese President Leopold Sedar Senghor into English, and they had become good friends. I was at Yof Airport outside Dakar when Cook arrived to take up his diplomatic post. Next to me was the Senegalese Foreign Ministry's Chief of Protocol, who wanted to have Cook pointed out to him. When I did so, the Senegalese looked at the man standing in the aircraft's doorway and said, 'But he's white. It's a fraud!'

I asked him what he meant, and he replied that, 'In Africa, if you have a drop of white blood, you're considered white. He's got maybe one drop of black blood, but that doesn't make him black.'

I then told him what my youngest son Chris had said not long before, when he had come home from school: 'I've got two brown teachers and one pink one.' The Chief of Protocol laughed, and we agreed that the little boy was closer to the truth than most adults.

Unfortunately, some of the best-laid plans go wrong. President Senghor was a pro-Western moderate and, as such, was anathema to several leftist groups. These included the Chinese Communists, who resented the fact that Senghor had allowed a Taiwan diplomatic mission to be installed in Dakar as a 'trade' mission. Taiwanese rice experts in the southern province of Casamance were teaching Senegalese rice farmers how to increase their annual production dramatically. But at one point it seemed likely that Senghor would be seduced by the PRC to take sides with Beijing, which he eventually did. This was the period when mainland Chinese visiting or working in Africa waved their little red Mao books at everyone and tried loudly to convert them to Maoism. The problem was how to convince

Senghor that the Chinese Communists were his enemies, not his friends.

A parallel problem at the time was that the French government, led by General de Gaulle, was unfriendly to US interests in Africa. For example, the French peddled rumours that the US Peace Corps was a CIA tool. This was utter nonsense; we were absolutely forbidden by Washington to use the Peace Corps, or to recruit any of its personnel. We decided that this French disinformation had to be shown up for what it was.

Ambassador Cook tried it, but evidently he was not persuasive enough. He and I discussed the problem and decided that there was no appropriate practical covert action to be taken about the French posture. That was a problem for Washington and Paris to sort out. But there was something we could do covertly to help steer Senghor away from the Chinese Communists. Even now I cannot explain what we did, because the methods are still under wraps, but it worked. The Chicoms were caught red-handed in a plot against Senghor.

Instead of bringing the plot to the surface as an outrage, however, Senghor let his advisors talk him into overlooking it. At the same time, some of his advisors decided that they should get rid of me. The best way, they reasoned, was to claim that it was I who was a mortal enemy of Senghor's, not the Chicoms. They whispered that I was planning to have the President killed, unknown to Ambassador Cook. Senghor had trouble believing this, so he shared the 'information' with Cook, who immediately asked me about it. I was able to demonstrate that it was without any doubt pure fabrication. Cook took direct action. He invited me to come with him and see Senghor. The two of us drove to the presidential palace in the Ambassador's limousine, flag fluttering, and walked into the palace side by side. Senghor was waiting.

'*Monsieur le President*,' Cook said to his friend. 'Here is *Monsieur* Doyle. I can assure you from the bottom of my heart that he is no enemy of yours. Quite the opposite, he is one of your admirers.' (This was true: I admired the way that Senghor, a member of the tiny Roman Catholic minority of Senegal, kept a precarious balance between the two major Moslem factions, thus keeping them from harming each other.) Senghor nodded and smiled, and we chatted about African politics for a half hour or so. I never heard any more about my supposed plot to kill him.

·

One of my espionage agents in Senegal was a senior police officer, whose job included interrogation of Communist prisoners. He kept us abreast of the on-going struggle between the government of Senegal and various Communist factions, including a few armed groups trying to infiltrate Senegal from Mali. His methods of interrogation were brutal, and he often came to our house late at night with his uniform splattered with blood. I can still see the expression on Ann's face whenever he showed up. She found the man unappealing and usually left the room at once. I shared her opinion, but there was no way, or indeed reason, to try to change Senegalese interrogation methods. They were very effective, and our service benefited from the results. Espionage officers often use assets whose mores are radically different from their own. Besides, this policeman was also a form of insurance that at least the police weren't trying to watch us. He would have known of any surveillance and warned us.

It was in Dakar that I first began to suspect that the Soviets were reading our mail. That suspicion was to be strengthened by the accounts of other officers, and it grew until it blighted much of my last decade in the Agency. Strong indications of a continuing and unidentified penetration or mole in the CS soon became a nightmare.

Unlike so many other espionage services of other countries, in the mid-1960s the CIA had no known history of being penetrated by the Soviets. We all understood, of course, that a KGB or GRU mole was always a possibility, but most of us in the CS thought that our colleagues were pretty much immune to ideological defection, and certainly very few considered that one of 'us' would be suborned by money. 'Us' meant the OSS/early-CIA corps of highly motivated and patriotic officers: people like Tracey Barnes, Dick Bissell, Bill Colby, Allen Dulles, Des Fitzgerald, Dick Helms, Tom Karamessines, Cord Meyer, Bronson Tweedy, Ann Whiting, Frank Wisner, and their admirers and/or followers – even their detractors – at all levels of the CS. (I have left Jim Angleton out of this list because his post-Philby paranoia made him distrust almost all his colleagues whether it seemed justified or not – see chapter 15.)

We had all seen and heard the Soviet bear; we knew how tough, slick and dangerous he was, and we were prepared to take him on any time, any way we could. That was the core of our motivation, whose roots went back to the fight against the various twentieth-century totalitarian regimes that had climaxed in the Second World War and provoked the Cold War. The idea of selling out to the enemy on ideological grounds was not part of our intellectual baggage, and to sell out for money was simply unthinkable. The fact that the world has a long history of people switching sides for money was something 'others' did, not 'us'. If that sounds old-fashioned, so be it – things were simply like that. We had all been brought up and educated to revere the nation, and the moral and social values that bound it together. So the idea that we might be penetrated by the Soviets was a shock. We were suddenly in the same boat as the British SIS had been when they discovered that Kim Philby was a Soviet agent.

My suspicions first arose in Senegal when we lost half-a-dozen Soviet Bloc operations under circumstances that made me wonder if someone was reading our mail. Several audio operations also went sour for no good reason. One involved a KGB officer who took his family to the beach every Sunday. We planned to break into his home and implant bugs there, and everything was ready, but each time the technicians came to the station to make the actual installation, the Soviet stayed home all day on Sunday. This happened four or five times, and eventually we could no longer justify the effort and expense of bringing technicians in to go against that target.

Another case involved the surreptitious placement of a microphone in a Soviet office occupied by a known KGB officer. The moment the bug was installed, that particular office became a storage room. The target, as if he had been warned, had moved to a different office. We recorded dogs barking, doors slamming, the clack of typewriters, traffic noises and the distant shouting of children, but no useful 'take'. There was another KGB officer whose office we bugged so skilfully that we figured the Soviets would never find it. They didn't, but they knew it was there; instead, they moved him to another room and his office became a broom closet. In another case, we bugged a Soviet office only to have the target – a male officer known for his garrulousness – stop talking to himself, or anyone else.

Then there was the failure of our security technicians – Ann called them the click and whistle boys – to find a bug that we knew beyond a doubt was in the ambassador's or the DCM's office. Two DCMs in a row had told me that they sometimes heard strange whistling noises which seemed to come from a corner of the office. At first it seemed hard to believe that the KGB would install a bug that had 'feedback' and whistled its presence, but the next DCM heard the same thing. We brought in the technicians three times, and they found nothing.

It was about this time that I doubled a Soviet agent – a man who was already working for the KGB but who now agreed to work for the CIA. This man reported that his KGB case officer was very keen to know who visited the US ambassador and the DCM; what day, exactly what time, and for how long. It was now clear that there was indeed a bug, and that the KGB could see visitors enter the embassy but didn't know who they were. Therefore, they couldn't match conversations they heard with the names of the visitors. Knowing who visited the ambassador and his deputy would place them in a good position: on the one hand, they could hold off at arm's length – or otherwise adjust to – those people who were obviously committed to the US, or those who were playing both sides; while on the other hand, the KGB could try to recruit appropriate people who visited the embassy and could be used as agents against us. Just as we were looking for access agents who could provide personality information on Soviet officials, they were seeking similar access agents against us.

The technicians almost always travelled together – two, usually youngish males with large briefcases. They always came by air and were preceded by an exchange of cables. They were easy to spot at airports if you knew what to look for and when, and it seemed to us that the Soviets knew this information. The next time a senior officer visited us, I asked him to carry an oral message. Would the technicians please arrive by road, unannounced by cable, after having sent their equipment by pouch beforehand? If possible, they were to check into different hotels and arrive separately at the office – on the same day, but not together. It worked, although by the time the bug was found I had left Dakar for a headquarters' tour.

It turned out that the KGB's listening post was in the same apartment/office building as our embassy. The KGB had rented an apartment that overlooked the glass-walled corridor leading into our embassy. They could see everyone who walked into the embassy and who visited either the ambassador or the DCM. We had checked the names of all apartment occupants listed in the building's foyer, but had failed to pay attention to Moslem-sounding names. The KGB had rented the apartment using a person from one of the USSR's Moslem states, whose name was indistinguishable from many West African names. The actual bug had been installed by a member of the US embassy cleaning crew, who had easy access to the upper floor of the embassy where all the classified offices were, because the embassy administrative people had put the same combination on the entry doors of both floors: the third floor where the unclassified offices were, and the fourth floor where the classified areas and files were. As far as I know, the KGB gained no access to our office, which we cleaned ourselves and kept securely locked.

Back in Langley, I was invited to attend a technical post-mortem of the KGB bug in the embassy. The technicians reported that the bug was made in Czechoslovakia by someone whose work they already knew. His tools had left distinctive marks while he had been drilling and carving out the space in a wooden bookcase strut in which the bug was hidden. The guts of the bug were also made in his distinctive style. The bug could listen for 3,000 hours on one battery, and – when the watcher in the upper apartment switched it to transmit – could send out its radio signals for 200 hours. All our employee – the KGB's agent – had to do was to exchange one wooden strut for another while he was cleaning the room and nobody was watching. And the KGB officer manning the listening post had to be sure to switch the thing off whenever our audio sweep teams arrived. But this time, as suggested, our technicians had arrived without cable traffic, by road. When they set up their gear, they had found the bug in the DCM's office immediately.

In addition to the audio cases, two or three non-technical cases of mine involving Soviets or East Europeans also went sour for no identifiable reasons. Also, one potentially recruitable double agent suddenly wanted no more to do with us. By the mid-1960s, I was fairly well convinced that someone, somewhere, was reading my operational mail and passing it to Moscow. Was this a penetration of our electronic communications? Were our safes being opened at night and the files read? Or was there a mole, perhaps even at headquarters? If so, logic said that he or she was probably inside the Soviet Division.

While I was puzzling the problem, a team of three Soviet Bloc (SB) Division officers visited quite a number of places, including mine. Their announced purpose was to 'discuss SB operations', but their real mission was to see if we had lost any Soviet Bloc cases under mysterious circumstances. The team was led by Tennent H. 'Pete' Bagley, then SB Division COPS (Chief of Operations) and soon to be its deputy chief.

My deputy and I sat with the SB Division team on the beach for most of three days, well away from prying eyes or ears, and discussed the problem. I was very impressed by Pete's knowledge of the KGB, his great enthusiasm and his strong sense of integrity. He and his colleagues were very pleased that I was able to add half-a-dozen cases to their list, which they said now numbered well over fifty other failed operations worldwide. They told me that they were even more convinced by our disclosures that there was a mole in the SB Division, and that they were extremely determined to find him or her. Pete's team continued with its tour of the world, while we in Dakar waited to hear that the mole had been found. We waited in vain.

Regrettably, field tours sometimes ended by being posted back to the United States for a tour of duty. Many of us saw this as something to be endured as stoically as possible. This happened to me in late 1966. A tour at headquarters had become inevitable in light of the children's educational and other familial needs. As a result, Ann and the five children left Senegal early to recover our house in suburban Maryland and to put the children in school.

I stayed on for a few weeks in Dakar and had one important visitor – DDO Des Fitzgerald, the popular chief of the CS. Des stayed in our house, where he was a very welcome guest whose enthusiasm was contagious. At one point I related to him an incident that had greatly bothered me. The Gambia had just become independent, and its leaders had sent discreet word to our embassy that they would very much like to attend the next UN general assembly, but that they didn't have the money. If the US would help, it would be much appreciated. Nobody suggested that the Gambian delegation would then vote our way, but as Gambians were sensible people, one could assume that that would have happened. The State Department had turned down our ambassador's request for the required funds – a small amount, about $4,000 if memory serves – and the ambassador had asked if the CIA could help. However, our cable to Langley went unanswered. When I told Des this, he exploded: 'Good God, do you realise how much we have to pay for some countries' votes? I'd have approved it right away if they had sent it up to me.'

Des apparently liked my work and asked me to accept a tour trying to recruit Soviets stationed in New York, but I asked to be excused because the family had just re-settled in Maryland. Des was sympathetic and agreed that I could serve a two-year tour at headquarters in Langley. Not long afterwards, he died of a heart attack while playing tennis in Virginia. He was a great loss to the Agency. DCI Dick Helms called him 'a gallant gentleman, unafraid', which was a well-deserved accolade.

15

The Soviet Bloc Division

Back in Langley, Pete Bagley told me that his team had continued their hunt for a mole. They had made a machine run and discovered that just one officer in the SB Division – one of the few with access to all the operational cases – had physically been in headquarters during the time all those operations went sour. Pete's suspicion, of course, focused on that person, but the matter was never resolved.

Soon after our arrival home, Pete urged me to transfer to the SB Division as Chief of the Africa Branch, and later to follow him to Brussels as his deputy. Glenn Fields, Deputy Chief of the Africa Division, warned me to 'read the small print', but that was as far as he was willing to go. I admired Pete greatly and accepted his offer, not realising that I was leaving the relative peace of the Africa Division for the pain and suffering of the SB Division.

Absolute certainty that a mole existed in the SB was being preached by the very men most likely to know we had such a problem: CI Staff Chief Jim Angleton, SB Division Chief Dave Murphy, and SB Division Deputy Chief Pete Bagley. They were among the most experienced KGB watchers, so their reputations and their certainty convinced the faction that believed in the mole. Central to their thesis was that the defector Yuri Nosenko

had been sent by the KGB to mislead us. The defector Anatoly
Golitsyn had warned us that this would happen, and it had. In
their view, Golitsyn was right and Nosenko was a Soviet plant.
(For more details, see Part Two, pages 227–30.)

There quickly arose a competing faction, which just as loudly
proclaimed that there was no mole and that Nosenko was all
right. The opposing (Jim Angleton) faction accused Nosenko's
supporters of being blind, of trumpeting the KGB line, or, even
worse, of being KGB agents. The two factions were soon at each
other's throats, with the result that SB Division operations were
temporarily paralysed, thus seriously wounding the Clandestine
Services.

Predictably, each faction broke into sub-segments, and soon
people in the SB Division and on the CI Staff were calling each
other KGB agents. DDO Tom Karamessines and DCI Dick
Helms stopped the fracas in the period 1968–9 by changing the
SB Division leadership. Dave Murphy went off to Paris and Pete
Bagley went to Brussels. Amusingly, Angleton himself was sus-
pected by at least two senior officers of being the KGB agent,
largely on the grounds that he had done so much harm to the
DO. He had, after all, fallen for Philby and for the worst of
Golitsyn, and then failed to find his mole.

Angleton was supported by both Karamessines and Helms,
neither of whom considered him disloyal or dangerous. He hung
on to his job until DCI Bill Colby finally fired him in 1974
because of his far-out and convoluted conspiracy theories, such
as his strong conviction that Averell Harriman was a KGB agent
and his certainty that the Sino-Soviet split was part of a huge
Communist trick to deceive the West while 'monolithic international Communism' made further inroads around the world. The
die however was irrevocably cast when Colby was informed by
the head of the French service – then called the SDECE – that
Angleton had taken it upon himself to warn the Frenchman
unequivocally that Dave Murphy was a KGB agent. Dave was of
Polish extraction, was married to a White Russian and spoke
fluent Russian. Angleton's charge, on top of his other theories,
was so preposterous that Colby not only fired him but told his
top aides – Ray Rocca, Newton 'Scotty' Miler and Bill Hood –
that they would have to find other jobs in the Agency, outside the
CI Staff. As a result, all three retired. More good men were lost.

All told, the DO had lost a couple of dozen true men, and no mole had yet been found.

We had always had a very strong *esprit de corps* in the DO. We trusted each other, and in the field we depended completely upon each other for our safety and security. Of course, we assumed that there might be hostile penetrations, but when operations had started going sour for reasons that suggested a Soviet-run penetration of the SB Division, the climate changed drastically. The trust that SB people had in each other was severely damaged and, in a sense, was replaced by anger – anger on the part of the anti-Nosenko faction that there were those who believed in this 'obvious' fraud, and anger by the pro-Nosenko faction that the other faction, which was in charge, was letting the mole scare hamper all our operations – especially those that were being developed or envisioned. There was also anger on the part of the other DO line divisions that the SB Division was tearing itself apart and, in so doing, was having an impact on all their operations against Soviet and East European targets.

As Chief of the SB Division's Africa Branch and later its European Branch, I was a close witness to this anger. Since the matter was never resolved, the anger persists to this day between the surviving mole theory supporters and those who debunked it.

In 1968, after I had taken over the European Branch of the SB Division, Angleton invited me into his office for 'The Briefing'. This highly touted and very special baptism was supposed to reveal to the uninitiated – such as me – the innermost CI secrets about the mole. I sat fascinated in his dark office, which had one feeble lamp lighting my end of it while Jim sat in virtual darkness. I expected him to go well beyond Bagley's blunt statement that, 'There is a mole, here's why we think so, and this is who we think it is.' I hoped for details of what we knew, and especially some indication of what the CI staff was doing to trap the mole. That there was a mole, that we were after him and that, meanwhile, we had better act accordingly, however, was apparently something that had to be discussed with utmost caution. Perhaps the person being briefed was the mole! Angleton spoke in a semi-whisper for about an hour. His words were ambiguous, his reasoning elliptical and, in the final analysis, he said nothing. Neither did he ask me about the cases I had lost under suspicious circumstances. In fact, he seemed entirely wrapped up in his

own cocoon of profound suspicion, a prisoner in his version of
T.S. Eliot's 'wilderness of mirrors'. Since this 'briefing' took place
before lunch, it was unlikely that he was struggling to make sense
after one of his frequent many-Martini lunches. I left his office
unimpressed. Bagley's direct approach, while it didn't provoke
any really skilled efforts to trap the mole, was refreshing compared to Angleton's convoluted paranoia. Sadly, he was a bright
man and a devoted officer.

In the late 1960s, the Chief of the SB Division instructed me
to tour the field stations in Africa and to evaluate their Soviet
operations, picking out the most likely recruitment targets. They
were to be given especially secure handling. I was to take along a
special cipher so that I could report to the Chief personally without my messages being read by anybody else – not even the field
communicators who sent the internally coded messages for me.
I was issued a private one-time pad, on which I could encode my
messages and give the communicators a bunch of five-letter
groups that made no sense to them. They would then encipher
the already coded text and send it to Chief SB for his 'Eyes
Only'. He would get the original and there would be no copies.
The Chief SB would then decide how to handle hot recruitment
attempts without their falling into the supposed mole's hands.
Also, a system of private communication channels for hot cases
was envisaged.

It was a logical way of trying to circumvent any Soviet penetration of SB at headquarters, but it infuriated the Africa
Division brass. They objected violently, threatening me with a
ruined career if I followed the Chief's – who was my current
boss – instructions. Since I knew that one day I would go back to
the Africa Division, my permanent operational 'home', I was
neatly caught between the heads of two semi-autonomous bar-
onies, as some called the DO area divisions in those days. I got
out of it by quietly promising to avoid using the cipher except in
cases of great urgency.

DCI Helms eventually intervened in the Great Mole Scare
(as it became known), and although in the eyes of the
Golitsyn/Angleton faction Nosenko's role was not at all resolved,
Nosenko was released from his solitary confinement in prison
and rehabilitated. Angleton, outflanked, was forced out of the
scene. In 1991, English author Tom Mangold produced an

excellent book, *Cold Warrior* (Simon and Schuster) about Angleton, which includes a detailed description of the Nosenko case, including his appalling treatment in his special prison cell at The Farm.

If KGB defector Oleg Gordievsky and former KGB Major General Oleg Kalugin can be believed, Nosenko shared with Golitsyn the honour of being at the top of the KGB list of those to be assassinated. You can argue that Kalugin and Gordievsky are deceptive, or that the KGB might have placed Nosenko at the top of a specious hit list in a disinformation effort to add ammunition to those who believed that Nosenko was genuine, but, not having access to all the relevant data, I could never really decide which faction was right. It was like watching the Republicans and Democrats today, each announcing diametrically opposed 'truths'. One thing did seem true, however: someone was reading our mail in Dakar.

The 'Angleton era' and the Great Mole Scare impacted on the DO in a manner that helped make the Ames penetration go undetected for so long. Nobody wanted a repetition of the paralysis of those years. But to proclaim that there was definitely no mole was dreadfully unwise because it cleared the way for Ames to carry out his betrayal with little apparent fear of being caught (see pages 241–4).

The day I took over the European Branch of the SB Division, the 1968 student riots and kidnapping of industrialists exploded on to the map of Germany, to be followed by equally violent manifestations in other Western European countries. Turbulent dissent was also rampant in the US, where a combination of Vietnam War protests and racial tensions caused widespread urban and campus disorders. The SB Division tracked KGB manipulations of the dissenters, and the European Division tracked the dissidents and the unrest they created. The FBI tracked dissent within the US, including KGB attempts to manipulate it. My European Branch was, however, somewhat removed from these events since our main thrust was to support on-going field operations aimed at recruiting Soviets and their East European allies. We were well aware of the turmoil, but were not directly involved. Instead, we directed all pertinent field stations to redouble their efforts to recruit KGB or GRU defectors-in-place, who would give us a better idea of what our principal enemy was up to. Over all this hovered the alarmingly evil spirit of the mole we felt sure was there but had not been found. Would he immediately tell Moscow about each and every recruitment we made and every defector we received?

The CS had moved from the Reflecting Pool to Langley in 1964 while I was in Senegal. The move hadn't been popular in the CS, since now overt and covert sides of the Agency would be together in the same building. One story that circulated displays the attitude of at least one case officer to the new building and its gadgets. This man was horrified by the vacuum tubes installed for moving paper around the building. It was efficient, but its security was questionable. So this irate adventurer went down to the cafeteria, bought a plateful of spaghetti with lots of sauce and launched it into the nearest vacuum tube. The system – full of moving cartridges with classified documents in them – had to be shut down while furious security and maintenance types squabbled over who would open it all up and look at the mess first.

For a long time it was so easy for the KGB to get into Langley that the KGB *rezident* in Washington was observed there at least twice lunching in the main cafeteria – looking and listening avidly. The KGB also contracted with one of the East European intelligence services to post observers with cameras outside the two entrances to Langley. For quite a while they photographed everyone entering or leaving, and their car licence plates. Signs announcing the CIA went up along the George Washington Parkway; they then came down and went up again. We used to wonder who it was who couldn't make up his mind whether the public had a right to know where we were – knowledge the Soviets and their friends had, of course, had from day one.

Eventually Security got fed up, tightened the rules on who could get into Langley and roughed up the hostile surveillance teams. That seemed to solve the more obvious of the problems, but morale in the CS had been further eroded by creeping bureaucracy. Divisions of opinion in the US about the Vietnam War were vividly reflected in the CS. I was overseas during most of the 1960s and early 1970s and so missed most of the on-going internal debate about Vietnam. There were those who were convinced that the war was a big mistake and was unwinnable; that the domino theory (if Vietnam falls, so does all of South-East Asia) was invalid, and that the US was just another

of the long parade of foreign invaders who were barely tolerated
if not actually attacked. The equally vocal proponents insisted
that the war would go well and that we would free North
Vietnam, as well as protect the South. My own suspicion was
that we couldn't win the war without the active support of the
majority of the Vietnamese people, and/or an even bigger and
more serious effort than President Johnson was putting into it.
Neither seemed likely, but we in the CS were not policy-makers.
Like our countrymen, we could vote for or against at the polls,
but pending elections the question of whether the war was to
continue or not rested with the White House and Congress. The
CIA followed the White House's instructions. Meanwhile, the
war went on, and many of the demonstrations against it – seen
from the perspective of Second World War veterans – seemed
unpatriotic.

The KGB, of course, jumped gleefully into the debate on the
anti-war side. KGB Chairman Yuri Andropov told his troops
that the CIA was the prime enemy. KGB covert action agents
egged on, supported and sometimes financed dissent in the US
and Europe: in academia (complete with orchestrated student
riots), in the media, among the film industry's celebrities and
among potential draftees into the military. Untrue or grossly dis-
torted stories were planted in left-wing newspapers all over the
world, 'proving' that the US in general and the CIA in particular
were up to every nefarious thing imaginable. Many in the West
went along with the KGB propaganda that the CIA was the real
enemy, not the KGB; and that the US was making war against
the people of Vietnam for its own imperialistic purposes. Events
like the US army's mini-massacre at My Lai, the National
Guard's killing of students at Kent State University and the
CIA's bloody Phoenix programme played into their hands.
People forgot that the US had become enmeshed in the war in an
honest attempt to stop a Communist takeover, which we knew
would cost the Vietnamese people dearly. The tragedy is that the
war itself was so badly handled that it crippled South Vietnam
(and to some degree the US) before a vengeful North Vietnam
took over the South.

Despite the pain of the mole scare and the other changes at
headquarters, a few amusing things happened during my
Langley tour. One day, a few weeks after we had left Senegal,

Ann and I attended a cocktail party given by a State Department friend and neighbour. One of the male guests introduced himself and began the conversation by announcing that he had just been the CIA chief in Dakar. He was home on leave, he told us, waiting for another 'dangerous' assignment. His statement was, of course, ridiculous since I had been the only chief there, and since we had faced no particular danger. We listened to the impostor weave a web of lies about his supposed exploits and encouraged him to greater heights of fantasy. It was clear that the man had never been to Africa and was not even a member of the CIA. I didn't challenge him on his story, or indicate that he was, unknowingly, posing as me, because there was no need for him to know that he had been talking to the real thing. The funniest aspect of the event was that our mutual host was a psychiatrist; I should have asked if the impostor was one of his patients.

Langley was a good place to pick up stories about the operational experiences of others. One of my favourite stories is about a heist that was pulled by one of our people in a city in Africa. The crowds in the streets were furious at both the US and the Soviets, and were attacking both embassies; they even succeeded in driving the Soviets out of their embassy, which the crowd then began looting. An enterprising CIA officer took advantage of the confusion to run over to the Soviet embassy, gain access to its most secret rooms and gather up all the classified documents he could find. He got them back to the CIA station without incident, and received a medal for his quick and courageous work.

Being blown – having one's cover exposed or penetrated – is disconcerting and may even be fatal. However, there was one case of an officer being blown where the blower was the DCI himself. Allen Dulles, DCI from 1953 to 1961, was known as the Great White Case Officer because he fancied himself as being well versed in all aspects of espionage. His management style was for his deputies to be responsible for all activities, thus leaving him a lot of time to play at being the gentleman spy. Now and then, however, he made mistakes. It was only natural, because his actual hands-on operational experience was limited to some very successful wartime operations he had run in Switzerland. One day he was visiting the chief of an Allied intelligence service in Europe. The CIA had good relations with the European service in question, but the relationship required the CIA to reveal its officers in the country to the host service. There was a reception one night put on by the friendly European service, and Dulles, chatting away to its chief and doubtless feeling no pain, asked him, 'By the way, do you know my man in XXX?' (the second city and principal port of the country). Dulles then named the man in question.

'No, I don't,' the chief replied, not showing his irritation. 'But you can be sure I will.'

The next day, our man in XXX, whom the DCI had been told was not declared to the host service, was made a *persona non grata* and had to leave the country.

One retired senior CIA officer recalls that when he was chief in Portugal, he was royally blown by the media. It was, however, a mixed blessing. On the one hand, he was suddenly open to verbal and physical attacks by leftist extremists, but on the other he was approached by a lot of Portuguese offering to help the CIA.

I also found that being blown could be a net advantage, particularly in newly post-colonial Africa. One could usually count on somebody in our own embassy snickering in public something like, 'Doyle is a spook, you know . . .' The result was that I was approached by total strangers, some of whom had something useful to offer. Most local security services in Central Africa either had no surveillance skills, or very primitive ones; they also had few assets, and their surveillance could easily be detected and subtly shaken off. This meant that we could operate with relatively little risk of being blown or of being 'sent' provocations by the local security services. (That was, of course, not at all the case where security services were highly trained and well equipped – the USSR being the most hostile and dangerous climate of all. It didn't pay to be blown there.)

By the time I left one African post, it seemed to me that everyone in town had been told that I was a CIA man. But there were no consequences at all; in fact, it tended to help rather than hinder operations. However, that was Africa over thirty years ago.

During this headquarters tour I went to The Farm (the principal DO training base) to take a course in defensive driving. It was just about the best course I have ever attended. By the time of our graduation ceremony, I felt much more confident that I could probably escape a terrorist roadblock alive, possibly even

quite unhurt. Some twenty of us were taught how to evade roadblocks, and how to ram another car or cars and get away with it.

The *piece de resistance* of the course was at the end, when,
having soaked up a lot of theoretical knowledge on how to ram
our way through terrorist roadblocks, we gathered in a field
where a short section of road had been built. There were bleachers on either side mid-way down the road, and a simulated
terrorist car – a battered wreck – was parked across the road,
entirely blocking it. Each student in turn was strapped into an
almost equally dilapidated car, helmet on head, and told to ram
the terrorist car just where we had been taught. The process
would both violently bang about the occupants so that they were
at least temporarily out of action and blast their car out of the
way. The intended victim's car could then drive on another mile
or so before a ruptured radiator made it overheat and seize up.

We all went through the test successfully. The last student was
a tiny, elderly African-American. After he had crashed into the
'terrorist' car and driven on beyond it, he stopped between the
bleachers, got out, took his helmet off his snow-white hair,
bowed, smiled hugely and announced to the crowd, 'I'm the
Secretary of State's driver, and I've wanted to do that for thirty-
five years.' He got a standing ovation.

The use of women as bait for vigorous (or not so vigorous)
males is as old as the two professions – espionage and prostitu-
tion. The KGB use of a 'swallow' to attempt to entrap Western
officials is well known. Much less common was the calculated,
long-term use of women by the CIA. I know of only one such
case. The intended victim was an elderly, very senior Soviet official who had made one enemy too many in the Politburo. He was
sent to a Third World country as ambassador, but as his wife
refused to go to such a primitive place, he went alone, as directed
by the Kremlin. He was lonely, his career was in tatters and his
marriage was on the rocks, so he began to drink. He quickly
developed a reputation inside the Soviet colony of talking to himself when he had had too much alcohol. His complaints against
the Politburo were muffled but obvious. Our station chief
decided that he was worth a serious effort. The plan was to res-
urrect him, and with our help make him so good at his job that
the Politburo would bring him back to Moscow. The resurrection
was to be performed by an attractive Western woman.

Somehow, the station managed to recruit a Russian-speaking New York prostitute to spend three months in a faraway place with one 'customer' in mind. Apparently, the idea of a paid 'vacation' appealed to her. She was duly installed in an apartment near the Soviet ambassador's house, and managed to meet him without the knowledge of the rest of the Soviet colony. As planned, she ended up in bed with him. They spent many nights doing what she was paid for, and she tried to induce him to talk. Far from reciting his troubles, however, he insisted on reciting Russian poetry in between bouts of weeping. Nothing could make him talk about anything substantial. Eventually, the station chief gave up, paid her off and sent her home.

There was once a Speaker of the US House of Representatives who had a very severe drinking problem. That much was public knowledge. Unknown to the public, however, was a more unsettling side to his drinking. I was at that time in contact with several members of the Soviet embassy in Washington DC, hoping to recruit one or more of them. On several occasions, during receptions at the Soviet embassy, I observed the Speaker – drunk as a skunk – surrounded by very attentive and happy KGB officers. They were listening avidly while he was telling them all about Capitol Hill and his role on it. In the process, he spilled out all sorts of secrets. There was nothing I could do, since members of Congress have immunity, and anyway he would have denied it.

At about the same time, I was developing a relationship with a Soviet diplomat, who invited Ann and me to dinner in his apartment. It was a relaxed meal, with excellent Russian food prepared by his very chic wife. During dinner, she looked across the table at me and asked: 'What do you do, David?'

On the spur of the moment I replied, '"Oh, I'm a capitalist.'

The reaction was amusing. Her husband burst out laughing, but she looked at me with horror. 'I've never met a capitalist before. I thought they were . . .' her voice faltered.

'Exploiters of children?' I suggested. 'Eaters of babies?'

Her expression made it obvious that that was exactly what she had been taught to believe. After a while, she got herself together and said rather weakly, 'I never thought I would hear anyone confess to being one.'

My efforts to recruit her husband came to nothing due to the crass but professionally effective interference of a KGB bore

(Boobie, we called him), who continually came up to me at receptions in the Soviet embassy and interrupted my conversations with my Soviet friend. Boobie also did his best to ensure that my friend stop seeing me socially outside the Soviet community. Boobie offered himself as a replacement, but it was clear that we would merely play the eyeball-to-eyeball game and would get nowhere. Other Soviet contacts looked more fruitful.

16

Brussels

In May 1969 – at my own request – I was transferred to Belgium. Pete Bagley was called away to Langley several times, leaving me in charge. The principal goal of our operations in Belgium between 1969 and 1971 was to recruit Soviets and their allies. We had no official interest in Western European politics, or even the student dissidents (except insofar as they were Communist pawns reflecting their masters' voices). Our entire optique was to discover what the Soviets and their allies were doing against us, and what we could most successfully do against them.

But our tour in Brussels was spoiled by the Great Mole Scare, and by a feud between some of the new management at head-quarters and Bagley. It was so bad that one senior manager came to Brussels and asked me to report privately to him on Bagley's activities. I did nothing of the sort, but it left a very sour note. It was, incidentally, the only time anybody in the CIA asked me to spy on a colleague.

In Brussels we encouraged – in fact, instructed – our officers to build up a ring of informants and agents around each Soviet human target. So we recruited people who could give us inde-pendent opinions and assessments of the Soviets from various perspectives. These access agents were foreign diplomats, appropriate government officials, businessmen, academics, neighbours of the Soviets – their doctors, dentists, electricians, plumbers and other contractors – and so on. They were extremely valuable sources on Soviet officials and their way of life, their buildings and apartments, their health, their personal habits, their friendships and dislikes, their hobbies and entertainment, and their strengths and weaknesses.

Despite the experience with Boobie, it was useful to talk to Soviets face-to-face. It was fascinating to see, hear and sense at first hand what our antagonists had to say about themselves and about the many profound differences that divided our ways of life. It was also useful to understand how they felt about Mother Russia and her history, and to listen to some of them clamber about within the invisible but rigid mental fences of their society, trying to convince us that we were wrong. Or to convince themselves that they were right. Or to avoid manifesting signs of discontent. Sometimes we could sense that they, too, would like to be free. Other Soviets however were turned off by the very freedoms we cherish, especially the licence to be 'undisciplined' – to tolerate hippies and other dissidents. With a good grasp of what made KGB people tick, one was better equipped to brief and manage the access agents with whom we surrounded them.

The Soviet espionage service right after the Second World War was quite different from the one that survives today. After the Second World War, in the 1940s and 1950s, most Soviets abroad, including known espionage officers, were relatively crude and unsophisticated. They could make little direct headway against sophisticated Westerners of operational interest to them, especially after they were stopped from using Communist Party members for espionage. Those uncouth thugs in their awful overblown suits were widely considered a joke. They had the heritage, however, of cunning work by pre-war *Chekisti*. The 1920s' and 1930s' deceptions – The Trust, the Rote Kapelle, the Cambridge Five, Richard Sorge's reporting from Japan, the clever Soviet use of US labour and the US Communist Party – were part of that heritage. The Chekists themselves, however, seemed to have become much cruder by the end of the Second World War. Perhaps the early successes were an anomaly in the first place, due largely to good luck plus the work of a few highly sophisticated and imaginative Chekists (later purged by Stalin).

Unlimited praise had been heaped upon 'the great Soviet exper-
iment' by the badly misled Western media and academic
trumpeters, helped by Soviet propagandists. Their noise blinded
most Western government eyes to the real nature of Soviet
Communism. That blindness materially helped early Chekist
operations to exist in the first place, and to survive unscathed
until after the Second World War. Western governments were
pitifully unaware of the size and effectiveness of the Chekists,
and the warnings of early defectors were virtually ignored. Only
after the Gouzenko defection in Canada, followed by the defec-
tions of American Communists, did the West (especially the
United States) begin to wake up.

Stalin's bloody purges of the late 1930s robbed the NKVD of
many of its best staffers. Then Hitler's cynical non-aggression
pact with Stalin robbed the Chekists of the services of a great
many actual and potential espionage and disinformation assets in
the democracies. Many existing agents and informants quit their
allegiance to Moscow and many potential ones turned away. The
war itself took the lives of a great many of the USSR's most
intelligent and effective people. The survivors tended to be a
rough lot, and they looked it. In only a few cases were their looks
deceptive, with some diplomats and spies being very good at
their work.

On the other hand, the USSR and its KGB were a tough nut
for us to crack: their society was so tightly controlled, and the
sanctions for espionage against the USSR so severe, that we
could make little headway against them. We had to make do with
the trickle of outright defectors who, apart from the rarities like
Oleg Penkovsky who stayed in place in Moscow and lost his life
as a result, were our only real window into the USSR and the
KGB. Those defectors we did get, those who were not 'sent',
were pure gold. They not only provided highly valuable information, but made it possible for Western intelligence and security
services to expose in detail the danger represented by the KGB
and its allies.

By the late 1950s, a significant change had started taking place
in the KGB people of the First Chief Directorate. The old
Chekisti, with their lack of liberal education, their crudeness and
overt brutality, were giving way to a new generation of fairly
sophisticated, younger case officers. They were bright, had some

understanding of the West, could speak foreign languages, had a vague idea of history, were able to assimilate a reasonable degree of foreign area knowledge and were tightly disciplined. But their rank and file still didn't really understand the West, or know how to recruit its citizens on behalf of their cause. By the mid-1960s, it seems to me, there had been another change for the better (from their viewpoint) in the general run of KGB personnel. The best of the younger case officers fielded by the First Chief Directorate were as good at their jobs and as sophisticated as the best we had.

In the 1960s, the KGB was directed to name, and attack, the CIA as its principal enemy. Soon after Andropov took over as Chairman of the KGB in 1967, he declared war on the CIA, especially the DO. He caused disinformation to be spread about the CIA, so that the world would consider it a 'government within a government' – a corrupt bully bent upon destroying democracy worldwide. This was a classic case of the criminal calling his victim a worse criminal. As mentioned before, it worked in a lot of cases.

Andropov also knew that the ideological clock was running out, and that the USSR and Communism were fast losing their appeal. No longer was the monster that Stalin had built – and which the old men who had succeeded him in the Kremlin were propping up – an object of admiration in the West. So Andropov preached to his troops about the monetary incentive: 'Always offer money to Americans. No matter how much they have, they'll always take more.'

When you look at the US navy mole Walker and his helpers, and at the Ames and Nicholson cases (see Part Two), it would seem that on the surface – and most unhappily – Andropov had a point. However, the general erosion of ethics and morals, and the rise of personal greed in the US, made his words even more accurate in the mid-1980s than when he had uttered them twenty years before.

There were other interesting incidents in Belgium. Ambassador John S. D. Eisenhower had just arrived in town, and his mother came over from the US to help him and his family get settled. Ann and the children didn't come to Brussels until after the schools in the US closed for the summer, so as a temporarily 'single' man I was asked to escort Mamie

Eisenhower to several receptions. I had heard and read 'news' stories about her so-called drinking problems, but in fact she was a charming lady who drank very sparingly, if at all.

On one occasion, a very senior Belgian official invited me to lunch at one of the isolated estates-turned-restaurants that are scattered around Brussels. We went there in his chauffeur-driven limousine, which he dismissed when we arrived. The car had barely left when my host, red-faced, noticed that the place was closed. He had not only forgotten to make a reservation, but that the restaurant was always closed on that day of the week. Acutely embarrassed, he looked for a telephone. There was none outside the building, which was locked. The driveway was very long, so we started out on foot. Just then a milk wagon drove up to make a delivery. The milkman had also forgotten that the place was closed. So my host begged a ride, and the three of us sat in the front seats of the milk wagon for the trip back to my host's office in the centre of Brussels. His humiliation did nothing to cement our relationship.

Another time I met the Soviet military attaché at a reception given by his US counterpart. The Soviet was very friendly, and we talked for some time about his career and the Soviet military in general. I invited him to lunch at our house. He came, and we talked at length. After lunch, I asked if he would drive me back to the US embassy. He agreed and, as I had hoped, he had not bothered to conceal the wiring of his hidden recording device; it ran along the seam of the carpet on the passenger side and should have been tucked under it. As he drove, he kept glancing at it and then at me, hoping that I had seen nothing. Not long afterwards, he accused our military man of introducing him to a CIA man. Our military attaché told me about it later. The Soviet had said, 'You didn't tell me [that Doyle was CIA].' The American had replied, 'You didn't ask me.' Evidently the Soviet hadn't done a name trace on me before coming out to lunch. When he did so afterwards, it was too late to recant what he had said. This was very unusual for a GRU officer and perhaps even career threatening, if he had reported it.

In the summer of 1971, we left Brussels without regrets. We had been very active against the Soviets, who at the time were also most active against us, so although it was by no means a dull or fruitless tour, we had the miserable shadow of the mole always hanging over us. The endless bickering over the mole scare, and the careers wasted or twisted because of it, had been dismaying. Upon our arrival back in Potomac, and while we were still unpacking, John Hart, then Chief of the European Division, offered me command of a small station in Europe. It was appealing, but on balance I turned it down and went back 'home' to the Africa Division with a considerable sense of relief.

The first part of my 1971–7 tour in Langley was spent running the branch that covered most of francophone Africa. The parish was huge – from Mauritania in the west, through to the Congo, Burundi and Rwanda, and east as far as Mauritius in the Indian Ocean. I visited each of our overseas offices and got acquainted with the staff, their operations and the environment. Again, the emphasis was on recruiting Soviets and other Communists, who were much more exposed and less protected in small faraway countries than they were in the industrial nations.

In 1972, I was promoted to GS-16 and became Executive Officer of the Africa Division, running the division staff. It was a job that allowed time to prepare for the next field tour: running a North African station, but it was not to be. Instead, I was offered a fifty per cent partnership in a successful private enterprise. It was very tempting, especially because in our next tour four of our five children would be attending schools in Europe, not North Africa. For other reasons, including the continuing misery of the Great Mole Scare, I decided to retire early and invest in the private business.

The reaction least expected was the great relief of not having to lock all the documents in sight away in a safe every night, and not to have any more state secrets to hold. I didn't have to wonder constantly if I had become one more victim of what French intelligence people call 'déformation professionelle': a personality twisted by the profession of espionage. I no longer had to watch the highly motivated and skilled inner circle of espionage in which I served eroding. There was no need to be directly concerned about a mole, or to watch unhappily as more and more loyal but under-motivated career officers reacted to the bureaucracy by keeping their heads down and avoiding risks until their eventual retirement. Such people were a minority, but they had their corrosive impact. Wild Bill Donovan's prediction was becoming a fact, I thought, and it was time to get out.

The sense of freedom and release was profound, but it didn't last. I missed the old life with all its frustrations. There's something about conducting espionage that gets under one's skin. I was invited back, but to return to the CIA was not really an attractive option – management was allowing itself to be bulldozed by arrogant young congressional staffers who invaded the place soon after I left. In addition, the damage done to all of us by the mole scare continued because so little useful work was done to resolve it.

PART TWO

TRAITORS

'A nation can survive its fools, and even the ambitious. But it can not survive treason from within. An enemy at the gates is less formidable, for he is known and he carries his banners openly. But the traitor moves among those at the gate freely, his sly whispers rustling through all the alleys, heard in the very hall of government itself. For the traitor appears not traitor – he speaks in the accents familiar to his victims, and he wears their face and their garments, and he appeals to the baseness that lies deep in the hearts of all men. He rots the soul of a nation – he works secretly and unknown in the night to undermine the pillars of a city – he infects the body politic so that it can no longer resist. A murderer is less to be feared.'

Marcus Tullius Cicero, 42 BC

17

Treason and Punishment

The lobby of the CIA headquarters at Langley has a sad tale to tell: a Book of Honour which displays stars in memory of the CIA personnel killed in the line of duty. Some fell victims to treachery, some to terrorism. Some of the stars have true names after them, but many of the victims, who well knew the risks they took, still cannot be identified. I knew many of these men and women, and can testify to their skills, courage and devotion to duty. There are hundreds of others who, like me, were luckier and lived to tell the tale – or some of it. The contrast between the hard work, the unique skills and often the sacrifice of the many for our country, and the treachery of a very few, is stark. That a dozen or so misled or greedy traitors can besmirch the work and damage the morale of so many good men and women is outrageous. Yet it happened and it probably will happen again, for there is no known cure for treachery. We must expect it and guard against it every day. That is the lesson some CIA managers forgot. They had to learn it again the hard way, from the treachery of Aldrich Ames and Harold Nicholson – and of others suspected but as yet undisclosed.

The case of Ames has been the subject of several books, including one by the traitor himself. None of those books adequately conveys the disdain of true CS men and women for traitors in general, and for Ames in particular. Their dismay, too, that some of his colleagues – especially his managers – made it so easy for him cannot be overstated. His cold-blooded fingering of Soviets he knew could then face death sentences was an act of utmost cowardly murder and treachery. All former CIA officers I've spoken to, as well as those still serving in the DO and other directorates, feel the same way. It also sickened much of the media and the general public. The treachery of Harold Nicholson evoked similar disgust and anger, although his treason lasted only four years, not the decade that enriched Ames.

More perhaps than any other government organisation, an espionage service requires the highest degree of loyalty from its staff. Agents' lives are essentially at risk so they, too, expect loyalty and protection from the service for which they work. Espionage services, and the officials and agents who work for them, must trust each other if they are to perform effectively. Treason, at no matter what level, breaks that trust: it is the most corrosive of all the many problems of an espionage organisation. Those who are betrayed, no matter their level in the organisation, are both infuriated and scared by it. They continually wonder who the traitor is – a friend perhaps, or the boss, or the person at the next desk.

When at last they know the traitor's identity, they are only partially relieved, for if there is one, why not others? Each officer wonders, 'How many of my agents have been identified by the mole and been turned against us?' Morale is sapped by the shock of both the nature of the treachery and the evil of the traitor. About the only good that comes of it is when appropriate steps are taken to lessen the chances of it happening again.

In the case of British traitor Kim Philby, and later during the Great Mole Scare in the CIA, the early steps taken were at times extreme yet never adequate. Later, the Ames case was marked by a widespread inability to believe what became obvious.

Defector-in-place Philby was a KGB mole in the SIS, the British equivalent of the CS. His treachery is well worth mentioning because of the impact it had on the CIA. Philby was SIS station commander in Washington, and he had a close liaison relationship with the CIA. A very naive Jim Angleton, who as chief of counter-espionage in the DO was in regular contact with Philby, told him a great deal of highly sensitive information about our operations. Philby, of course, thanked Jim warmly and passed it all along to the KGB. One of the first warning signs was when our APPLETREE agent teams were parachuted into Albania and were met by hostile reception parties; they were then arrested, interrogated and put to death. More were seized as they parachuted, or infiltrated by land or sea, into Eastern European countries. The main reason for these failures turned out to be the treachery of Philby and some of his colleagues, the rest of the infamous Cambridge Five, who had been recruited at university in the 1930s. – Philby was already a Soviet agent when he joined the SIS in 1941. Apparently, his motivation was entirely ideological. His personal tragedy was that the KGB kept him officially at arms' length during his many years of exile in Moscow. According to espionage author Phillip Knightley, another reason for Philby's profound unhappiness was the fact that the KGB did not warn Julian and Ethel Rosenberg that the FBI was about to identify them as Soviet agents. They let the Rosenbergs be caught rather than endanger Philby, who was privy to the FBI VENONA communications intercept files which were identifying Soviet agents. Philby had the grace to feel guilty about this betrayal.

Philby's detection as a Soviet spy impacted enormously on Angleton, who became extremely paranoid. The ghost of Philby haunted Langley long into the 1970s and beyond.

As I have already related, the long and very damaging mole scare that began in 1961 and went on for some ten years caused havoc, and is still basically unresolved. That lack of a firm conclusion helps explain, but does not excuse, the managerial attitude that favoured Ames when a mole was next suspected, from 1985 to 1994. The uproar led by Angleton during the Great Mole Scare was so severe and so unprofitable that it caused a change in the DO management's approach to counter-intelligence (CI). CI became less important, which helped make the Ames case more likely to happen and able to succeed for so long. Because of the significant influence of the Great Mole Scare on later management, its background is worth a quick look.

It began in December 1961 when KGB officer Anatoly Golitsyn (aka Klimov) showed up without warning in Helsinki, Finland, and announced to our representative there that he wished to defect. Golitsyn had been second on the 'most likely to defect' list made up by a previous (1954) KGB defector, the late Pyotr Deriabin. Golitsyn, a controversial and rather extreme figure, was so difficult that eventually he lost most of his audience. His temperament and ego were such that he really only wanted to deal with President Kennedy and other heads of state. He was, however, a most useful source on the KGB and its agents in the West. His bona fides were not the problem: to most of his handlers and his wider audience they were impeccable. It was his political messages and advice which were an increasing problem.

Golitsyn claimed, among many other things, that there was a KGB mole in the Soviet Bloc Division of the DO. That warning was taken at face value because it seemed to fit perfectly with what had gone wrong with a lot of the SB operations. In the 1960s, quite a few operational cases against Soviet or East German targets went sour – like ours in Dakar – under circumstances which strongly suggested the existence of a mole.

In 1962, in Geneva, a KGB defector-to-be named Yuri Nosenko began serving up what appeared to be very useful, accurate information about KGB activities. He identified to his CIA handler, Pete Bagley, several KGB agents inside the US and British military establishments. Among other things, his leads included information that enabled the British to catch John Vassall, a homosexual Admiralty employee who had been blackmailed by the KGB in 1956. Vassall had sold the KGB great quantities of highly classified British and NATO military secrets. He was caught and imprisoned in 1962.

However, when Nosenko actually defected outright in 1964, his two principal messages were considered very doubtful by Bagley, Angleton and a number of other senior and mid-level officers. As one of them described to me, Nosenko's two principal messages were: firstly, that the KGB was not behind US Marine Corps defector Lee Harvey Oswald's assassination of President Kennedy – in fact, it had no operational file on, or contact with, Oswald; and secondly that Nosenko knew of no KGB mole in the CIA. Therefore there was none.

That the KGB was not actively behind the assassination of Kennedy was, on balance, believable. Indications pointed to Cuba's President Castro and/or US gangsters who detested the Kennedys. But that there was no KGB operational file on Oswald seemed patently absurd: Oswald had defected from the

US Marine Corps. He had been a corporal stationed at Atsugi Naval Air Station in Japan, from which the U-2 spy planes flew. As such, he would have been a prime target for KGB debriefing. Despite his low rank and relative lack of access to the U-2 area at Atsugi, he would still have been worth a serious interrogation. Therefore, a KGB operational file on him would have been opened. Yet Nosenko claimed that there was no such thing. Instead, he said that the KGB had ignored Oswald. – In the Cold War climate of the 1960s, this didn't make sense. Oswald had got official permission to enter the USSR and had got a job there. He had been allocated an apartment, married a Soviet citizen in Minsk (she was the niece of a prominent Soviet official) and had eventually been allowed to leave the USSR with her. Every one of those supposed privileges was directly controlled by the KGB: it operated the Soviet Border Guards, it owned Intourist and watched foreigners like hawks, and it approved all passports for internal and external travel, all immigration and emigration, all housing and all employment in the entire USSR. By proxy, it could control many of these factors throughout Eastern Europe. Doubt about the KGB having no operational contact with Oswald was reinforced because of his appearance at the Soviet embassy in Mexico City shortly before Kennedy's assassination. Oswald was seen going in and out of the Soviet embassy. He was supposedly asking for permission to go back to the USSR, but what else was discussed in there is still unknown. In any event, it seems unlikely that, given his background, his Soviet wife and his pro-Castro activities, Oswald was not at least interviewed by a KGB officer while he was in the embassy. Yet curiously the various conspiracy theorists leave Oswald and the KGB out of the question of who wanted President Kennedy dead.

That there was definitely no KGB mole in the CIA was hard to believe coming from any source; coming from Nosenko, it seemed to his detractors to be ludicrous. He could not have been certain, and he instantly became very controversial. Golitsyn's supporters in the SB Division, recalling his clear warning that a defector would be sent to discredit him, took sides against Nosenko. Among the debunkers were Angleton, SB Division Chief Dave Murphy and Bagley, who had initially handled Nosenko and at first thought him to be authentic. The SB officers who believed in

Nosenko's bona fides did so because the information he brought
was, they claimed, too valuable to the Soviets to have been given
away to authenticate him. They had a good case.

However, the anti-Nosenko faction implied that the pro-
Nosenko faction was, in effect, supporting a KGB mole by
refusing to believe that such a creature could exist. Those were
fighting words in anybody's language. The SB Division was thus
split into two fiercely antagonistic camps. The split bubbled over
into other parts of the DO, even the Africa Division because
Africa was a continent where KGB officers were easier for us to
approach on a one-to-one basis than anywhere else. Many sound
operations and potentially good ones were damaged by the con-
troversy, and fine careers were tarnished. Rumours spread and
good agents broke away for fear of being identified to the KGB
by the mole. Liaison with the intelligence services of foreign
countries suffered. In headquarters and the field, officers dis-
trusted each other and called each other every nasty name in the
book. It was, for all of us in the DO, a time of great trial.
Operations were inhibited and yet little was done to unearth the
mole by cunning. Rather, the jaws clamped on Nosenko, who
never broke in over three years of hostile interrogation in solitary
confinement, while the Golitsyn partisans tried to crack his story.
Nosenko was either a masterful deceiver, or he was telling the
truth as he saw it. In either case, he proved himself to be a very
tough cookie mentally. Physically, the conditions he suffered
were abominable, and they cost him his teeth and his health.

Even if Nosenko had been telling the truth as he saw it, it was
still likely that there was – unknown to him – a mole inside the
CIA. Therefore, every possible resource, including the FBI,
should have been put to trapping him or her. But the leaders of
the Golitsyn/Angleton faction did not act with the skill and cunning needed to isolate and smoke out the suspected traitor.
Among other things, they didn't use the enormous counter-espionage resources of the FBI to help sniff out the mole, or even the
full resources of other CIA elements such as the Office of
Security. For reasons of 'turf' protection, potential widespread
embarrassment and professional paranoia, the problem was
pretty much 'contained' within the DO – stupidly so.

When the pro-mole faction lost and its heads rolled, the
anti-mole faction ran the show – and the mole sailed on

unmolested, just as Ames would do a decade later. (Recent publication of Vasilii Mitrokhin's 'archives' in Professor Christopher Andrew's *The Sword and the Shield* [1999] seriously strengthens the case that Nosenko was a legitimate defector after all. However, whether or not there was a mole at that time remains a mystery which, I believe, only the very top level of the former KGB can uncloak. Unfortunately, it seems unlikely that the survivors of that small group would have any interest in doing so.)

Memories of that scare are very vivid and make it possible for those who lived through it to understand all too well the pain that so many DO officers felt during the nine years from 1985 to 1994 when Ames was actively spying. A traitor was clearly in their midst, unhindered and untrapped, while top DO management derided the idea – and once again contained the problem within the DO for years.

Just imagine what it is like to have spent months, maybe years, convincing a Communist to become our agent, then training and nurturing that person as he or she risks death for our joint cause, only to have some scoundrel sell your agent for money! It is hard to describe exactly what it is like to look around and wonder if your operations are going to be handed over to Moscow by a colleague or colleagues.

With so many cases lost under mysterious circumstances, it was natural during the Great Mole Scare that a main topic of whispered corridor conversation was whether or not there was a mole inside the Division. I can still remember clearly the sickening feeling that one of the colleagues I was dealing with daily might well be a KGB asset. Sensible CIA personnel always assumed that we might be penetrated. That was the main reason for the polygraph, for compartmentation and for the need-to-know principle. But when there is a definite possibility, even a strong probability, in your mind that a mole exists – maybe in the very room you work in, perhaps a friend as well as a colleague – things change. The assumption of a possible mole becomes a harsh reality. There is a sort of horror that underlies everything all the time, a sense of quasi-despair because everything you do may be known in Moscow within hours.

Inexplicably, a sound trap was never set, not in the 1960s nor in the 1980s. It was only in the early 1990s when a trap was finally set and was eventually sprung on Ames in 1994.

The early Cold War treachery of Kim Philby, and more recently of the US navy's John Walker, the CIA's Edward L. Howard, Aldrich H. Ames, Harold J. Nicholson, and the FBI's Earl E. Pitts, did great damage not only to their former colleagues but to the images of their respective organisations.

Ames and Nicholson weren't the first moles to have been discovered in the CIA, although between them they did by far the most damage. Their prime motivation – despite later efforts to rationalise their actions – was money. As we will see, in the case of Ames, treachery was his way to pay off debts and feed his own and his wife's shopping sprees. Nicholson sold out his colleagues and their agents in order to pay bills and to atone for neglect of his family by buying luxuries for his children.

One new effort to spot moles early is called Project SHADOW (AFIO Periscope, April 1997), which has so far studied 120 espionage cases looking for common traits. The study concluded that greed alone is not the only motive when a loyal officer turns traitor. The sale of secrets is usually the culmination of a 'long simmering emotional' crisis during which 'the symptoms are often obvious, identifiable, and even treatable' before the damage is done. The study also found that three out of every four traitors went to the other side and volunteered to work for them; fewer than a quarter were recruited by hostile intelligence services. Money was a significant motivation for about half of the volunteers, but more than forty per cent said (apparently believably) that they spied for other reasons: 'disgruntlement', 'revenge', 'thrills', 'self-importance'. Activities such as Project SHADOW should in future make it easier to spot and treat potential traitors before they act.

The Agee Case

Former CS case officer Philip Agee caused one of the first publicly visible cracks in the DO facade, an early harbinger of the future in which there was worse to come. Agee was not a classic mole, but an operations officer who became disenchanted, left the Agency and wrote a 1975 'tell-it-all' book, *Inside the Company: CIA Diary*. In it, he blew a great number of CIA staff and agent assets. His disloyalty to the CIA shocked us all, but at least he was initially motivated more by ideas than by money. As with Ames and Nicholson, alcohol contributed to the fact that Agee's career was a shambles.

Agee now gives public talks regularly, whenever and wherever he can, as part of his long crusade against the CIA. His book clarified his motivation: he wanted to expose and defeat the CIA's role in supporting corrupt and greedy Latin American governments. With little foresight, he wrote, 'Why be a secret policeman for US capitalists when the system itself is disappearing?' Fortunately, it is the Communist system which is disappearing, in large part because most of its managers were finally exposed as being even more brutal, incompetent and corrupt than most of the regimes they tried to overthrow.

There were indeed cases where the CIA supported thoroughly disreputable leaders just because they were anti-Communist. I doubt anyone really liked doing it, but the CIA's leaders and the National Security Council felt it necessary. However, an honourable man would not have broken his pledge and revealed who was doing what, where and how – thus putting many people in great danger. Like all of us, Agee signed a secrecy agreement when he joined the CIA. He should have protested all the way to top management and resigned if that didn't work. He might then have gone public against what the CIA was instructed to do by the US government, but not with details of operations, staff personnel and agents.

One of Agee's explanations in his book for violating his secrecy agreement was that, 'One way to neutralize the CIA's support to repression is to expose its officers so that their presence in foreign countries becomes untenable.' The repression he cited was, however, not nearly as insidious and overwhelming as Communist repression in the Soviet republics, mainland China and most of Eastern Europe.

Appendix 1 of his book listed a great many CIA case officers and agents, and has been called an incitement to murder. Lives were lost as a result. He also revealed that the State Department's 'stud book' – its biographical register – listed CIA officers as FSR (Foreign Service Reserve) rather than FSO (Foreign Service Officer). Therefore they could easily be identified and targeted. The problem was that a lot of non-CIA personnel were also listed as FSR, and they too found themselves targeted as a result. The 'stud book' is now classified and thus no longer available to the public.

It might be of interest to look at a couple of other quotes in Agee's book. When he was in hiding, he wrote that his money had run out and that 'research still pending in Cuba was canceled'. That 'research', he has admitted, was for the DGI (Dirección General de Inteligencia, Cuba's intelligence agency), which in turn was financed by the KGB. The KGB and the DGI traded information back and forth. It was undoubtedly from these sources that Agee got the bulk of his 'research' information – i.e. who was chief in Lima, who was the new chief in an East Asia country, who were their agents – which he then used in his campaign against the CIA.

He also accused the CIA of being a secret police force, by writing: 'American capitalism, based as it is on exploitation of the poor, with its fundamental motivation in personal greed, simply cannot survive without force – without a secret police force.' The CIA is in fact tightly overseen by Congress, has absolutely no police powers and demonstrably can't keep all its own secrets.

Agee left the CIA in 1968 after twelve years of service, mostly in Latin America. He spoke of those years as follows in his book: 'For most of my career in the CIA I felt that I was doing something worthwhile.' He became unhappy because, in his view, the US government, hence the CIA, supported Latin American conservative regimes which catered to the rich minority and cared nothing for the poor majority. In some cases he was right; the regimes were terrible. Many US citizens were not in favour of our supporting brutal regimes and greedy people in order to counter Communist efforts to replace them, but there was often no other option.

Agee claims to have left the CIA for noble reasons. The last straw, he writes, was when he overheard the torture of a Latin American political prisoner he had helped send to jail. But in reality Agee's career was a failure, and his final pre-defection fitness report noted that he was 'definitely less than satisfactory . . . making little or no effort to fulfill [his] obligations to the organisation'. He quit during a period of personal turmoil that included divorce, alcohol abuse and sexual entanglement with a woman who was reportedly a DGI agent. It was strikingly like the Ames experience years later in Mexico City.

The DGI paid Agee in cash, $20,000 to $30,000 at a time, because 'he only likes green'. It was KGB money, paid to a man who says he disliked the KGB.

Communism's track record speaks for itself. In the USSR, it killed at least twenty million of its own citizens in the forced collectivisation of the 1930s. In China, it cost over thirty million lives in the 1960s alone, courtesy of Mao's collectivisation and his 'Cultural Revolution'. In North Korea, Romania, East Germany and Poland, to name a few, it killed, jailed and tormented millions more before the people rose up and rid themselves of the self-styled 'revolutionary socialists'. Agee, too, uses those deceptive words to describe Communism. However, he avoids the obvious fact that Communism strangled not only human rights but the economies of the countries it invaded.

Far from being a showcase for socialism/Communism, 'socialist' Grenada which Agee lauded in his book was the only Caribbean island where people were deathly afraid of their leaders. I visited Grenada in 1979. The frightened faces of the people on the streets and peering from curtained windows, and the absence of laughter, singing and music, were striking. So was the almost complete absence of people of any age on the streets of the capital at high noon on a Sunday. The contrast with the other Caribbean islands I had visited was stark.

Agee decided that there were only two options: to continue to uphold the rich minorities, or to back the Communists – i.e. to help Cuba's KGB-assisted effort to overthrow Latin American regimes and replace them with repression of a different hue. He opted for the latter. He discarded all other ways to resolve his dilemma. It was either black or red; there was no middle ground. But he made a poor choice; red was even worse than black.

Major Florintino Aspillaga Lombard, DGI, defected to the US in 1987. According to the *Los Angeles Times* (8 October 1992), Aspillaga said that Agee received a total of 'a million dollars or more' from the DGI for his work against the CIA. He also confirmed that Agee was a 'paid agent of the DGI while posing as an independent critic of US intelligence'. The money the KGB gave him was specifically to support him, according to Aspillaga.

Former KGB Major General Oleg Kalugin's book *The First Directorate* confirms unequivocally that Agee worked for the

Cuban DGI, and contains an amusing note that Agee first offered himself to the KGB in Mexico in the early 1970s, only to be turned away as a suspected CIA provocation, an operational stupidity that quite rightly infuriated Kalugin.

According to AIM (Accuracy in the Media), in 1975 an Agee-backed publication called *CounterSpy* published the name and home address of Richard Welch, the CIA station chief in Athens. The Leftist *Athens News* then reprinted the material. In the June 1975 edition of *Esquire* magazine, Agee wrote: 'Eventually, perhaps, CIA people can be neutralized faster than [the CIA] can hire them for mischief abroad.' Two days before Christmas 1975, terrorists ambushed Welch and murdered him in front of his wife. As a result of his treachery, Congress passed the 'Agee' law (50 USCA s 421, 422) making it a Federal criminal offence to identify publicly a US covert intelligence agent. Dick Welch was an honourable man engaged in espionage to help protect the Western way of life from the brutality, censorship and deceit of Communism.

Agee has now been bypassed by events. The 'revolutionary socialism' he espouses is in worldwide disrepute, and the treason he committed made him for a long while more detested in the DO than Benedict Arnold (the famous traitor in the American War of Independence) – until 1994, when that dubious distinction passed to Ames.

It is a great shame that the similarities between Agee and Ames were not recognised by DO managers before Ames was given the keys to the kingdom: the job of protecting all CS operations against Soviet and Eastern Bloc targets.

The Stockwell Case

John Stockwell was born in the former Belgian Congo (now Zaire) of US missionary parents. He joined the CIA in the 1960s and became a case officer, but eventually became disaffected and resigned some twenty years ago. After he quit, he went to war against the CIA. To this day, he is still giving anti-CIA lectures all over the United States to unaware audiences who lionise this 'courageous' man for turning on the CIA. Unfortunately, they do not know what lies inside his decorative exterior.

I first met Stockwell in 1968 during a headquarters tour of duty. He was then a case officer in the Africa Division, and I was much impressed with his background, his personality and his potential. He was tall, athletic (Black Belt Karate, I believe), very good looking, very talented and personable. Above all, he knew a good deal about the Congo and had grown up there - if memory serves - speaking Chiluba, Swahili, Chokwe and French. His only apparent deviation from the norm was that in the office, unlike any of his peers, he wore an open sports shirt and an amulet or *grigri* on a chain around his neck. I thought it refreshing that he did his own thing no matter what his superiors might think.

He had been selected to go out to the Katanga and was serving there when two of us went out to Africa on a fact-finding mission. Howard was chief of operations of the Africa Division, and I was chief of the Africa Branch of the Soviet Bloc Division. We toured much of the African continent assessing CIA operations against Soviet installations and personnel in Africa.

We had just fourteen hours to spend in Lubumbashi (previously Elisabethville) and our flight from Kinshasa landed in the late afternoon. Stockwell met us at the airport and drove us to the Leo II Hotel, where we left our luggage. We then went to his house for dinner and the usual operational discussion. Mrs Stockwell was a delightful hostess, he was a charming host, and after dinner we went through the usual routine, with the men talking shop.

But it didn't go the way such evenings usually went. In my experience, DO case officers, and especially station or base chiefs, never dwelled on their personal fears of physical danger. Doing the job regardless of risk was a given, and the entire evening should have been devoted to the problems of Stockwell's base, the effectiveness of his operations and his plans for new operations. However, it wasn't. Stockwell spent most of the evening whining about the risks to his life that he encountered daily. Howard and I tried to steer the conversation back to operations, but it was no use.

Howard and I were disappointed. We went back to the hotel for an hour or so of sleep and caught the morning plane back to Kinshasa. We talked about Stockwell during the two-hour flight. It was clear that the job had got to him and he was running scared. We didn't like the idea of ruining his career, of seeing him become a desk man in Langley, but camaraderie was less important than effectiveness. We finally agreed that Howard, as one of the Africa Division's management, would discuss the situation quietly with the chief of the Clandestine Services, DDO Tom Karamessines. We felt certain that Stockwell would be relieved and brought home to serve out his time at a desk in headquarters, but it didn't happen. Tom K (as we called him) didn't pursue the case. Instead, Stockwell was sent to Luanda, Angola, as chief. Apparently his tour there got the better of him, and he became totally disaffected. His case is another illustration of what can happen when espionage service managers ignore disaffection, and when the disaffected violate their secrecy agreements and go public.

From Barnett to Howard

Former CIA staff officer David H. Barnett was one of the first CIA traitors to be caught, and probably the only one before Ames and Nicholson who clearly did it for money. A KGB officer named Lieutenant-Colonel Vladimir M. Piguzov told the CIA that in Indonesia, in the late 1960s, Barnett had been one of his agents. Piguzov reported that Barnett had sold the identities of some thirty CIA case officers and agents to the KGB.

Barnett's handler after Piguzov was Major General Oleg Kalugin, who met him in Vienna, paid him $80,000 and directed him to get back into the CIA. Barnett managed to do so as an independent contractor (i.e. not as an officer on the staff), but was imprisoned in 1980 after Piguzov blew him. According to Kalugin in *The First Directorate*, Piguzov was himself arrested and executed in 1986 after Edward Lee Howard (see below) blew him in 1985.

Others were also uncovered. Larry Wu-Tai Chin, who was already an agent of the Chinese Intelligence Service, was accepted into the CIA in 1952 on a contract. He was naturalised a US citizen in 1970 and became a staff employee with top-secret clearances. His fluent command of three Chinese dialects (out of the total of fifty-two dialects in China) made him very useful and he was considered the best translator in the Agency, receiving a Career Intelligence Medal. For some reason he was made aware of sensitive DO information, including details of clandestine operations in China, and he reported back to the Chinese in great volume. The FBI arrested him in 1986 and he confessed, was tried, found guilty and imprisoned. A few days later he committed suicide in prison.

Karl Koecher managed to pass a CIA polygraph examination in 1973 and was hired as a contract employee translating Russian material. However, he was already secretly working for the CIS (Czech Intelligence Service). He was given a CIA top-secret security clearance and was thus able to provide the Czechs with large amounts of classified information, some of it very sensitive. The CIS in turn fed the material to the KGB. Koecher's material led the KGB to detect and arrest Aleksandr D. Ogorodnik, a very useful CIA agent inside the Soviet Foreign Ministry. Ogorodnik escaped the KGB's hands by committing suicide with an L-pill which the CIA had given him. Koecher and his wife Hana, also a CIS agent, were arrested in 1984 by the FBI.

In 1985, CIA secretary Sharon Scranage pleaded guilty to disclosing the names of CIA officers and agents to her Ghanaian boyfriend.

Also in 1985 a disgruntled former Soviet Division junior case officer named Edward Lee Howard defected to the USSR. Howard, now a fugitive from US justice, had been slated for assignment as a case officer in Moscow. During preparations for the posting, he was briefed about several Soviets working for the CIA as clandestine agents, and was given very sensitive information about the special tradecraft used in the USSR by the CIA. Howard, whose personal flaws resembled those of Ames, was fired by the Agency in 1983 as unfit for the Moscow post – or any overseas post, for that matter. He took it upon himself to punish the Agency in early 1985 by giving the KGB identifying information on those Soviets he knew were CIA espionage assets. Several of these moles were arrested and executed. According to Kalugin, it was Howard who first told the KGB about General Nikolai Polyakov, a CIA mole in Moscow, who was arrested, tortured and executed in 1986. (Kalugin's book was however written before Ames was identified, and he may therefore have fingered Howard to protect Ames, who knew more than Howard about Polyakov.) Howard also told the KGB about CIA counter-surveillance techniques, methods that had been worked up at great effort and were successful until then. For example, he gave away such goodies as the fact that CIA officers were using 'pop-up' dummies in their cars to appear to replace officers who rolled out of the cars as they rounded corners. The officers could then get away undetected by KGB surveillance, to meet agents or to service drops. In fact, Howard and his wife used that very technique to escape FBI surveillance, thus allowing him to escape to the USSR (shortly after KGB officer Vitali Yurchenko defected temporarily to the US and fingered Howard and NSA employee Ronald Pelton as KGB agents).

Howard also apparently told the KGB about CIA officers crawling down into the Moscow sewers and using sophisticated audio techniques to monitor the offices of high-level Soviet officials, or offices where vital scientific work was underway. According to Kalugin, Howard now lives in the Moscow area and is drinking himself to death. His life must be rather unrewarding unless he has joined the Russian mafia.

Ironically, Howard's defection took place in the same year in which Ames says he gave the Soviets the rest of the DO's family jewels in the Big Dump (see page 247). So many US officials were found to be spying for the USSR in 1985 that it came to be known in parts of the government as the Year of the Spy. Howard's treachery was permitted to obfuscate Ames's treason. It took the Agency far too long to sort the two cases out by discovering that Howard could not have known about some of the cases Ames sold.

Ames and his Managers

Former CIA officer Aldrich Hazen Ames was finally caught in a trap in 1994 and confessed to treason in the form of espionage against the United States. From 1985 to 1994 he had spied first for the USSR and then for Russia. To many US Intelligence community insiders and supporters, Ames outdid Benedict Arnold by a wide margin. Among other things, Ames caused a dozen people to be executed. He should have been charged with murder in the first degree; instead, he is serving life in a federal prison without the possibility of parole. The ultimate irony is that the US taxpayer must now feed, clothe and house this serial killer until he dies.

His wife, Maria del Rosario Casas Ames, is also in a federal prison, serving a term of up to five years. Their only child, a son, is now a Colombian citizen and lives with his maternal grandmother in Bogota.

One year after Ames's arrest and confession, polygraph tests were still being administered by the combined CIA/FBI damage assessment team. These tests, administered in the penitentiary, indicated that Ames was still lying about when and why he started working for the KGB, whether he had disclosed all of the more than 1,500 CIA and other espionage and counter-espionage operations he sold to the KGB, and if he knew of another mole.

The Ames mole scare lasted far too long while successive DDOs proclaimed that there was no mole. Unquestionably there was laxity, stupidity, inattention, over-defending of turf, and inadequate internal and external co-ordination at all levels in the CIA's handling of Ames. But it was principally the unbelievably head-in-the-sand tone set by successive DDOs that enabled Ames to get away with it for so long. The failure of top DDO management to put more resources into the mole hunt after they knew that there was a penetration is mystifying because by all accounts they were otherwise bright and devoted officers.

Blindness does not mix well with intelligence and is a catastrophe in the management of espionage. Such blindness on the part of heads of the CS in the 1980s greatly helped Ames, as did such statements as: 'There was not, there is not now, and there never will be a KGB mole in the Clandestine Services.' This remark was made to me personally in the mid-1980s (after my retirement), in all seriousness, by the then DDO, chief of the CS. Our conversation was in the context of the Great Mole Scare, but we now know that Ames was already a highly paid KGB penetration of the Soviet East (SE) Division of the CS and was already selling CIA secrets to the Soviets. The DDO's words must have given great comfort to Ames, who now had every reason to believe himself relatively immune from all dangers but the polygraph. He was even able to beat the polygraph courtesy of incompetence and poor inter-office co-ordination.

When I returned home to Honolulu, I told my wife Hope –

herself ex-CIA – what the DDO had said. When I finally convinced her that he had not spoken in jest, but rather that he had
seemed quite annoyed that I could think there might be a mole,
she agreed that the organisation we had both worked for had
fallen into strange hands. With its guard down, an espionage
service is asking, almost begging, for penetration by the opposition. And that is just what happened.

In June 1986, CIA Director Bill Casey tried to inject some
common sense into the scene, but failed. He sent a letter to DDO
Clair George taking strong exception to the DDO's 'unwilling-
ness to accept even as a possibility a DO officer committing
espionage for the Soviet Union'. Casey went on to state that the
DDO and the chief of the SE Division deserved censure, and
that DO Division and staff chiefs 'must be more alert to possible
CI cases in the ranks'. Casey held the DDO personally responsible for correcting 'deficiencies in process, organization, and
attitude that contributed to [the Howard] catastrophe'. But things
didn't change. At least two other DDOs viewed the possibility of
a mole as next to zero. They were not alone. In fact, the introduction of the House Permanent Select Committee on
Intelligence's *Report of Investigation: The Aldrich Ames Espionage
Case* began with this quote from a senior CIA official: 'We have
never found a real "mole" in CIA, we have not found any full
time staff officers who were recruited by the Soviets and served
them while they worked for CIA . . . there has never been an
agent of the Soviets in the center of the CIA itself. We may have
failed to find such an agent, but I doubt it.'

The Committee's report goes on with an irritated comment:

> In November 1985, when these assurances were given by
> CIA's most senior counterintelligence officer to the Senate
> Select Committee on Intelligence, the CIA had already
> been penetrated by the KGB through the treachery of
> Aldrich Ames. The CIA's most valuable assets in the
> Soviet Union had already been compromised. The arrest
> of Aldrich Ames in February 1994 for spying for the
> Soviet Union and, later, Russia shocked the CIA and
> appalled the American people. Since then much has been
> reported – by the press, by the CIA, and by Congress –
> about the failure to find the source of the compromise of

significant Soviet cases in 1985 and 1986. This report is
critical of the conduct of the investigation into the compromised assets and the attention paid to it by senior
management, especially in the period from late 1985
through 1991. Although the case against Ames was successfully concluded, the Committee believes that it could
have been brought to a close much sooner. The report also
addresses the failure of those responsible for the conduct
of the investigation to keep senior CIA and FBI managers
fully apprised of its progress, and the failure of three DCIs
to ensure that the statutory obligation to keep the Congress
fully informed of a significant intelligence failure was met.

Like the two DDOs mentioned earlier, the CIA's most senior
counter-intelligence officer (the Chief, CI Staff) who made the
foregoing comment to the Committee should have known better.

One problem with taking the position that there is no mole is
that a very valuable agent of the KGB might be so compartmented that only three or four KGB officers would know the
agent's identity and the nature of his or her product. The agent's
product might be so disguised by Moscow that other KGB officers would not even divine the existence of such an agent. There
has been at least one recorded case of a very sensitive Soviet
agent who was recruited and run by a Politburo member without
the KGB's and the GRU's knowledge. Soviet defectors, therefore,
no matter how many or of what seniority, might not know of a
highly sensitive Soviet penetration of an organisation like the CIA.

Another problem with proclaiming an espionage service free
of moles is that such a position undermines the very need for
security measures such as compartmentation and the need-to-
know principle. It also ensures that people like Ames can carry
classified documents out of CIA buildings with impunity.
Therefore no insider, certainly not the DDO or his peers, should
ever make such a claim.

The House Committee report's summary noted that, 'while
the esprit de corps of the DO contributes to the DO's strong
sense of mission, it also fosters attitudes which can be overly
self-protective and insular'. However, the report's introduction
softened the blow with an accolade for the men and women of
the Agency:

Shock and disappointment at Ames' treachery and at the
missed opportunities to have stopped him sooner are all
the more profound because of the high regard [the
Committee] has for the men and women of the CIA. They
frequently work under extraordinarily difficult circumstances to perform a critically important mission,
providing this country with an intelligence capability
second to none. Few would deny that many CIA personnel perform at a standard unexcelled in the US
government. Nevertheless, the Committee must also
forthrightly state where it has found individuals and elements of the organization as a whole to have fallen short
of that standard.

Ames was able to spy unhindered because, even after the possibility of a mole was becoming accepted, the problem was once
again 'contained' within the CS. Efforts by DO officers to find
the mole were not encouraged by management , and once more
FBI and other resources were left unused because of 'turf' protection and professional paranoia.

Treason is the only crime defined in the United States
Constitution (Article III, Section 3): 'Treason against the United
States shall consist only in levying War against them, or in adher-
ing to their Enemies giving them Aid and Comfort. No Person
shall be convicted of Treason unless on the Testimony of two
Witnesses to the same overt Act, or on Confession in open
Court . . . The Congress shall have power to declare the
Punishment of Treason, but no Attainder of Treason shall work
Corruption of Blood, or Forfeiture except during the Life of the
Person attainted.' Congress was so angered by the Ames case that
it used its constitutional privilege to include in Public Law
(103–322 of 13 September 1994) provision for making certain
categories of treason in peacetime capital crimes. The death
penalty can only be used, however, if the culprit 'knowingly created a grave risk of substantial danger to the national security' or
'knowingly created a grave risk of death to another person'.
Although the wording is too loose, this law should help restrain
some future hunters seeking easy foreign money in exchange for
government secrets. But the death penalty won't cure the problem of treachery. Moreover, it is impractical in any society, and

impossible in the United States, to stamp out treachery; instead, we must accept its inevitability and make it more risky and less appealing. In other words, potential treachery must be discovered and contained as early as possible.

Treachery has intrigued mankind since long before Judas Iscariot sold Christ's identity. Most traitors driven by personal gain of some sort seek to establish a moral defence of their immorality, to justify or rationalise their actions. Often that defence takes the form of righteous bitterness for having been badly treated – or for perceiving bad treatment or lack of appreciation. This occurred in Ames's case. He worked up a well-rehearsed 'ideological' rationale for his actions, interspersed with admissions that it was due to simple greed. He blew two agents inside the Soviet embassy in Washington because they might have fingered him (see page 247), but that self-protective measure came after he had already turned traitor. His principal motive for treason was money, his solution to a long-simmering emotional crisis: a very obvious string of professional disappointments and personal problems.

For reasons that may reveal more about my own bias than about the motivation of traitors, I believe that most of us in the DO – especially during the Cold War – assumed that a supposed mole in the CIA would be motivated by things other than money: by honest conviction, or perhaps misplaced loyalty, but not by personal greed. That still seems to be the general reaction in the DO today, despite Project SHADOW's claims that money as a substantial motive was present in only about half the cases of those prosecuted for treason since the Second World War.

A close look at Ames not only shows how easily a mundane personality can drift into treachery, but how readily the signs of his treachery were glossed over by his managers. At first glance he is a rather unlikely traitor. He was born on 26 May 1941 in River Falls, Wisconsin, the eldest of three children. His parents, Carleton and Rachel Ames, were both teachers. Carleton Ames joined the CIA in 1952 and served in the CS (then called the Directorate of Plans – DDP) for one Far East tour, after which he was relegated to CIA headquarters to serve out his time without any additional overseas service. It was there that I met him. He was a nice enough fellow, but he had a serious drink problem – one which also afflicted his brother and one of his sisters (who died of acute alcoholism). Perhaps Carleton and his siblings were unable to cope with the hauteur of their father, Jesse Ames, a former lumberjack turned college president, who was the patriarch of River Falls and was a strong-minded auto-crat with strict ethics.

Aldrich Ames tried acting, but could not make a career of it. He did summer work for the CIA, then a period in the Agency's records section, before finally joining the CS as a career trainee in the class of 1962. He served for thirty-two years, with tours of duty in CIA headquarters, Ankara, New York, Mexico City and Rome. Like his father, 'Rick' Ames was a lacklustre performer with a serious drinking problem.

Most CIA operations officers I've talked to since the case broke on 21 February 1994 believe that KGB attention was about the only way that Ames could feel flattered and wanted by espionage professionals. The KGB stroked his self-inflated ego and allowed him to feel needed, respected and admired, none of which he got from most of his DO colleagues.

But was Ames really respected by his Russian handlers? As Plutarch says, 'I love treachery, but hate the traitor' (*Caesar*, Romulus 17). The Russians say that he was, but one must wonder how real that respect was. In 1985 when Ames first sold out to them, KGB officers were already slowly understanding what a total failure their regime was facing; five years later when the USSR collapsed, and Ames was still plodding on in their pay, they must have known that he was motivated by money – the least appealing of all motives for treason.

Ames had a classic profile of disenchantment. He was going through both a personal and a professional crisis. He owed money and couldn't afford to pay off his debts or support the lifestyle he desired. Nor was his career a success. In 1985, after twenty-three years in the CS, he wasn't going anywhere and he knew it. He had a very high opinion of himself which the CIA did not share.

By his own account and those of many of his CIA colleagues (and indeed his second wife Rosario), Ames was operationally sloppy. He was unable to recruit agents, was reluctant to work unless a task interested him and was often drunk on duty. He was, in the minds of his supervisors if not his own, a terminal GS-14 – a $69,800 pay grade roughly analogous to a lieutenant-colonel in the military – a mid-level officer going nowhere. (In the military such a person would be forced to retire, but not in the CIA.) However, his perception of himself was at variance with the way most others saw him. Except for a few sympathisers and his drinking buddies, his colleagues' views (voiced after his arrest) mostly ranged from 'made no impression' to 'I didn't trust him'. Ames's failed career angered and embittered him. Like his father before him, he felt unappreciated despite his self-perceived talents. More importantly, he needed money because his extravagant wife, Rosario, caused him severe financial problems. Although he was bright and – after KGB money paid for cleaning him up – personable enough, he knew that all but one of his supervisors rated him low on the scale, and it infuriated him. Unfortunately, little of this was reflected in his file.

Sadly (and most curiously) none of his managers bothered to ask him sympathetically what the trouble was. Instead, this known misfit was given the very sensitive post of chief of the SE Division's CI (counter-intelligence) Branch. In that position, he was in charge of being sure (if one can ever be) that all CIA and some Allied agent operations against the USSR and Eastern Europe were not doubled or otherwise tainted, and he therefore had automatic daily access to all CIA operations in this area. How he was placed in such a demanding job remains a mystery; the officer who first recommended Ames for it regrets it to this day.

Now a very hungry and angry Ames was guarding the CS's most sensitive area. While management kept him locked in there for years, he sold its secrets to the Kremlin. Sure that he could get away with it, his first act of treachery was, he claims, a scam: in 1985, he sold two dubious agent cases to the KGB for $50,000. Although he makes light of it, any unauthorised sale of anything belonging to the CIA was and is illegal.

Next came the Big Dump: his sale of classified documents, the total of which eventually equalled a stack of papers some 24 feet high. He sold about 1,500 covert intelligence operations to the enemy. Inexplicably, the Kremlin quickly rolled up the agents he had blown. Over a dozen CIA and FBI agents were tortured and executed in Russia alone, plus others in Eastern Europe. Two of these, Sergei Motorin and Valeri F. Martynov, who had been in the Washington *rezidentura*, were FBI agents and were especially dangerous to Ames.

After these losses, the Agency slowly reintroduced strict

operational compartmentation, especially in the SE Division, but it was too late to catch Ames. He was already deep inside the SE Division's CI Branch and trusted by his colleagues. The fact that the KGB was willing to pay him, or set aside for him, a total of over $4 million is a testament to the importance that a notoriously stingy organisation attached to his product. Even though Ames displayed all the signs of a penetration agent, it is incredible that he was able to remain in the DO, at home and in the field, for another nine years before being caught, protected by the management's belief that there was no traitor.

I have discussed the Ames case with a number of former CIA colleagues and with some who are still serving in the CS – top-level managers as well as mid-level officers. We all find it very hard to understand why Ames and many other mediocre employees – i.e. the drunks, the inept, the lazy, the undisciplined and the untrustworthy – were tolerated in sensitive positions for so long. As former CIA Inspector General Fred Hitz put it, 'We carried our walking wounded much too far.'

Other factors favouring moles in the DO included management inattention up and down the line, lack of adequate internal and external communication and co-ordination, and lack of the simple discipline of being aware. Paradoxically, these managers were otherwise bright, seasoned professionals whose skills and careers contributed significantly to the best qualities and successes of the CIA. But in the Ames case, when management at last perceived the problem, the size and nature of it were recognised too slowly. Inexplicably, the DO's investigation into the loss of all those agents was treated with no urgency and not given the utmost priority. Other things were considered more important, although it is hard to conceive what could have been more urgent for the DO in general and its SE Division in particular.

Casey's admonitions to the DDO and his other senior officers do not appear to have significantly affected the meagre efforts to resolve the 1985–6 compromises engineered by Ames. By the mid-1980s, tight compartmentation of sensitive agent operations and other espionage and covert action activities had become severely eroded, and literally hundreds of officers – many with no real need to know – were aware of highly sensitive information. Ames gathered corridor and lobby gossip like a vacuum cleaner. Classified papers and cables floated around the DO with few effective controls, and copying machines were open to all. More recently, there was also widespread internal access to computerised files, and Ames stole reams of documents from the CIA's computers by copying them on to floppy disks, which were found in his house when it was finally searched. Therefore, once inside the Agency, a penetration agent could have a field day – which is just what Ames had.

On leaving the CIA headquarters at Langley, the guards at the doors could be counted upon to nod, smile, or even say a polite 'Goodnight', but they never asked to see what was being carried out. Admiral Stansfield Turner was the first DCI to institute spot checks at the exit doors, and it made him very unpopular because looking into an individual's packages or briefcase was widely (and quite unwisely) seen as a personal affront. After Turner's directorship (March 1977 to January 1981), things returned to 'normal'. Therefore, Ames was able to carry out a vast amount of paper with impunity.

The KGB at first found it almost impossible to believe that Ames could get away with what he did, but he was eventually able to convince them of the Agency's laxness. Later, when computers became *de rigueur*, he had to teach his computer-illiterate Russian handlers how to read the new product he sold them.

Had Ames set out to be caught, he could hardly have done a better job. He flaunted his new affluence, failed to report contacts with Soviets, tossed evidence of his treason into his rubbish, ignored phone security and used old-fashioned tradecraft. Meanwhile, had his DO top managers deliberately tried to avoid catching a mole, despite clear evidence of one, they couldn't have done a better job.

All this wasn't lost on the working case officers in the field and at headquarters. The DO is staffed by many hundreds of highly intelligent, well-motivated, skilled and effective people, who take great risks and keep their silence. Therefore, when in February 1994 the Ames case exploded, this gifted group of people reacted with fury. Ames had caused all their valuable work to go down the drain and led to many lives being lost. As a result, morale within the DO fell dramatically and many bright, young officers left the Agency in disgust; others who remained had little faith in its top management (of whom only two said '*mea culpa*') and work efficiency decreased. The CIA moved one more notch in the direction which General 'Wild Bill' Donovan had predicted so long before.

Problems of management and leadership were all too common in the DO of the 1980s and early 1990s. Faulty management deluded itself and hated rocking the boat, while many of the troops regarded their leaders with scorn if not suspicion. Until 1991 when they started working together, substantive and effective co-ordination between the SE Division, the CIA Office of Security and the FBI was more occasional than the rule. The fact that CIA co-operation with the FBI was marginal was a very big mistake, and the traitors took full advantage of it.

Reliance on the polygraph – many of whose overloaded operators were inadequately trained and improperly briefed – was too great, and yet paradoxically its results were often ignored. Ames was actively protected when troubling lie detector test results were excused as being of no consequence. It is interesting to note that three of the known moles in the CIA – Koecher, Chin and Ames – successfully passed Agency polygraph exams administered while they were spying.

One senior CIA officer who is still serving had some pungent things to say about the DDOs of the Ames era. In a private communication to me, he wrote: 'Top management permitted people who were arrogant, vindictive, and operationally blind to become chiefs of the Clandestine Services. Once there, these men surrounded themselves with a coterie of clones who did their bidding without question. These clones and cronies included various division chiefs in the DO, the "barons" of the CS. Not one was seriously punished.'

Whatever one's views, it is a fact that there was a lack of management interest in and support for counter-intelligence, believed by senior CIA officers to be the result of the aftermath of the paranoia of the Angleton period. There is some truth to this. During Jim Angleton's twenty years as Chief, CI Staff, a career in CI was considered acceptable but not the best way to glory unless you were one of Jim's chosen few. After Angleton's departure in 1974, dedicated counter-intelligence officers were not adequately appreciated or rewarded and, therefore, became harder to find. Just as a career in military intelligence was long considered a blind alley by the rest of the military, a career in counter-intelligence was considered a dead end in the DO. Good officers avoided doing a tour, let alone making a career, in CI. Even in the years just before Angleton's crash, assignment to CI work was not seen as an especially good career track for DO officers because it meant getting involved in a bitter dispute. It became even less popular afterwards, when Jim and his works were so denigrated. CI was more or less put on the back burner, which was never the proper place for it. That this extraordinary window of opportunity for the KGB was left open even briefly by successive DDOs is hard to understand, but that they left it open after they knew there was a mole is incredible. Even those DO officers – notably Jeanne Vertefeuille – who did search diligently for the mole received little support from their superiors until it was too late.

Ames has been asked why he didn't separately negotiate each case he sold, and why he didn't vaguely describe each CIA agent he knew about and set a price on more complete information. This could have bled out the operation for years. It would have been potentially much less dangerous for Ames, and perhaps would have brought him much more money in the end. He could simply have begun by sacrificing the two greatest threats to his own welfare: Martynov and Motorin. However, he has not given any clear reasons for making the Big Dump rather than parcelling out his product, but whichever way you look at it, it was a dumb way to sell the government's secrets.

Another example of Ames's ineptitude, if we are to believe him, is that he fully trusted the Soviets to protect their agents carefully. He says that the roll-up of agents which followed his sell-out was apparently directed by the Politburo. There were just too many Russian traitors active at one time. Had Ames had the wit to bleed out his treachery over a number of years, his revelations would almost certainly not have caused Politburo intervention.

The KGB Role

One side's traitor is, of course, the other side's asset. One would expect that the Soviets would take as much care of their treasure-trove as possible, making sure that the information wouldn't be used in such a way as to expose the fact that they had a mole. Yet as we have seen, the Soviets rolled up Ames's victims right away, making it clear that they had either penetrated the Soviet Division of the CS or the Agency's communications system.

The KGB, compounding the error, failed to control Ames. Having acquired this most valuable asset, it handled him sloppily. It allowed him to use arcane contact and agent communication methods, a risky business which eventually enabled the FBI to catch him red-handed. The KGB claims that it regularly cautioned Ames to be careful, but its actions belie its words. It rolled up (or was forced to roll up) and executed assets he had fingered without warning him beforehand. It simply let him find out for himself that he was in danger. No matter how compelling the Soviet reasons for making it obvious that they had a mole in the DO's SE Division, one would have expected the KGB to warn him ahead of time of the coming danger. Logically, it would have given an agent of such value the opportunity to organise his defence from detection, or to defect outright to the USSR, or to take refuge in Brazil. It failed to do that, and it also failed to require him to use sophisticated counter-surveillance and agent communication methods.

It did not make him cut down his drinking or be careful how he spent the large sums of money it gave him in $100 bills. It didn't require him to be careful about storing information he had stolen, or the messages exchanged between them. In reality, it lost control of him, and for some reason made little effort to regain it despite the danger he now faced. As his motivation was the money they paid him, it could have controlled him, but it simply didn't. This was unusual for the KGB, and is one of the several mysteries of the case. One possible answer is that Ames progressively became of less value, and the KGB could afford to let him be caught to cover a better asset inside the CS.

On balance, it seems quite unlikely that the KGB, on its own, would have exposed Ames so soon after the Big Dump without a truly compelling reason. Even if the KGB feared that one or more of the CIA agents fingered by him would, if not quickly dealt with, uncover a better Soviet asset in Washington, it would normally have gone about it slowly and carefully. It is, therefore, possible that what Ames says his KGB case officer 'Vlad' told him is true: that the Politburo somehow prevailed over KGB Chairman Viktor Mikhailovich Chebrikov and forced the roll-up of the agents. If the Politburo did indeed take that extreme stand, it is a mystery why the KGB was unable to persuade them differently. After all, Chebrikov (like his predecessors) was himself a member of the Politburo and had enormous influence in the Party and the government. Why did he acquiesce, instead of resigning, in what must be one of the most bizarre ways of treating a valuable agent in the history of espionage? Even the most primitive espionage service understands that one doesn't risk one's best agent by quickly grabbing everyone he fingers. Chebrikov, with all the KGB's extensive files on his fellow Politburo members at his disposal, should have been able to fight the matter and win. Chairman Yuri Andropov surely would have.

Or was the entire Politburo, including Chebrikov, so sickened by what the Big Dump revealed that they panicked? That, too, seems unlikely, although it is what Vlad was hinting at. Unfortunately, we may never know for certain why the KGB put – or was forced to put – what appeared to be their most valuable CIA agent at such great risk. Even the possible explanation that they had to protect an even better mole is a bit thin because they had no idea what access to secrets or influence Ames might have secured later in his career. Whatever their reasoning, their actions would normally have quickly sacrificed Ames. It was only because of world-class bungling in the CIA that he was able to survive as long as he did.

Equally inexplicably, at no time did the KGB try to enhance Ames's career, which it could have done in multiple ways: for example, by feeding him first-class information, or having him supposedly recruit a very important Soviet source with excellent access to the highest levels, skilfully mixing good information with bad. Instead, it acted as if he were disposable.

All in all, had the Soviet government and the KGB between them tried to blow Ames, they could hardly have done better.

Meanwhile, Ames hopes to be exchanged for a US intelligence asset whom the Russians are holding, although it is very doubtful that this will happen. Although we have exchanged Soviet spies for US spies, including the famous Francis Gary Powers whose U-2 was shot down over the USSR in May 1960, it seems most unlikely that the US would have any incentive to seriously consider exchanging Ames rather than having him serve out his life in prison.

It is amusing that retired Colonel Viktor Cherkashin, who in 1985 was the deputy KGB *rezident* in the Soviet Embassy in

Washington, claimed to have recruited Ames, for which he received the Order of Lenin in 1986. Cherkashin called Ames 'a man of great self-control and courage' (*Nevavisimaya Gazeta*, Moscow, 15 June 1996) and urged the Russian government to ask the US government to help Ames – whom, he claims, was not the disrespected slob that his colleagues knew. However, those colleagues knew better. Cherkashin was taken in by Ames's acting ability.

Some 'correct' thinkers inside and outside the Washington Beltway will doubtless be swayed by Cherkashin's dubious claims and Ames's self-serving comments from jail. Hopefully they won't be able to convert Ames into a hero – and the CIA into even more of a villain than they portray it now. It's a testament to our times that such a reversal of opinion is entirely possible.

An example of claims that are doubtful and may be related to the Ames case, or another mole, is in a book recently published by two former KGB officers, Colonel Valentin Aksilenko and Major Yuri Shvets. In a television interview, they maintained that:

> We in the KGB considered Americans unrecruitable. They are proud of their country, proud of themselves. To recruit an American was a fluke. So we just sat around [in the Washington KGB *Rezidentura*] and waited for a walk-in. Or we wrote up news media stories and sent them to Moscow marked Top Secret. There is a long history of fake agents manufactured by KGB officers. One such was Henry Kissinger, who was codenamed LORD. He was never an agent. One KGB officer met him and chatted about foreign affairs when Kissinger was still a professor. When he became a White House security advisor, we claimed we had penetrated the White House. His supposed product came from news stories. In the twenty years from 1970, Washington *Rezidentura* did not recruit a single American agent.

Each of the two authors claims to have recruited one agent only, neither of which was US born. One was a Peruvian janitor who obtained some valuable information from waste-paper baskets in defence contractors' offices, an easy mark, while the other was an Australian-born journalist, who vehemently denies being a KGB agent.

The claims of past non-recruitment of Americans seem to me quite suspect, especially in the current climate where money is king and government is widely discredited. Other Chekist defectors have reported that there is a history of fake cases engineered by KGB employees, but still others have revealed significant successes against the American target, not walk-ins but people developed and recruited from scratch.

It would seem more likely that most *Chekisti* today consider US citizens in general, and intelligence personnel in particular, very difficult to recruit but certainly not impossible. Former KGB Chairman Andropov pressured his troops to offer Americans money, which was sensible since the desire for money plays so large a part in our society. But apparently recruitment for money alone was not tried all that often by the KGB and was even more rarely accepted by its American targets. The Andropov edict was not a factor in the treachery of US navy officer John Walker. The KGB didn't walk up to him and offer money; he went to them and asked for it. Nowadays, the Russian Federation's SVR, unlike the USSR's KGB, has no cause other than the love of Mother Russia to attract potential spies.

Whatever the truth, it is very hard to believe that the KGB was so unsuccessful in Washington for twenty years. The *Chekisti* specialise in lying, and so presumably do most of its former officers. What better motive could they have than lulling the US populace back to sleep? If I were a Russian intelligence officer operating in the US now, that's exactly what I'd be doing. It is far easier to conduct espionage in a relaxed climate of societal opinion than in one where there's suspicion. To steal US industrial and technological secrets is still a major Russian espionage goal which requires recruiting American citizens. The Soviets before them, and now the Russians, have done very well in that field. In future, money will presumably play an even larger role in the temptation and recruitment of US traitors than it has in the past.

The Nicholson Case

Like Ames, Harold James Nicholson was apparently motivated entirely by monetary greed, but seems to have been willing to risk the death penalty for a relative pittance: $300,000. But unlike

Ames, the Nicholson case was solved more quickly because the FBI was in on the case from the start, and his problems with the polygraph were taken seriously.

One senior officer still serving in the CIA, who worked with Nicholson, told me that he thought he knew him quite well. Nicholson was not very good at his work and so by the age of forty-six had only reached a mid-level management rank, between GS-14 step 8 and GS-15 step 2. Like Ames, he had problems with women and, to some with extent, with alcohol. My source thought him a nice enough fellow and was completely surprised to learn that he was a traitor. Although the damage Nicholson did was not comparable in nature or quantity to that done by Ames, it was – especially in terms of the CIA's Asian operations and personnel security and assignments – certainly severe. After his arrest, Nicholson agreed to explain in detail what secrets he had given to the Russian Federation. In exchange, a plea bargain got him a lighter sentence (twenty-three years) than the life without parole he would otherwise have suffered.

In the summer of 1997, *Insight* reported that there was at least one more traitor in the CS as yet not apprehended for lack of evidence. Other reports insist that several Russian defectors have claimed that, in addition to Ames and Nicholson, there were more traitors working for Moscow. All this emphasises the simple fact that treachery is part of human nature and very much a companion of espionage. Nobody should ever deny its existence, or lower security standards, or fail to search aggressively for it.

PART THREE

VALUE VERSUS ETHICS

' . . . intelligence . . . should be conducted with the minimum trespass against national and individual human rights . . . [and] despite all the opportunities – and temptations – that it offers for malpractice, intelligence can be an honourable pursuit.'

R.V. Jones, *Reflections on Intelligence* (1989)

'Your successes are unheralded, your failures are trumpeted.'

President John F. Kennedy inaugurating the new CIA head quarters, Langley, 28 November 1961

Whereas the rest of the world takes espionage for granted, it is typically American to be concerned about the ethics of an open society conducting espionage. The US navy's code-breaking efforts before the Second World War drew this remark by Secretary of War Henry Stimson: 'Gentlemen don't read each other's mail.' In fact, gentlemen in the US have done just that since George Washington; our first Commander-in-Chief and first President regularly used espionage and covert action (often called 'dirty tricks') to further his country's cause. He even ran several spies himself, who helped him win the War of Independence. Spies also played a serious part for both sides in the Civil War. President Woodrow Wilson ran covert operations into Mexico, as did President Roosevelt into several countries during the Second World War. All US Presidents since Roosevelt have been fascinated by (and in one case apprehensive of) the clandestine tools at their disposal: espionage and its sub-set, covert action.

Had Stimson helped instead of hindered the effort to break the Japanese codes, their surprise attack on Pearl Harbor on 7 December 1941 would have gone very differently. Stimson's views should have gone permanently out of fashion after that attack, but even now there are those who would have us cease conducting espionage. It is perhaps morally cleansing to oppose spying, but it is impractical to dispense with it if you want to try to discover the whole truth. Conducting foreign policy, and even going into war, without having spied out an enemy's true intentions and capabilities may be morally uplifting but it has never been even remotely sensible.

According to the very strictest personal moral code, the opponents of espionage are right about its ethics: it is reprehensible for one person to open and read another's private mail. However, while that position is all very well on a personal and national level (American law makes eavesdropping a crime unless court-approved), it ignores the needs of national security in an imperfect world. However unhappy some people feel about it, national security has to take precedence over ethics – a view which, I discovered while lecturing, a surprising number of people do not accept.

Obviously, the ethics of state espionage can be condoned only by the vital national need to see the present and the future as clearly as possible. A sound espionage effort acquires and disseminates accurate knowledge and foreknowledge of events that impact upon everybody. It is a basic national instrument for anticipating danger and a necessary first line of defence, as it has to be for any serious nation. It is vital to determine beforehand what dangers are in sight for our country and its allies. Nobody sensible wants to be caught by another Pearl Harbor or by 'suitcase' nuclear bomb attacks on their cities, or surprised by a massive terrorist explosion like the one at the Trade Center in New York.

We must clearly understand the intentions and capabilities of those who may pose a threat to us. Their capabilities may be fairly clear from overt sources, but, as we have seen, their true intentions are much harder to determine and can often be perceived only through espionage using paid, trained and controlled human agents.

Espionage using human beings, therefore, is as necessary to sound intelligence as stealth and camouflage are to the military, or a concealed gun is to a police detective. We cannot simply rely on imagery, the world media and other open sources to expose the facts and to flag the dangers and problems up front. These overt sources are vital to intelligence analysts, but they can be wrong, or biased, or follow a hidden sponsor's wishes – sometimes all three. It is mostly through human beings that we can discover what a troublesome nation's leader has in mind. If he talks to others about his ambitions, worries and plans, then we need either a person who hears him, or a hidden microphone (which is often impossible to install). If he communicates mostly in writing, even electronically, then we must try to read his mail. The same is true for those trying to replace that leader. We must track them closely and know in advance what they stand for and how likely they are to succeed, often by recruiting their closest confidants or personal advisors. Without using such human assets, we walk with only one eye open, and no sensible citizen wishes his government to navigate in a dangerous world with one eye closed.

Given all this, the question is not whether we need to conduct espionage, but whether the CIA's Clandestine Services are up to the task today. Or have they become so demoralised by adverse events and publicity as to be permanently crippled? Many people who are prepared to support US espionage as such (Senator Daniel Patrick Moynihan included) have commented that the entire CIA must go. They see the Agency as wasteful, deceitful, useless, unethical and essentially out of control. There have certainly been incidents of waste, unethical deception of our presidents and congresses, espionage failures and institutional lack of discipline. The Ames and Nicholson cases have added more fuel to the fire, as have past failures such as the Bay of Pigs and past discomforts such as the perception that some private or corporate interests were being served by CIA activities.

However, these events, while deeply troubling, do not represent the rule in the Clandestine Services. That they are too often portrayed as such is a failure of the CIA to defend itself adequately, as well as a failure of large segments of the media and academia to do their homework well and without bias. The CIA is seen as guilty unless it can prove its innocence, despite the obvious fact that it cannot prove its innocence without exposing its operations to those with no need to know.

As in most organisations, there is both good and bad in the CIA. Unfortunately, it is the bad news which always seems to surface, while the good news is rarely leaked. For example, while dwelling on the CIA's problems, few commentators have repeated the accolade for the men and women of the CIA in the House Permanent Select Committee on Intelligence's *Report* (see page 244).

In 1996, the Committee's *Staff Study* also highly approved of the performance of CS officers under difficult conditions and noted that, 'The DO of the last few years appears to be at least as and possibly more successful than it has ever been.' However, the risks in espionage are, of course, high. The *Study* also correctly points out that, 'A safe estimate is that several hundred times a day [across the world] DO officers engage in highly illegal activities (according to foreign law) that not only risk political embarrassment to the US but also endanger the freedom if not the lives of the participating foreign nationals....' In other words, a typical twenty-eight-year-old GS-11 case officer has numerous opportunities every week, by poor tradecraft or inattention, to embarrass his country and president and to get agents imprisoned or executed.

In May 1994, the Intelligence Community Management Staff identified HUMINT (the principal function of the DO) as 'the most important source of intelligence for the subjects treated'. Other studies have placed the product of the CS second only in importance to open source and State Department reporting; SIGINT, IMINT and military attaché reporting followed. DO reporting is usually considered at the top in the fields of terrorism, narcotics, weapons proliferation, economic matters and on a broad range of events in Europe, Africa and Latin America.

These positive achievements are often obscured when the media shows its bias against the CIA. A good example of bad 'news' surfacing and doing gratuitous damage was the spate of media reports on the supposed failure of CIA analysts to predict the collapse of the USSR. In 1995, the *Wall Street Journal* and the *New York Times* reflected widespread belief in the media that the CIA was oblivious to the deteriorating societal and economic conditions in the USSR. That of course mainly referred to the annual National Intelligence estimates, which use the CS as one source among many. Despite remarks in Senator Moynihan's book *Secrecy* (1998), there is another side to this. A group of non-governmental economic experts, evaluating the CIA's analyses of the Soviet economy for the House Permanent Select Committee on Intelligence, reported on 18 November 1991:

Most [such] reports were equally satisfactory: accurate,
illuminating, and timely. In fact, we find it hard to believe
that anyone who has read the CIA's annual public reports
on the state of the Soviet economy since 1975 could possibly interpret them as saying the Soviet economy was
booming. On the contrary, those reports regularly
reported the steady decline in the Soviet growth rate and
called attention to deep and structural problems that
pointed to continued decline and possibly stagnation.

Another damaging myth is that the CIA assassinated President
Kennedy and then managed a secret *coup d'etat* in Washington.
This is without any foundation either in fact or in logic, but
many people believe it – especially the young, the impression-
able, the conspiracy theorists, and those who distrust or hate
their own government or even their own country. Leaks in
Washington being what they are, any CIA hand in a presidential
assassination would have quickly become public knowledge
because too many insiders would have had to be involved. The
eventual publicity given to President Eisenhower's efforts to have
the CIA get rid of Fidel Castro and Patrice Lumumba attest to
the difficulty of keeping secrets in Washington. The amazing
thing is that we have been able to conduct espionage at all in such
an atmosphere.

People who question whether we need espionage in the first
place are simply not thinking logically. There is no substitute for
knowing as much as possible about any danger to the nation.
Others, more discriminating, support espionage but question the
value and ethics of covert action. The reality is that a government's
two eyes can be open only with both intelligence and espionage
(including covert action). Too many recent US presidents – the
prime customers for the product of our modern intelligence operations – have said that they couldn't do without the CIA's
intelligence, and the espionage and covert action products of the
CS. President Clinton and his predecessors have affirmed that
covert action – the President's unique ability to act covertly to
change things overseas in the national interest – is necessary.

Since the late 1940s, most of US state espionage has been
conducted by the CS, which has consequently been the object of
intense curiosity, and much of the media (along with academia)

have been consistently irritated by the CIA's refusal to talk more openly about its operations. But state espionage is not simply another of man's endeavours that is cloaked in mystery by its practitioners for their own purposes. The fundamental difference is that state espionage should be, and usually is, designed to serve national rather than narrow interests. It has sometimes dovetailed with, or even assisted, US private business and organised labour interests, but there is usually a discreet *quid pro quo* that makes the association mutually beneficial.

It is true that in a perfect world state espionage should never include special interests such as business, labour, the Mafia, covert partisan politics and the artisans of the drug trade. It is equally true that in a perfect world state espionage (if it existed at all) should never employ agents who are human rights abusers. But we live in a very dangerous world, and if those people are the only ones who have the inside knowledge we need, then they should be used.

No serious government can afford to be as open about its espionage activities as it can about most of its other activities, although, as Senator Moynihan writes in *Secrecy*, US government secrecy has long been far too widespread and is applied to vast numbers of documents which don't warrant such classification. As a result, government and political leaders have often been seduced by 'secret' (and sometimes inaccurate) information that does not take into account overt information that may be at odds with it. This, Moynihan claims, has led to leaders making mistakes, such as spending huge amounts rearming against a USSR which was openly weakening and, in fact, heading towards collapse. In my experience, some of what the CS classifies is given too high a rating. In the early 1950s, many documents were classified as 'Official Use Only'; some were 'Restricted' or 'Confidential' while maybe half were 'Secret' or higher. Twenty years later, you couldn't find anything classified less than 'Secret', even if the document repeated some overtly available information. That said, certain CS information must always be 'Secret' or higher, including *inter alia* what might reveal identities, methods, electronic communications and operations. Therefore, despite declarations about more openness, the CIA will have to – and should – go right on protecting its clandestine sources and covert methods, if little else. The tension between much of the media and academia on the one hand, and the CIA on the other, is natural and will continue. It will go on breeding distrust as well as frustration and disinformation, but is as inevitable as it should be understandable.

In reality, the CIA produces reams of quality intelligence which can be hinted at. For example, should one state if any particular operation has been a success? I believe that the answer is 'Yes'. Our early work contributed a great deal to the inability of the Communist Parties in Italy and France to attain supreme power, and we built up and maintained espionage stay-behind networks in case the Soviets overran Western Europe. We provided extensive knowledge and foreknowledge of important events that were not otherwise covered, and covert action helped several Latin American nations to remain out of Communist hands. Against all odds we recruited some Soviets, which was very hard indeed in their closed society. For years, our espionage operations provided excellent intelligence on the Soviet military scene. Just how important that intelligence was is illustrated by the Soviet rush to arrest, interrogate, and execute or imprison the spies fingered for them by Ames. As I've already remarked, this was a panic move; the logical reaction would have been to roll them up slowly, trying to make each in turn work for the KGB against the CIA – for example, feeding the US with carefully tailored disinformation.

Covert action – secret action to change events or opinions – is a sub-set of espionage and cannot be undertaken without a presidential 'finding' to approve it beforehand. When it works, it passes either unnoticed or unattributed, and nobody outside the small inner circle of US national security cheers. When it fails, however, it does so loudly and is then used against the CIA.

Covert action undertaken to achieve anything less than important national security goals is clearly not acceptable in an open society. If, however, covert action is the only means to achieve an important national security goal, then an open society must set aside its ethics and undertake the action. But covert action is really only practical if its ultimate goals are in line with congressional (and hopefully national) consensus on the aims of foreign policy.

The other side of the coin is that since national security is the basis for state espionage, it is natural to ask whether the CS really does perform a vital service for the nation. Has its performance been useful, and did it outweigh its failures? Can the CS do as well or even better in the future? If the answers are 'No', then other solutions are needed.

The dilemma is, of course, that the work of state espionage cannot be put before the public for judgment because it cannot become known to our opponents. CIA successes cannot often be paraded publicly because human assets and methods would be exposed. Therefore, assessment of the value of what the Intelligence community and the CIA in general have accomplished, and how the CS in particular has performed, must be entrusted solely to those who need to know.

As I've already related, from 1953 to 1955 I headed the Projects Branch of the old Foreign Intelligence Staff, and every foreign espionage project we had passed across my desk. Even then the quantity of good espionage projects and their quality were very high. I was never again in a position to know the totality of what we were doing or to assess its total usefulness, but President Bush was. He put it well in a 1997 letter to Larry King (which King aired on his show *Larry King Live*). Bush's words were about the CIA as a whole, but they definitely apply to the men and women of the DO:

> I was . . . very proud to have been the DCI at a very complicated period. Now, the CIA is under attack again . . .
> Some suggest the Agency should be in the State
> Department. Some say we no longer need the types of
> intelligence the CIA provides the President. How wrong
> these views are . . . I detest those on Capitol Hill who
> know little of what the CIA really does, and yet who criticize it all the time. I will never forget the young
> undisciplined arrogant staffers from the Hill, who came
> out to a CIA under fire in 1975 and treated everyone in
> that fine Agency as some kind of crook. They compromised the legitimate security considerations of the Agency
> and they set back our liaison relationships around the
> world and they devastated the morale of perhaps the finest
> group of dedicated public servants this country has. I
> hope that this never happens again. And further I hope
> those who want to downgrade the CIA will not be permitted to use the case of one treasonous individual, Mr Ames,

to further impugn the integrity of the CIA or the ability of its people. I was DCI, but I was also a President. I would hate to have contemplated doing my job as President without the benefit of the intelligence provided by the great career people at the CIA, and indeed throughout the rest of the intelligence community . . .

President Bush, having held those two positions, knows what he's talking about, but CIA critics will still read this and jeer at him. Probably nothing will convince them to the contrary.

At its best, espionage helps tells the policy-makers what will occur in the future. At its worst, it has sometimes failed to produce good intelligence, or it has been misleading, or it has been ignored. There is no question that events like Iraq's invasion of Kuwait could have been avoided by having, and properly using, knowledge gained clandestinely to complement knowledge obtained overtly. Few would argue that the CS and its allies failed in not penetrating the top decision-making level of Iraq's government before, during and since the Gulf War. However, I can recall no serious intelligence failure (on the scale of North Korea's surprise attack on South Korea, the Bay of Pigs, the Ayatollah's seizure of Iran, or Saddam's invasion of Kuwait) that was attributable to the rank and file of the CS.

In no case does the ethical argument against espionage win. Whatever the CS has or has not done in the past, its failures or those of the Executive should not lead us to cease conducting espionage because a strong national espionage organisation is still vitally necessary. Past failures should simply impel us to spy better and use its products better. Whatever is decided as a result of the ongoing debate in Washington about the future of the CIA, a first-class clandestine service – no matter what its name, or where it pitches its tent – must exist somewhere within the intelligence community; otherwise, we have lost one of our basic national instruments for anticipating danger and doing something about it.

Ironically, espionage by democratic governments (which, incidentally, very rarely fight each other) against expansionist, autocratic governments or extremist religions helps defend the rights of those critics in the democracies who speak out against espionage. The counter-terrorism function of the FBI, the CIA and other US government entities very definitely helps to protect not only the lives but the rights of its critics.

In October 1996, responding unwisely to congressional pressure, DCI John Deutch sent a WWSB (a message to all CIA stations and bases around the world) requiring them to take special care in contacting potential sources of information who 'might be guilty of civil rights violations'. Such a message, ambiguous as it was (for example, does 'might' mean in the past or at some future date?), resulted in strong reactions from field case officers. Most ignored it, hoping it would go away. Faint-hearted case officers bent over backwards to comply, thus restricting their developmental cases to those few humans who were demonstrably clean in human rights terms. Imagine what that meant in such countries as China, Uganda, Myanmar or Indonesia. If you can only contact visible and government-targeted opposition elements who ooze 'political correctness' and human rights respectability, you increase the danger to them while producing little intelligence of value because they are not in 'the loop'. I'm quite sure how I would have reacted if the WWSB message had come to me in Senegal. The first candidate to be considered would have been the blood-splattered policeman who beat his Communist prisoners to get them to talk. Although I felt negatively about him as a person, his information was both unique and useful. To have dropped him would have meant losing a good source without changing a thing because he would have continued beating his prisoners. But then, of course, it would have been inconceivable to receive such a message in the 1960s. I would probably have cabled home, as one chief did in Asia, asking, 'HAS HQS FALLEN INTO ENEMY HANDS?'

Case officers who actually engage in the craft of espionage are perceived by some as personally unethical. This is both unfair and inaccurate. In any open society which needs to keep an eye out for all dangers, a few people have to break the ethical code so that the vast majority can be free to adhere to it. Those who do should of course adhere to our basic ethical code in everything but their professional espionage activities. That is what I and my colleagues were taught to do, and it is what we tried to do. Other than anomalies like Ames and Nicholson, the men and women of the DO were and are ethical people using unethical means to confound totally unscrupulous opponents. To do this and keep one's own ethics untarnished is not easy, but by and large we managed to succeed.

We applied several quite separate sets of ethical values as regards our espionage activities. The first was the ethics of our profession as conducted within the CS: we didn't lie to each other, steal, cheat, or otherwise act unethically. We had a strict code of ethics that forbade using the dirty tricks we were taught against each other or against our own country. Insofar as our families and friends were concerned, we had to lie – or at least obfuscate the truth – to protect cover stories, agents and methods. We told other US government organisations only what they needed to know in order to do their work. If it was necessary to lie, it was only to protect our operations. It wasn't always easy.

To quote Ambassador Viets, a State Department official, the life of a successful espionage officer involves an 'almost unspeakable paradox, on the one hand holding yourself to a personal code of ethics, as a representative of the institution, and on the other hand dealing in this murky world in which ethics and morality often are meaningless'. The United States is lucky that the DO has so many people who fit that bill.

Against the opposition – the KGB and its allies – we happily used every dirty tool to counter them. Even though the USSR no longer exists, the post-Cold War world is still full of danger. The US must therefore continue to have an espionage organisation fully equipped – including in the use of covert action – and appropriately staffed to go after information that may save us from serious damage. The men and women who form the core of the DO, which consumes a minuscule percentage of the intelligence community's budget, are an important part of the US's national defence. They are a valuable national resource that must be kept; there must be more discipline and focus, but they must not be scattered or dropped. It would be very difficult, time consuming and expensive to put together another group like the DO.

The Culture

Much has been said and written about the DO culture and how it made things easy for traitors. As a former insider, I can testify that there was always a fervent hope that none of us would ever sell out to the opposition. But that hope was accompanied by acceptance that we could very well harbour a mole – perhaps even several. The first mole scare reflected the paradox between the dream of 'not one of us' and the question, 'I wonder who it is?' At the height of that scare, people said that they did not believe there was a mole, not that there couldn't be. By contrast, as we have seen during the early years of the Ames treachery, top CS management actively discounted the possibility even when it had become a very strong probability. Now, of course, the CS culture accepts the probability – even the inevitability – of moles and actively works to uncover them. Latent moles will always be tempted to sell out, but the forces arrayed against them have been seriously strengthened. People are on guard now, and top management is with them.

There was also a strong tendency to keep personnel problems contained within the CS, as happened in the Great Mole Scare and the Ames case. This, too, seems to have been reversed, as can be seen by the inclusion of the FBI in the CS activities against moles and terrorists and various other world scourges.

By the 1970s and the 1980s, the sense of common adventure, intense eagerness and relative informality of the early days of what is now the CS were greatly diminished. This came about partly because of bureaucratic growth, with bureaucrats taking over from innovators. The DO, it seemed to me, lost some of the toughness of mind and spirit that an espionage organisation needs to stay lean and focused. I have yet to talk to a DO officer who does not agree that it had become too big and too bureaucratic, with too diffuse a mission. Ex-CIA Inspector General Freddy Hitz put it this way in a speech to former colleagues: '[The] CIA's sense of mission was gigantic during the Cold War. We need to recapture that elan....Only then can we hope to once again attract the highly qualified young applicants we need . . .'

The changes in the DO were perhaps partly inevitable because the United States had changed so greatly. Since the 1960s, the US national culture (as distinct from the DO's micro-culture) has put less emphasis than before on the values that promote loyalty. There has been a steady erosion of the sanctity of thrift, hard work, the family and individual endurance. Personal responsibility is less appealing to many than blaming everything or everybody else. Activists of all stripes try by the most sinister means to make sure that their voices are the only ones heard, and the public seems more and more willing to accept even the most outlandish conspiracy theory no matter what the facts. Perceptions of cronyism, favouritism, racism and unfairness have caused deep distrust of all levels of government. The US Congress is widely perceived as a nest of career charlatans captured by lobbies, and the Administration as a band of unprincipled deceivers trying to stay in power by raising funds from any source. We seem to have spawned a 'me first' generation with little sense of community and loyalty to their country, even though many of them benefit enormously from the nation's many gifts. Not unexpectedly, being in the nation's service is of less interest to young people than feathering their own nests.

Against this backdrop, there have been increasingly ominous signs that the changes in the mores of society have impacted substantially on the CIA. Since the late 1970s, there has been a steadily growing number of cases of CIA people who have been discovered giving aid and comfort to those who would harm our country. The changed mores in the country made it easier for disaffected members of the CS to blame others for their omissions, and to consider treason as an acceptable path to take. As standards of patriotism, integrity and personal responsibility steadily declined, so the number of people increased who had to be quietly ejected from the CIA (including the DO) for treason or other crimes.

Substance abuse – i.e. drugs and alcohol – have become more in vogue, although alcoholism in the DO was not a widespread, or serious, problem up to the early 1970s. Those few who drank to excess on duty were relieved from sensitive assignments. However, judging by the Ames and Nicholson cases and recent statements by female case officers, alcohol abuse – especially by chiefs of station – seems to have increased markedly by the 1980s and 1990s. Several CIA managers have stated that alcohol abuse 'was not uncommon in the DO during the mid-to-late 1980s', and therefore Ames's drinking did not stand out since 'there were employees with much more serious alcohol cases'.

The machoism of male case officers and managers has apparently also increased, causing a problem for the women in the CS. The tradition of women in senior positions, both in operations and at home, goes back to the OSS, which had a substantial number of extraordinarily bright and effective female officers at all levels, some of whom performed with great courage in the most dangerous field espionage jobs. Others were successful senior managers at OSS headquarters. From the outset, the CIA promoted competent and motivated women from the traditional ranks of secretaries and intelligence analysts to case officers. Most of the male case officers treated these women with respect. Although it was easy to find good case officer material among the women in the DO, it was often difficult to find good operational environments for them. Much of the world then was (and still is) so male-dominated that it was difficult, in some cultures even dangerous, for female case officers to try to recruit males, or otherwise impact on a male world – especially if they were alone. But a surprising number did so very well.

Quite naturally morale has been lowered at Langley, especially among those who care about it. Former DCI Deutch (who himself contributed significantly to poor DO morale) confirmed the problem over and over after Nicholson followed Ames into the spotlight. However, the view from lower down is more specific. I recently received this note from a former colleague still serving in the CIA:

> There is no doubt that the environment is changing. We have people with limited experience making decisions about critical things. We have keen, enthusiastic, but young analysts who don't remember the cold war, but are making analyses about what is happening in China and Russia. Now, when you have a situation where ranking people won't even take the polygraph, this too will open up the likelihood that others may balk – and get away with it – simply because it isn't universally applied. It all seems so messy to us older types. As the institutional memories of those who served for a long time are gradually lost, new institutional memories will be born, and many years down the road, if there is someone to compare them, we will find they are miles apart . . .

Ames and his inattentive managers contributed to the steep decline. Those managers are just as responsible for it as Ames was because they didn't fight the trends in the CS that reflected the changes in national mores. They tolerated the mediocre and knowingly fed three Presidents with tainted intelligence, thus deliberately deceiving them. Unless America gets its core values back, there will be other traitors selling their secrets to the highest bidder. This will mean that fewer people will risk being our agents. The vital element of trust between Langley and the White House will also vanish if Presidents continue to be deceived; and too many congressional leaks of espionage activities to the media will erode mutual trust in all directions – between Congress and the DO, between the DO and foreign security services, and between the DO and prospective agents.

Taking these factors to their logical, if rather ludicrous, conclusion, the country might eventually have to conclude that it cannot successfully conduct espionage even if it wants to.

Whither the CS?

So where does all this lead? Will the CS revive itself and its reputation, or will it continue its decline? So far the Administration seems to be willing to let it try to repair itself, but if the White House and Congress fail to support a truly vigorous revival of the DO, it will inevitably shuffle along in something of a daze.

To restore itself, and improve upon the spirit and the skills that were at its core for its first few decades, will take some doing, but it can be done with excellent management supervising exceptional personnel. The DO of today needs all the good, young people it can get, yet it is having trouble finding enough of them; even so, recruiting standards cannot be allowed to sink. A firm recruiting policy is needed that admits only the very best men and women. The US still contains a healthy percentage of loyal, motivated, young people with the skills and aptitudes the DO needs. A huge effort therefore should be made to spot, assess and recruit such people to replace the gaps that have appeared in the DO ranks. DO personnel should be encouraged to think innovatively and to discard excessive bureaucracy. Managers will have to resist the previous pitfalls of hiring mediocre people just to fill empty posts. The 'walking wounded' should never be tolerated in espionage, no matter how many of them have to be removed to safer jobs or fired. One bad apple in a sensitive position can wreck the work of a thousand true people.

A revived DO will need, and in turn could help revive, the national mood that once viewed the CIA and its work as a positive asset and not as a national question-mark or worse, but this will take a supreme internal and external effort. Even then, it may simply be too visible to do its work in secret. It is unlikely to happen, of course, but it is interesting to speculate that it might be best for the CS to be removed from the CIA and to go under real cover – instead of leaving it in the goldfish bowl of Langley.

Why should a bright young American today consider joining the CS? Because the CS management finally seems to have learned its lessons. Moles are being hunted and trapped, potential moles are being identified and steered to safety, the FBI is being used properly, and sensitive information is being treated more securely. Much greater care is being taken to avoid activities that bring charges of involvement in the drugs trade, of deceiving Presidents, of end-running Congress, or of covertly helping US commercial interests. But above all, regardless of how well or badly the CS did during its first fifty years, the United States needs a first-class set of covert eyes, ears and hands in order to make foreknowledge of danger its first line of defence.

Index